Six Sigma: Continual Improvement for Businesses

Six Sigma: Continual Improvement for Businesses

A Practical Guide

William T. Truscott
Ph.D., B.Sc. (Eng.), C.Eng., M.I.Mech.E., M.I.E.E., M.R.Ae.S., F.S.S., F.I.Q.A.

BUTTERWORTH
HEINEMANN

AMSTERDAM   BOSTON   HEIDELBERG   LONDON   NEW YORK
OXFORD   PARIS   SAN DIEGO   SAN FRANCISCO   SINGAPORE
SYDNEY   TOKYO

Butterworth-Heinemann
An imprint of Elsevier
Linacre House, Jordan Hill, Oxford OX2 8DP
200 Wheeler Road, Burlington, MA 01803

First published 2003

British Library Cataloguing in Publication Data
A catalogue record for this book is available from the British Library

Library of Congress Cataloguing in Publication Data
A catalogue record for this book is available from the Library of Congress

ISBN 0 7506 57650

For information on all Butterworth-Heinemann publications
visit our website at www.bh.com

Typeset by Newgen Imaging Systems (P) Ltd, Chennai, India
Printed and bound in Great Britain by Biddles Ltd, *www.biddles.co.uk*

Contents

Preface

Survival is not compulsory

Edwards Deming

Let us put 'Six Sigma' aside for the moment. Instead, let us reflect on some real-life scenarios in a number of quite different organizations.

Take the machine shop whose machines are not exactly new. They have great difficulty meeting the tolerances and are continually pressed to meet almost impossible delivery dates in the presence of varying degrees of unscheduled scrap and rework and the corresponding high levels of inspection and re-inspection. Profit margins are low, even when things are going relatively well and negative when they do not. Then there is the foundry that makes overhead cam manifolds for the motor vehicle industry. On just this one product line alone the effect of scrap and reworks impregnation adversely affects the 'bottom line' to the tune of over £58 000 per year. Recognize the electricity power insulator manufacturer where the actual ongoing yield of its main-line glass fibre product was 34% compared with a break-even yield of 52%.

Observe the trouser assembler who, following complaints from a major retailer, decided to double-up on his already 100% inspection in order to placate the customer. This has the effect of turning a marginal profit into a loss. Contemplate the steel tube producer who buys steel strip by weight and sells tube by length. Targeting and control of outside diameter and wall thickness dimensions affect the 'bottom line' by as much as £250 000 per annum. Take the brick press-works who make refractory bricks for the steel industry. In order to meet minimum density standards, and as a result of inadequate control of variability in pressing, some 21% excess material is given away on each brick. Consider the subsidiary of a large company who assembles hybrid electrical/hydraulic/mechanical units using functionally critical components acquired from various approved sources. Extensive goods receiving inspection is undertaken because of the amount of product received that is not to specification (over 8% on average).

Look at the health service that is attempting to reduce ever growing patient waiting lists whilst containing the situation brought about by the shortage of beds and resources required to treat existing patients. Take the loss making railway service who are aiming to minimize late running of trains and cancellations in the face of simultaneously achieving much greater safety standards.

From the purely personal point of view, take the harassed quality champion who has been hired expressly to initiate, nurture and deploy projects to improve quality. Instead, he spends his whole life fire fighting. This fire fighting is not on even his own list of priorities, which is growing by the day, but on those given to him by his supervisor at the daily morning briefings. The odd days out at quality motivational seminars/workshops, intended for personal development, compound the issue both from a task and individual perspective.

The list is endless. These are not worse-case scenarios. They appear to represent present-day standard practice in very many organizations that are held in high esteem by their peers, customers and other interested parties. These organizations have also recognized the need to adopt a policy of, and pursue practices leading to, continual improvement. Sometimes this awareness has been self-initiated. Sometimes it has arisen from the need to conform to prescriptive requirements by major customers, or legislative authorities, in order to stay in business or meet their statutory responsibilities.

The first premise on which this book is based is that 'continual improvement is a vital ingredient in any organization in order just to continue to survive in the climate of today'.

The second premise is that 'All work activities consist of processes. Continual process improvement is achieved by a focus on, and timely response to, the voice of the customer (needs and expectations) and the voice of the process (performance and identification of opportunities to improve effectiveness and efficiency)'.

Contemporary Gallup studies (Tritch, T., 2001) show that the bulk of members of an organization switch off mentally to some degree whilst at work. Only some 22–33% claim that they are fully involved in their work and 12–19% feel actively 'disengaged'. The larger the organization the worst the situation. It is considered that in small work units (e.g. project teams), of fewer than 10 people, engagement[1] will soar if properly managed. This leads to two further premises. The third premise is that 'The active engagement of a critical

---

[1]Engagement means more than just involvement. It also requires motivation: the encouragement of a culture in which members feel wanted; the setting of goals; the development of core competencies and the matching of value enhancing tasks to talents.

mass of its members in pursuing the goals of an organization would significantly improve the performance of that organization'.

The fourth premise is that 'Continual-improvement activities are enhanced by establishing priorities, developing the appropriate competencies of members of an organization, encouraging member involvement in focused team-based project-improvement activities and establishing an infrastructure to ensure continuance of the improvement effort'.

The fifth premise is the 'recognition that an increasing number of major organizations, who are themselves committed to continual improvement through Six Sigma, have the expectation that their suppliers are likewise committed'.

The sixth premise is that 'the mention of the term "Six Sigma" to statistically aware people usually provokes an extreme reaction either for or against'. Why is this? Those against are often from the statistical fraternity. They use the 'iffy' statistical basis for quality measurement developed and applied by its originators as the principal reason for their views. This has given rise to such phrases as 'cowboy quality' and 'peddling of quack medicine'. Some even dismiss Six Sigma in a peremptory manner as 'having no statistical relevance'. However, there is also a view held that this dubious statistical foundation can actually work to its advantage by inducing managers to disregard previously held assumptions about acceptable failure rates. And, after all, the Captains of industry and commerce, not statisticians, are the identified customers here whose needs and expectations are to be satisfied.

The seventh premise is that 'Fundamental changes in the metrics used in conventional Six Sigma initiatives are essential to provide valid benchmarks of performance'.

Those for it hail it as the 'breakthrough management strategy revolutionizing the world's top corporations'. Such enthusiasm is sometimes tempered by the thought that what has been demonstrated to work well in a multibillion dollar corporation such as General Electric may not be suitable for small- and medium-size organizations This thought may well be extended to large organizations, which are normally split into a number of different entities, operating units and functions, if the continuing total commitment of the chief executive is not forthcoming. After all, Jack Welch, who was at the helm of GE at the time, was unique with his extremely successful management style. When 'Neutron' Jack proclaims that: 'Six Sigma is the most important initiative GE has ever taken. It is part of our genetic code of our future leadership'. Of course, it works in GE!

The eighth premise is that 'Total commitment to any specific initiative, throughout a large organization may not be forthcoming for a variety of reasons. This apparent handicap can be turned to advantage by the evidence that people in smaller work units are much more likely and willing to participate'.

This book addresses the questionable statistical foundations of 'Six Sigma' and proposes alternative simple, yet statistically sound, performance metrics. It also provides the key to creating the necessary tailored focus, competencies, leadership and organization, in small- and medium-size companies, and work units/sections/departments within large organizations, to reap the benefits from sustained deployment of Six Sigma.

The eight premises forming the basis of this book are:

1 Continual improvement is a vital ingredient in any organization in order just to continue to survive in the climate of today.
2 All work activities consist of processes. Continual process improvement is achieved by a focus on, and timely and effective response to, the voice of the customer (needs and expectations) and the voice of the process (performance and identification of opportunities).
3 The active engagement of a critical mass of its members in pursuing the goals of an organization would significantly improve the performance of the organization.
4 Continual-improvement activities are enhanced by establishing priorities, developing the appropriate competencies of members of an organization, encouraging member engagement in focused team-based project improvement activities and establishing an infrastructure to ensure continuance of the improvement effort.
5 Recognition that an increasing number of major organizations, who are themselves committed to continual improvement through Six Sigma, have the expectation that their suppliers are likewise committed.
6 The mention of the term 'Six Sigma' to statistically aware people usually provokes an extreme reaction either for or against.
7 Fundamental changes in the metrics used in conventional Six Sigma initiatives are essential to provide valid benchmarks of performance.
8 Total commitment to any specific initiative throughout a large organization may not be forthcoming for a variety of reasons. This apparent handicap can be turned to advantage because people in smaller work units are normally much more likely and willing to participate.

If you can, spend a bit of time to think about the subject of continual improvement before deciding how you are to achieve this. In this day and age you do not probably have a choice about getting on-board. However, you probably do have a free choice in the initiatives you deploy. The possible exception is if you have a major customer insisting that you adopt a particular approach. The odds are, at the moment, that this will be Six Sigma. This is because of its current popularity particularly with major procurement organizations. In any case, whatever approach is chosen, it is considered worthwhile to tailor the initiative to the individual needs and culture of your own organization rather than go for a stereotyped 'off-the-peg' deployment route. Consider also the medium- to long-term implications. Do not settle for an approach that will most likely be thrown out of the window at the next, or next but one, market downturn, downsizing or management change. This is what this book is about. It spells out the alternative approaches to continual improvement. If you do choose to adopt Six Sigma, or a variant, this book sets the scene. It covers the range of interpersonal and technical skills required to proceed, the driving infrastructure, and the kind of culture necessary for these new found skills to be fostered and incorporated in the blood-stream of your organization. These features will enable you, not only to make a rational choice on tailoring your approach but also to deploy the Six Sigma initiatives successfully to meet the needs and expectations of your own organization.

This book is intended for anyone interested in continual improvement of performance throughout any type of organization, large or small, in whatever sector. Just skip those parts not relevant to your current need.

Bibliography

Tritch, T. (2001). Think big, act small, *Gallup Management Journal*, **1** (3).

Chapter 1
What is Six Sigma?

Six Sigma is the most important initiative General Electric has ever taken

Jack Welch

Six Sigma in perspective

Six Sigma focuses on establishing world-class business-performance bench-marks and on providing an organizational structure and road-map by which these can be realized. This is achieved mainly on a project-by-project team basis, using a workforce trained in performance-enhancement methodology, within a receptive company culture and perpetuating infrastructure. Although particularly relevant to the enhancing of value of products and services from a customer perspective, Six Sigma is also directly applicable to improving the efficiency and effectiveness of all processes, tasks and transactions within any organization. Projects are thus chosen and driven on the basis of their relevance to increased customer satisfaction and their effect on business-performance enhancement through gap analysis, namely, prior quantitative measurement of existing performance and comparison with that desired.

Six Sigma, in current business usage, has a dual meaning. Six Sigma provides, on the one hand, a world-class standard or benchmark for product and service characteristics and for process parameters. On the other hand, Six Sigma refers to the structured process itself aimed at achieving this standard of near perfection. These two meanings contrast with the precise statistical meaning of the term.

Success in Six Sigma is dependent on active senior management leadership and mentoring, an established infrastructure including, the so-called 'judo-like black and green belts', a continuing project focus on 'bottom line' opportunities and results, with established teams trained in using a structured approach and methodology to achieve positive results. Six Sigma does not normally require significant capital expenditure other than for investment in the training and development of the participants in the process. It does, however, require long-term commitment from management in the ongoing process of continual improvement through active interest, support and review and the provisioning of appropriate resources. However, financial benefits should begin to be experienced with the completion of the first set of projects undertaken. Results from organizations committed to the Six Sigma initiative indicate that the financial benefits make a very significant effect on the 'bottom line'.

Principal facets of Six Sigma

What is it about the term Six Sigma that evokes such extreme views?

Much of the reason probably lies in the confusion surrounding its conceptual meaning and differences in interpretation of this multifaceted expression. In this respect, it is essential to clearly distinguish between Six Sigma – the statistical model, on the one hand, and Six Sigma – the improvement process, on the other. The statistical model comprises three principal constituents: the standard sigma statistic, the Six Sigma metric (measure) and the Six Sigma performance benchmark. The Six Sigma improvement process is also made up of three essential elements: its project-by-project approach, Six Sigma organizational infrastructure and its development of core workforce Six Sigma competencies. Figure 1.1 illustrates these principal facets of the Six Sigma business initiative. Each aspect is now discussed.

Six Sigma: the statistical model

The Six Sigma statistical model is intended, by its originators, to serve a triple purpose. This is to provide: a universal performance metric, or measure, that can be applied to any product, process or service regardless of its relative complexity; a world-class performance benchmark; and the marketing name

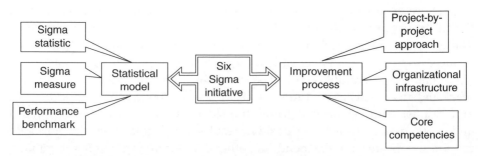

Figure 1.1   Principal facets of the Six Sigma business initiative

for the Six Sigma improvement initiative. The statistical model is essentially made up of three elements as indicated in Figure 1.1. These are the:

- *Sigma statistic.* This refers to the universally used statistic, the statistical measure of variability, termed standard deviation, and called *'sigma'*. It forms the basis of the statistical model.
- *Sigma measure.* This Sigma is *not* the same as, but is indirectly related to, *sigma* and provides a numerical performance measuring scale.
- *Performance benchmark.* A Sigma value of 6, as used by many Six Sigma practitioners, represents a so-called world-class performance standard of 3.4 defects per million opportunities.

A discussion of the Six Sigma statistical model is considered from three viewpoints: overall appreciation level; technical level; and statistical level. Those readers who purely wish to have a general impression of the essential value and application of the Six Sigma statistical model will probably contain themselves to the overall appreciation level discussion in this chapter. However, it is imperative that those who are, or intend to be, associated with Six Sigma in any 'hands-on', or influential, sense read also the critique, discussion and response at the technical level in Chapter 7. Such readers may also consider it beneficial to consider, and reflect upon, the statistical issues covered and recommendations made in Chapter 8. This will enable them to take the appropriate countermeasures and make the improvements necessary in the original Six Sigma statistical model (that is in widespread use) to improve its efficiency and effectiveness in a diagnostic sense in their area of operation.

Appreciation-level discussion

The statistical model provides the marketing name for the Six Sigma improvement initiative. The originators of the Six Sigma initiative use a unit of measurement, a 'Sigma', to measure performance, the higher the number of Sigma the better the performance. For example, a 6 Sigma process is rated better than a 5 Sigma one.

An advantage of the Sigma measure is its simplicity and practicality. This appeals to all those who do not wish to get too embroiled in statistical niceties, but just want a simple readily understandable scale of performance measurement. The fact that 6 Sigma denotes something better than 5 Sigma and that 5 Sigma is better than 4 Sigma, and so on makes good practical sense to a number of people and they are quite happy to run with it.

The relationship between Sigma value and faults per million opportunities and equivalent percentage yield, used in standard Six Sigma practice, is shown in Table 1.1. A more detailed table is shown in Table 7.2.

Many quotes are made to appeal in the emotive sense to emphasize the need for improvement in the Sigma value from current values to world-class values. Two examples are given in Table 1.2.

Table 1.1 Relationship between Sigma value and faults per million opportunities and equivalent yield

Six-Sigma Sigma value	Faults (or events) per million opportunities	Yield (%)
1	691 462	30.85
2	308 538	69.146
3	66 807	93.319
4	6210	99.379
5	233	99.9767
6	3.4	99.99966

Table 1.2 Effect of Sigma value on expectations of different everyday event results

Process Sigma value	Expectation of	
	time without electricity per month	aircraft landing/takeoff incidents in each direct return flight
2	207 h	8 per 10 flights
3	45 h	24 per 100 flights
4	4 h	25 per 1000 flights
5	9 min	9 per 10 000 flights
6	8 sec	12 per million flights

In the United States of America, such quotes abound. For activities taking place at Sigma levels of between 3 and 4 there would be some 50 newborn babies dropped per day, 5000 incorrect surgical procedures per week, 20 000 lost articles of mail per hour, and so on.

It has been said that a computer is 'a device to turn a clerical error into a corporate disaster'. There may be good reasons for this statement when one considers that there is said to be, on average, one software error in every 55 lines of computer program. This equates to a Sigma line value of between 3 and 4. Think of the effect of this on the air traffic control system in the United Kingdom, where at Swanwick alone there are more than 2 000 000 lines of computer code. Compound this with computer upgrades, staffing problems and the fact that flight controllers complain that they have difficulty in distinguishing between figures and letters on screen. Is it surprising that there were 3500 h of flight delays registered in one recent week? On the understanding that the amount of software is doubling every 18 months or so, and that, historically, the defect density is remaining virtually constant, this inevitably leads one to a very pessimistic conclusion. In the absence of some form of intensive improvement initiative such as Six Sigma, the computer industry and its customer base are likely to continue spawning known and avoidable failures such as those mentioned. If this initiative is not taken the computer will continue to be 'a device that turns a clerical error into a corporate disaster'!

Six Sigma: the improvement process

Process focus

In today's business environment, a process focus is essential as each and every activity, function or task within an organization can be considered to be a process. In focusing on the process, a number of concepts and principles should be borne in mind. These are:

1. the mindset of today is one of prevention and continuous improvement;
2. process improvement focuses on the end-to-end (concept to customer) process;
3. process improvement stems from a disciplined and structured approach;
4. processes have internal customers (e.g. downstream recipient) and external customers (e.g. end-users);
5. customer expectations drive process improvement;
6. every business is made up of processes;
7. every person manages a process;
8. every person is simultaneously both a supplier to someone and a customer of someone else;
9. every process has inputs and outputs;
10. every process has resources and controls;
11. process characteristics affect output;
12. processes cross organizational boundaries;
13. processes are often independent of hierarchical organizational structures;

This leads to a concept, a need and the answer to two very pertinent business questions:

Concept
Every process generates information (voice of the process) that can be used to control and improve its performance.

Need
To develop informed perceptive observers using appropriate methodology.

To answer two very pertinent business questions that require answers
What is the performance of the process?
Is there evidence of process performance improvement?

Figure 1.2 illustrates a model of an actual integrated process consisting of a number of stages. It shows the opportunities for monitoring at various within-process stages to provide information in order to control, measure and improve

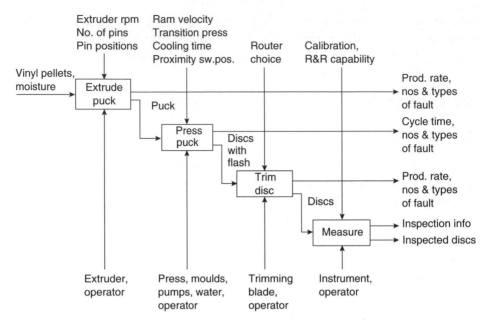

Figure 1.2 Video disc pressing: flow diagram of integrated multi-stage process

process performance. Such monitoring is most beneficial when it takes place on process parameters that have a significant impact on the output of each stage of the multiple process prior to the output being produced. This facilitates the achievement of first-run capability at each stage.

Figure 1.2 shows the distinction between the strategy of control associated with post-process monitoring and the strategy of improvement possible with the Six Sigma process focus approach. Real-time monitoring and the seeking out of inter-relationships between in-process parameters such as ram velocity, transition pressure, cooling time, pin positions on extrusion, proximity switch position, router choice, extruder type and trimming blade status with product characteristics provide opportunities for improvement. Whilst Figure 1.2 relates to a manufacturing process, the same approach is applicable to any process, in any organization.

Multiple-stage processes demand very high stage performances

Figure 1.3 shows that it is imperative to have very high stage yields (very high Sigma) to achieve even a modest final output yield even in this basic process. It also illustrates the difference in performances between the more realistic first-time yield and the conventionally used logistic yield where rework is hidden.

The overall process performance is now shown in two forms for comparison. In the Six Sigma initiative, the more realistic first-time yield is used as this

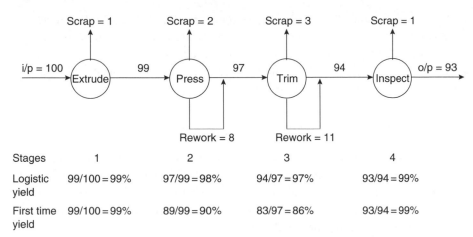

Figure 1.3 Logistic yields compared with first-time quality capabilities or yields of a multi-stage process. Note 1: logistic yield = (good output/input) × 100%. Note 2: first-time yield = $[(N - W)/N] \times 100\%$, where N is the number of items entering the process and W the waste, that is, the number of items that are not processed right first time whatever the ultimate disposition (e.g. reworked, scrapped)

uncovers waste hidden by the more generally used logistics yield:

$$\text{Overall logistic yield} = \text{apparent yield} = 93/100$$
$$= 93\% \text{ (nearly 3 Sigma process)}$$

$$\text{Overall first-time yield} = \text{real yield} = (100 - 1 - 10 - 14 - 1)/100$$
$$= 74\% \text{ (just over 2 Sigma process)}$$

Figure 1.3 shows that whilst stage yield look quite respectable, overall yields of the integrated multi-stage process are much less attractive. It also shows that the logistic yield, at 93% overall, is much more optimistic than the actual first-time yield, at 74% overall. This example illustrates the value of the use of overall first-time yield to identify Six Sigma process-improvement opportunities, to exploit these and to verify the effectiveness of any changes made to the process. They also show the need for an overall management perspective when dealing with multi-stage processes rather than the narrow-stage view often taken by discrete functional departments.

With the process focus as a starting point for improvement in Six Sigma, key questions are asked:

- *What is the process or task?* How do we monitor performance? How much scope is there for improvement?
- *Who is the customer?* How do we monitor customer reaction? What issues/inhibitors are there?
- *Who is the supplier?* How is supplier performance monitored? What issues/inhibitors are there?

- *What resources are deployed?* What are their effectiveness and efficiency?
- *What controls are exercised?* Are they appropriate to the customer expectation and compatible with the capability of the process?
- *What makes the process tick?* In what way do process inputs and process parameters affect the process output?

Six Sigma process-improvement management

Traditionally, managers are required to control and handle breakthroughs that arise largely through advances in technology and changes in business direction brought about by market and other perturbations. The modern Six Sigma manager is also expected to initiate and manage improvement projects on a continuous basis as a regular part of the job.

The Six Sigma improvement process refers to the mechanism of break-through to world-class standards of performance across the whole enterprise. It is focused on 'adding value'; one in which organizations seek out opportunities to improve efficiency and effectiveness with a view to enhancing profit margins, competitiveness and customer satisfaction:

- it achieves results through a highly focused system of problem-solving and process-improvement projects;
- it is implemented through a standard road-map for each project undertaken;
- it is an initiative that aims at channelling and unifying the efforts of everyone in the organization towards the Six Sigma goal;
- an infrastructure is created to make it work and keep on working;
- it is equally applicable to all processes in an organization and to any organization;
- it is based on scientific method utilizing practical and directed statistical thinking and methodology.

Figure 1.4 illustrates these main features in a pictorial manner.

Are we doing such things already? Perhaps not as much as we think. Consider the following questions in this respect. Does our culture and infrastructure promote or inhibit continual improvement? Do a critical mass of people in our organization successfully practice continual improvement? Are they equipped to do so effectively? If the answer to any of these questions is no, or yes in part, then the Six Sigma improvement process should be well worthy of close attention.

Six Sigma: the project-by-project approach

There are many possible different approaches to the project-by-project approach to improvement in organizations. The standard Six Sigma project road-map proposed here is a generic one. It consists of eight steps:

1 *Identify* the project.
2 *Define* the project.

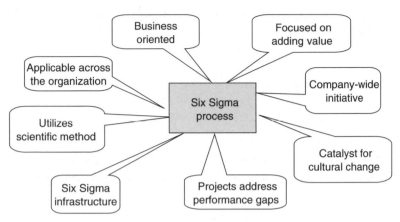

Figure 1.4 Key features that make the Six Sigma initiative different from other approaches

3 *Measure* current process performance.
4 *Analyse* the current process.
5 *Develop* the improvements; pilot and verify.
6 *Implement* the changes; achieve breakthrough in performance.
7 *Control* at new level; institutionalize to hold the gains.
8 *Communicate* new knowledge gained; transfer solution to similar areas.

Two questions could be posed at this stage.

First, why are these steps different from the DMAIC (define–measure–analyse–implement–control) approach proposed by the originators of Six Sigma? Three further steps have been introduced for a number of reasons. 'Identify' is added as the first step because it is of vital importance that Six Sigma projects are chosen so that they are specifically directed at the achievement of business objectives. This is the principal distinguishing feature between the Six Sigma and Quality Circle approach. The fifth step 'develop' is added to distinguish it from the analysis phase. These are two quite different matters. In the step 'analyse', one is analytical whereas the step 'develop' demands creativeness. The eighth step 'communicate' is added to address the benefits of possible exploitation of the specific local gains made by transferring the project solution to other areas of the business.

Second, what is singular about this approach that distinguishes it from the many others that have been developed over the years? The answer is that there is very little between the Six Sigma approach and the best of these. In point of fact the eight steps recommended in the Six Sigma project approach here is indeed culled from these and hence represent best practice.

The most important issue here is to standardize on the generic method used throughout the organization. There should, however, be a difference in

Table 1.3 Differing standard project steps depending on the nature of the project

Problem-solving	Process improvement
Identify the problem	Identify the process
Clarify the problem and approach	Define flow of activities
Measure the extent of problem	Establish ownership: measure
Analyse and determine causes	Probe the process
Develop preventive action plan	Develop improved process
Implement to prevent recurrence	Implement improvement
Control: maintain gains	
Communicate: transfer knowledge gained to other areas	

sub-routines depending on the nature of the project. This will arise for two principal reasons:

- Whether or not the project is concerned with 'problem-solving' or 'process improvement'. The differences are outlined at this stage in Table 1.3. They are both dealt with in detail later in the book.
- Special projects that have their own methodology. Examples are experimentation, failure mode and effect analysis and quality function deployment. These are all covered later in the book.

Six Sigma: the organizational infrastructure

Martial arts

What is the relationship between a business-improvement process such as Six Sigma and the martial art of Judo? What is its relevance? Before discussing this it might be useful to reflect on why and how martial arts come into the picture at all.

In the west, 'martial arts' are generally thought of as war-like arts, of battles and conquests, of victors and vanquished. Take a typical 007 film where James Bond goes off to train with a master for a few days and comes back extremely proficient in some particularly lethal form of martial art. Martial art means much more in Japan. It is a way of life. The practising of a martial art can be a lifelong quest for personal fulfilment, the path to physical and mental liberation and, above all, to spiritual growth. An effect that martial arts, as practised in Japan, can have on persons introduced to a martial art is that they see seasoned practitioners performing feats well beyond their own current capabilities. In so doing that person often takes on a completely new perspective on the art of the possible of what he or she can, and cannot, accomplish. Following training, new participants will find themselves performing similar feats. This leads to a new belief in ones own possibilities.

Judo and Six Sigma

There are many types of martial arts. These include boxing, wrestling, Kung Fu, Karate, Jujitsu and Judo. Why Judo? Judo is formed from two Chinese words, Ju and Do. 'Ju' is a Chinese character meaning 'pliable' or 'adaptable'. 'Do' denotes 'way of life'. Judo is the art of self-perfection. The ultimate aim of Judo is to: 'perfect oneself by systematic training so that each person works in harmony within oneself and with others for the common good'. This perhaps is a good enough reason, in itself, to explain why Judo comes into the picture as far as Six Sigma is concerned.

There are, however, many other rational reasons for this decision. First, Judo is standardized throughout the world whereas, for example, there are some 1500 styles of Karate and over 700 forms of Jujitsu. Second, Judo in its pure form, in marked contrast to other forms of martial art, is not about beating an opponent. Having said this, Judo has been an Olympic sport since 1964. This use of Judo, as an instrument of aggression and domination through combat, is looked upon as a corruption of true Judo. On the other side of the coin, the popularity of Judo has been considerably enhanced in the sporting context by it being brought into the Olympic arena. The founder of Judo, Dr Jigoro Kano, has summed up the essential altruistic nature of Judo thus: 'the ultimate aim of Judo is to perfect yourself and to contribute to the well-being of mankind'. It is the intention of Judo training that an individual will secure improved physical and mental fitness. Mental development will be displayed through increased self-confidence, self-discipline, improved decision-making skills, enhanced empathy and spirit of fairness. Third, Judo is increasingly being looked upon in a multifaceted way: as a fun sport, an art, a way of life and a Six Sigma discipline, amongst others. Judo, in one form or another, is being practised by millions the world over. It is an inexpensive all-year-round activity that appeals to people of either sex and any age group drawn from all walks of life. Fourth, Judo recognizes a person's degree of knowledge, ability and powers of leadership by a system of ranks. Rank is denoted, in part, by the colour of one's belt. In Six Sigma, the colours yellow, green and black are deployed in order of increasing seniority.

A comparison of the similarity between Judo and the Six Sigma business initiative is given in Table 1.4, which attempts to summarize in a rational way the reasons why Judo concepts and practices are used in Six Sigma.

Six Sigma

The Six Sigma infrastructure makes the approach unique. It has an infrastructure based on martial arts judo belts that:

- provides the driving force for all Six Sigma activities;
- ensures a business orientation by focusing efforts on 'bottom line' results;

Table 1.4 Similarity of concepts between Judo and Six Sigma

Concept	Judo	Six Sigma
Marketing	New disciplined way of life Applicable to all and sundry	Disciplined new business initiative, applicable to, and with participation by, all members of the organization
Motivational	Exciting Popular sport Sets adrenal going	New, exciting business idea with popular sporting connotations Awakens and stimulates latent abilities
Personal awareness and development	Development of the individual Set pattern of 'Judo' training in standardized stages	Development of the individual Waves of training in Six Sigma competencies
Efficiency	Concept of maximum efficiency from minimum effort	Concept of maximum efficiency from minimum effort regarding project cost/benefit considerations and project selection, conduct and management
Key objectives & primary aims	Mutual benefit of all mankind	Improvement in performance of one's own organization coupled with an enhanced personal 'quality of life'
Hierarchy infrastructure	Defined system of ranks in recognition of a person's current knowledge, abilities and leadership skills	Defined system of ranks in recognition of a person's current knowledge, abilities and leadership skills Black, green and yellow belts

- shows that top management is actively committed to continuous improvement using Six Sigma as the platform;
- creates a favourable environment for involvement through employee participation in effective teamwork;
- ensures that those involved are familiar with, and practised, in the methodology;
- is concerned with the progressive deployment of the Six Sigma process;
- recognizes the contribution that all members of the organization can make to the success of the organization and provides the means by which this can be achieved;
- facilitates and act as champions and standard bearers for Six Sigma throughout the Company.

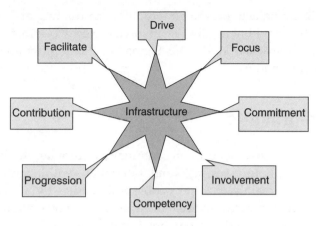

Figure 1.5   Key roles of the Six Sigma infrastructure

The standard Six Sigma infrastructure consists of:
Champions
Master black belts/mentors
Black belts
Green belts

The actual infrastructure and number of roles will be dependent on:
– the size and complexity of each participating company
– the stage of maturity of deployment of Six Sigma

Figure 1.6   The key players in the Six Sigma infrastructure

The key roles of the infrastructure are illustrated in Figure 1.5 and the principal players are described in Figure 1.6. The infrastructure and its key members are discussed in detail at a later stage.

Six Sigma: the core competencies

Two aspects relating to the competencies of people engaged in Six Sigma need consideration. First, a wide range of skills, tools and techniques are likely to be deployed in Six Sigma projects. These involve soft (people) skills, as well as the so-called 'hard' skills, such as the use of technical and statistical tools. Second, it is a basic tenet that no one should be required to work beyond the bounds of their competency. Competency can be defined as the key knowledge, skills, abilities, behaviours and other characteristics needed to perform specific tasks.

Competency profiles are used to develop performance-based learning objectives. A consequence to this is that it is standard practice for all persons engaged in Six Sigma activities to go through a set training and development programme. This would normally also involve project work that culminates in certification as a particular kind of Six Sigma belt. Such programmes are dealt with in Chapters 5 and 6.

Chapter highlights

- The Six Sigma initiative focuses on continually improving the efficiency and effectiveness of all processes, tasks and transactions within any organization. This is achieved mainly on a project-by-project basis by a critical mass of members, trained in performance-enhancement methods, within a receptive and company culture and perpetuating infrastructure.
- Two principal facets of the Six Sigma initiative are the statistical model and the continual improvement process.
- The Six Sigma statistical model provides a universal measure of process performance called a Sigma measure. The higher the value of Sigma the better the performance. A value of 6 Sigma corresponds with 3.4 adverse events (e.g. faults) per million opportunities. 6 Sigma is generally considered to be world class. This world-class standard of 6 Sigma provides the marketing name for the Six Sigma initiative. It is suggested that many, if not most, organizations operate at around 2–4 Sigma. This has the effect of generating considerable waste and customer dissatisfaction.
- The Six Sigma continual-improvement process is based on the premise that each and every activity in any organization is looked upon as a process. Every individual process has a supplier, a customer, resources and controls. Every organization consists of a myriad of inter-related processes. The improvement process focuses on business critical issues and opportunities with the intention of enhancing profit margins, competitiveness, customer satisfaction and generally adding value. It is made up of three primary components.
- The Six Sigma continual-improvement process is made up of three primary components: the Judo-like organizational structure of belts, the development of core competencies in participants and the project-by-project approach.

Chapter 2
Why should organizations implement Six Sigma?

No one keeps his enthusiasm automatically. Enthusiasm must be nourished
with new actions, new aspirations, new efforts, new vision

Papyrus

Response to change: competition: waste

Overview

Six Sigma recognizes that we live in a rapidly changing and increasingly competitive world. Customers' needs and expectations are continually changing.
Economies are also on the move. In the early 1900s, some 70% of UK workers
were in agriculture, now there are less than 2%. In the early 1950s, just under
50% of UK employees were in manufacture or production, now the figure is just
20% or so. The UK economy is now becoming dominated by the service sectors
and public administrations, which are claimed to have a higher proportion
of waste than manufacture. This is not necessarily a reflection on relative
management performance but rather on the nature of the process. For instance,
the yield of a manufacturing process is generally expected to be high. The
consequences of failure are immediately transparent. Not so, say, in a sales process.
The proportion of actual sales to sales interest or enquiries is likely to be much
lower. Failure to make a sale is not so transparent and obvious. In consequence,
the scope for improvement is much higher than for the manufacturing sector of
an industry or function of a single organization.

   Change is a breeding ground for problems, inefficiency and lack of effectiveness in all business processes. This gives rise to an adverse impact on the
'bottom line'. The more pronounced the speed and extent of change the greater
the adverse effects. These arise from things such as poor choice and inadequate
control of suppliers, immaturity of designs, inadequate process capabilities,

Table 2.1 Estimate of average cost of waste in terms of type of organization and Sigma level

Type of organization	Cost of waste	Sigma level
Average service	30–40% of sales	3
Average manufacturing	15–30% of sales	4
Good practice	5–15% of sales	5
Best (world) class	Less than 1% of sales	6

cutting corners generally and quick operational fixes. It is not then surprising that estimates for financial losses due to lack of 'doing things right the first time' in organizations are of the order shown in Table 2.1. Table 2.1 also shows how the Sigma measuring scale is linked to approximate estimated average cost of waste as a percentage of sales for different organizations.

Many people would argue that they do not have so much waste as this in their organization. They could be deluding themselves as most of this is hidden. Waste has been likened to an iceberg, only the tip is visible, the majority is unseen. Hence, the percentages quoted in Table 2.1 are probably greatly under-estimated. Waste consists of wasted people, wasted effort, wasted space, waste time, waste product and so on. In a complex product, process or organization, a single malfunction can bring the whole system to a halt. In a manufacturing environment, product-related waste is more easily recognized. In service organizations, and support functions in manufacturing companies, waste is less conspicuous. It demands Six Sigma type projects to search out waste and identify and exploit opportunities for improvement.

Typical findings of special Six Sigma type project probes

Surveys have confirmed the actual state of affairs in many sectors. Who would believe, on first thoughts, for instance, that such surveys have found that:

- Twenty-five per cent of tax bills sent out by the Inland Revenue are incorrect.
- There was a 50% error rate in processing completed forms in some Inland Revenue offices:
  - a principal error concerned a 13-digit taxpayer identification code – leaving one taxpayer to pay the bills of another.
- Twenty per cent of the £282 million the Department of Health spent each year on 5000 office personnel was wasted. Instances are:
  - it took 20 civil servants to answer a letter. It had to go through a 72-stage process before it could be signed, sealed and sent;
  - each House of Commons question took 25 Whitehall civil servants 285 min on average and 79 separate transactions to handle;

- – at least three civil servants took minutes of meetings, which were then reviewed by six more before being passed back; in all this required 53 transactions;
- – it took 120 person-hours and £2693 to prepare for a single committee meeting.
- Fourteen million letters a day arrived late or not at all in the UK:
  - – only 69% of first-class mail arrived the next day;
  - – one million letters a week never arrived; most were either delivered to the wrong address or simply dumped.
- Staff errors cost UK organizations £5 billion a year due to literacy and numeracy alone:
  - – Eight out of 10 companies surveyed said failings in reading, writing, verbal communication and simple arithmetic reduced efficiency, hindered adaptation to new technology and contributed to a poor image among customers;
  - – lost business and rectifying mistakes cost small companies (less than 100 staff) £86000 per year and large companies some £500000 per year; half of this loss was on putting right orders that were incorrectly produced or dispatched;
  - – cancellations and loss of business due to errors or misunderstandings accounted for £1.8 billion;
  - – employing staff whose function was to check and approve the work of others cost £530 million.

It should be noted that these figures are survey estimates prior to, and as a basis for, improvement action.

Consider also the computer-based information technology (IT) situation. Fiascoes are continually being reported. In the United Kingdom, Whitehall has been beset with a number of high-tech information technology disasters. Twenty-five such disasters have been identified by members of the British Parliament. These include the National Insurance Recording System that was intended to pay pensions. It ran over 4 years late and cost the taxpayer nearly £90 million to put right. Then there was the Passport Agency's attempt at computerization that left half a million people waiting more than 7 weeks for passports. This cost the taxpayer nearly £13 million. A Benefits Agency anti-fraud system involving the use of smart-cards that would have cost £1.5 billion collapsed in mid-stream. A £319 million contract to computerize the criminal courts has been cut drastically due to software problems, delays and spiraling costs. A well known and respected university also has almost been brought to its knees by taking a knock of £10 million due to a botched attempt to install a new computerized accounting system. At a different level, a user who analysed failures of his Windows 95 operating system recorded one fault every 42 min and 28% reboots.

Other organizations throughout the world are similarly plagued. The entire eastern seaboard of the United States of America lost its telephones for several hours, due to one misplaced statement in a software fix, at a reported cost of some $1 billion. Ariane suffered a disastrous launch due to a similar computer fault that was previously experienced by the shuttle Endeavour.

Opportunities

On the other side of the coin, the nature, extent and severity of such problems give much greater opportunities for improvement and profit enhancement. The size of an organization no longer guarantees continuing success. Neither does a long-established reputation for first-class management, quality and value for money, by itself, guarantee continuing success into the future. Take Marks and Spencer, for example, which has had to rediscover itself. Business managers are becoming aware that the 'excellence' of yesteryear, become the 'commonplace' of today and the 'cast-offs' of tomorrow. Today's and tomorrow's successful organizations will be 'lean' ones, fleet of foot, who anticipate and respond to both internal and external customers needs and expectations. They will have discarded excess baggage, and outmoded principles, procedures and practices, and adopted a world-class approach such as the Six Sigma business strategy.

Whilst most organizations have functional hierarchical structures, products and services are realized and delivered by an interaction of business processes operating cross-functionally. The Six Sigma initiative recognizes and builds on this with its process approach to business improvement.

Six Sigma could not have arrived at a more timely moment. It offers a new way of life whatever the business sector, and whatever the type of organization. It offers a unique solution to many of the opportunities that arise today and can be expected to continue to take place in the future. In such a situation, organizations must quickly adapt or die. Six Sigma provides a ready means for such an adaptation.

Company transformation case study

Background scenario

Take the new Chief Executive who needs to 'turn' a Company that:

- has made a £869 million loss in the past year;
- needs to sell non-core businesses to reduce debt;
- is shedding a significant number of employees with the consequent weakening of the confidence of the remaining workforce in the Group's future;
- continues to trade in a difficult environment with prospects of recovery exacerbated by the tragic events of September 11;
- has a track record of persistent under-performance;
- is embattled by a severe cyclical and economic downturn.

What does he do?

Perform strategic review

What is one of his first significant decisions? A strategy review was launched to determine the best option for creating shareholder value and achieving returns that compare favourably with those of the Group's global peers. The review was rigorous and radical with no preconceptions about the future size or shape of the Company. In conducting the review, customers, business partners, employees and industry experts were listened to at length. Data were collected and analysed relating to markets, competitors, business opportunities and historic performance. Above all, as many as possible of their own people were involved in the review process. A number of strategic alternatives were then tested for their fit with customer demands, their potential for rapid recovery and their ability to deliver the overriding requirement of enhanced shareholder value.

Create a vision: set corporate goals

Following this comprehensive and far-reaching strategic review, he set out a bold vision and ambitious targets to establish a route to profitable growth. To achieve these, he identified the need to cultivate and 'grow' the commitment and contribution of his workforce through the systematic development of latent talent. He also recognized that this required to be coupled with the introduction of a disciplined and highly focused process through which to channel their ensuing contribution to corporate goals. The successful implementation of these two innovative features would ensure that the organization had both the people and processes to achieve the required step change in business performance.

Select critical business functions: establish performance metrics and targets

What next? How best to implement these policies? First, it was considered necessary to determine key areas for concentration of improvement activities. In the strategic review four areas had been established as key to the business. These four areas were *customer development, service delivery, project management* and *lean supply chain*. Second, key performance metrics in each of the four areas were conceived. Key metrics for *customer development* include customer satisfaction and retention, and employee satisfaction. Among targeted customers expectations are a sales growth of 1–2 percentage points, 1–2 points margin improvement and 50% reduction in customer attrition. The prime goals in *service delivery* are to increase countercyclical service revenues by 5–15% of total sales and to improve service margins by 5–10 points as well as achieving higher rates in contract renewals and problem resolution. In *project management*, early pilots indicate the company is on track to achieve increased margins of 2–3 points in the current year on existing projects. Over the subsequent 3 years, the aim is to improve gross margins across the whole project portfolio – currently one-third of all revenues – by up to 10 points, generate positive cash flow through staged payments and contribute strongly to customer retention. The *lean supply chain* initiative is targeting reductions in cost, inventory and the number of suppliers and the formation of stronger strategic partnerships. Its long-term objective is a 1–2 point in overall Group margin.

Systematically transform the business

Create project-based company-wide programme deploying performance-improvement teams

Having established the focus areas, performance metrics and overall benchmark criteria, by what means are these to be achieved? The organization decided that delivery demanded a systematic transformation of the way they did business. They set out to place this change in the hands of all their employees by way of a project-based company-wide programme deploying performance-improvement teams. The rationale for this was that this would provide employee ideas for local and cross-business performance improvements of the structure and skills necessary to deliver results to the 'bottom line'. Over 1000 project leaders are being trained to take on specific projects. Over 650 potential performance improvements, nominated either spontaneously from the business or in response to strategic initiatives are already being tracked. This programme is intended to run up to 4 years.

Principal aims, approaches and features in each of the areas of focus are:

1 *Lean supply chain.* A review of the Group's £2.6 billion spend and 20 000 supplier base indicates that the quickest way to achieve savings is in the reduction of inventories and the identification of commodities that can be sourced on a Group-wide basis. Some 60 sourcing teams are being established to achieve this. The Group's hundreds of 'Six Sigma black-belts', specialists in improving performance, will tackle problem areas and spread 'lean' initiatives. Supply chain management throughout the Group will be continuously benchmarked in a effort to drive improved business performance and the spread of best practice.

2 *Project management.* It is known that an increase in profit margins can be achieved by delivering on time and to budget. Project management champions have been nominated across the Group. Four areas form the immediate field of focus. These are: the correction of underperforming projects; placing each project under the stewardship of an accountable senior manager; improving bid and tender management; and preventing changes to project scope. It is intended to develop consistency in project excellence through training and mentoring packages for hundreds of project managers.

3 *Service delivery.* A key to improved customer satisfaction and the provision of high-quality earnings lies in the strengthening and expanding the nature of the Group's customer relationships. To drive this the service initiative team is building a Group-wide network of experts. It has benchmarked best practice internally and externally to create a model encompassing technical support, call centres, spare parts logistics, field operations, dispatch and marketing.

4 *Customer development.* The development of closer relationships with the Group's 165 000 customers is considered to be an essential part of the drive

to improve business performance. This demands a clearer understanding of key customer issues, to manage customer relationships more effectively and to consistently deliver to customer expectations. To achieve this, a customer-development team is engaging with every business to improve their planning, sales processes and customer information systems. As well as a focus on strategic accounts, the aim is to raise the capability of the Group in all customer relations by driving best practice across the businesses and removing barriers to cross-selling.

Business expectation

At the end of this time, the Company expects a minimum annualized profit benefit of £200 million. Any upturn in the global economy or the Company's particular markets will increase this figure. In the first year of operation, the minimum profit enhancement considered tolerable is £50 million net. This represents a one-for-one return on the budgeted programme costs in the period. However, the aim is to double that return. This programme is designed to provide the engine to spread best practice across the organization and ensure effective management of a large number of initiatives. An Intranet-based tracking system has been developed to monitor projects and share expertise on a transparent Company-wide basis.

Reference: Invensys summary financial statement: 2002.

Results achieved by organizations already committed to Six Sigma

General results

Experience has shown that in the application of Six Sigma, some 25% reduction of the cost of non-conformance (CONC) alone can be expected to be achieved by projects aimed at 'low hanging fruit' that is there for the plucking, say, by green belt led teams. A further 65+% requires a higher degree of diagnostic effort, say, by black belt led teams. This leaves a small amount of non-conformance related projects with a higher degree of technical intractability that require a greater up-front investment to secure a positive result. This is illustrated in Figure 2.1.

Of course, there are also the upstream and value-enhancement projects to tackle that have higher leverage. These will relate to the optimization of the offering in terms of customer needs and expectations, and the application of Six Sigma to value analysis/engineering of the design and realization (manufacturing, assembly, operational and service). This aspect is covered in Chapter 4.

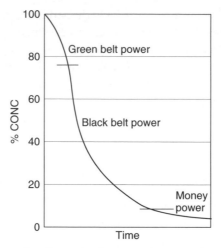

Figure 2.1 The journey to Six Sigma by the cost of non-conformance route

Specific results

Results from organizations committed to Six Sigma indicate that the financial benefits make a very significant effect on the 'bottom line'. An early USA convert to Six Sigma, the Chief Executive Officer of General Electric at the time, Jack Welch, quoted

> Six Sigma is the most important initiative that GE has ever undertaken. It is part of the genetic code of our future leadership.

Whilst the crest of the Six Sigma wave is high and powerful, as yet, in the United States of America, somewhat less than 15% of the *Fortune 1000* are using it in a significant way. The American Society for Quality (ASQ) are fully committed and running with it. They have trained more than 1500 people in over 150 organizations and are promoting the Six Sigma initiative with vigour. In the United Kingdom, the Institute of Quality Assurance have established a training liaison with ASQ on Six Sigma.

In the quoting of claimed savings, readers will appreciate that these figures are, in the main, generated from within a particular organization. As such they have not, generally, been subjected to independent scrutiny or validated by responsible third parties. Hence, readers are advised to compare claimed Six Sigma savings with business benchmarks. For instance, Schneiderman (Howell, D., 2001) has posed a question relating to the Six Sigma claims of Motorola. He asks where did the billions of dollars saved by Six Sigma go? It does not appear to be reflected in its overall business performance relative to its peers.

Of course, quite a different question could have been posed. What or where would Motorola be now if it had not deployed Six Sigma? One might also ask what of the failures in instituting Six Sigma? There obviously have been some, but actual admissions are hard to come by. In any event such failures appear to be related more to the lack of top management leadership and involvement, rather than through weaknesses in the Six Sigma approach itself. In some cases, this has been due to a forced management preoccupation in ensuring survival of the organization in the face of a sudden cataclysmic downturn in the business situation. This may be quite understandable from the point of view of traditional management, but does not reflect an appreciation of the potential of Six Sigma as exemplified in the Invensys company transformation case study described earlier in the chapter.

There are considerable savings claimed through the practising of Six Sigma. Motorola, the initial champions of Six Sigma, credit it with over $4 billion manufacturing cost savings and a doubling of productivity over a period of 6 years. General Electric has claimed the following benefits from the application of Six Sigma:

- reduced quality costs from 20% to less than 10% of sales;
- saved $300 million in the first year of Six Sigma, rising to $2 billion in the third year;
- operating margins stuck at about 10% for decades soared to 16.7% in less than 3 years.

These results come from the most treasured business in the United States of America, then run by 'the manager of the century', Jack Welch. Neutron Jack took GE, an unfashionable conglomerate, from $14 billion in 1980 to $530 billion. In Welch's own words, GE became the 'fastest elephant at the dance'.

At Allied Signal, the CEO, Larry Bossidy, has been quoted as saying:

> We have taken the basic Six Sigma skill of reducing faults and applied it to every business process, from inventing and commercialising a new product all the way to billing and collection after the product is delivered. Just as we think we've generated the last dollar of profit out of the business we uncover new ways to harvest cash as we reduce cycle times, lower inventories, increase output and reduce scrap. The results are a better and more competitively priced product, more satisfied customers who give us more business and improved cash flow.

At *Allied Signal*, thousands of employees have been trained in Six Sigma with the goal of increasing productivity by 6% per year. In actuality, it is claimed that an increase of some 14% was achieved with a saving in excess of $2 billion in direct costs. This represents about 6% of sales revenue. At Polaroid, the CEO, Gary DiCamillo, announced his vision for the 'Polaroid Renewal' initiative as 'improved product quality, an expanding customer base, increased profitability and continual growth'. The initial results were a 50% reduction in time to bring

Table 2.2 Effect of a 50% reduction in waste on profit margin

Item	Initial situation	After Six Sigma project
Sales	£10 m	£10 m
Cost of Sales	£9 m	£8.65 m
Waste	£0.7 m	£0.35 m
Profit	£1 m	£1.35 m
Profit	10%	13.5%

Note: actual figures have been rounded for clarity of understanding the concept.

product from inception to market, whilst adding 6% to its 'bottom line' each year. The business reorientation within Asea Brown Boveri with Six Sigma resulted in a 68% reduction in fault levels and a 30% reduction in product costs, which led to a near $9000 million savings per year.

Such breathtaking accomplishments can only be expected in an organization totally committed to the Six Sigma business strategy and that has successfully deployed it. However, very significant savings are being realized by European organizations who are dipping their toes in the Six Sigma water. The effect of the halving of detected waste in an already good practice European organization is shown in Table 2.2. It is seen that it has the same effect on the 'bottom line' as increasing sales by £3.5 million. This indicates that such Six Sigma projects can be particularly effective even in a static or declining marketplace.

Six Sigma does not require significant capital expenditure other than for investment in the training and development of the participants in the process. It does, however, require long-term commitment from the management in the ongoing process of continual improvement through active interest, support and review and the provision of appropriate resources. However, financial benefits should begin to be experienced with the completion of the first set of projects undertaken. Results from organizations committed to Six Sigma indicate that the financial benefits make a very significant effect on the 'bottom line'.

Response to competition

A leading product manufacturer, Company x, is totally committed to Six Sigma world wide. From a competitive standpoint the reasons for this are illustrated in Figure 2.2. It is predicted that world-class competition will have further enhanced customer satisfaction within 5 years. The historical trend within the

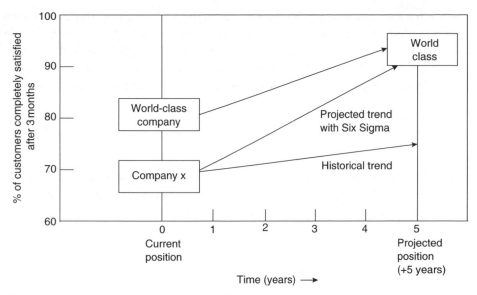

Figure 2.2 Recognition of need for Six Sigma to beat competition

organization is inadequate to other than maintain the present situation. The conclusion was that a world-wide Six Sigma initiative was needed to increase the projected trend in customer satisfaction to world-class standards.

Another example is from the automotive field. BMW recognizes that it and its supply base are constantly confronted with the complex demands of a global market. As such this requires:

> adaptation to permanent change and a constant optimization process.

There is a constant customer expectation of cost reductions. This means higher supplier 'base competencies' in terms of cost performance (year on year cost reductions and productivity improvements); quality performance (consistently within specification); and delivery performance (on time, in full). Implications for suppliers are the need to develop such competencies, to commit to continual improvement and to invest in people and skill development. In return, suppliers can expect business continuity leading to long-term partnerships.

Improving employee involvement and engagement

New technologies are continually emerging and the scope and speed of the 'information revolution' is radically changing the shape of our life and jobs. Employees are no longer expecting job security for life as a right. Even in Japan the 'job for life' culture is on the change. There the *madogiwazoku* (those who have been retained in limbo) are coming to terms with the new practice of *katatataki* (getting the tap on the shoulder that says farewell). Employees are realizing that job tenure is increasingly related to the continuing success of their organization, which, in turn, depends on their increasing contribution to the organization:

> This gives rise to an employee expectation for opportunities for 'in the job' competency development coupled with the empowerment to make improvements happen.

Are their expectations currently being met? Studies indicate not in many organizations. This provides another two good reasons for implementing Six Sigma. Six Sigma is aimed at achieving both competency development in, and empowerment of, employees.

Continuing high cost of quality

It is generally accepted that most organizations are not aware of the extent of their quality costs. To determine the potential viability of Six Sigma in reducing quality costs, it is first necessary to quantify these costs in monetary terms. A business will then be in a position to assess the predicted impact of Six Sigma on the reduction of these costs. It is suggested that those contemplating the introduction of Six Sigma in their organization, together with those who are already committed and are prioritizing projects for deployment, first assess the nature and extent of their quality costs. A number of models are available for this.

What are quality costs?

Just what is meant by quality costs can be the subject of unlimited discussion. There are three principal quality cost models that breakdown quality costs into distinct components. These are:

- the PAF (prevention, appraisal, failure) model;
- the process COC (cost of conformance) and CONC (cost of non-conformance) models;
- the Error Source model.

These models are illustrated in Figure 2.3.

PAF model

In the PAF model, the costs are:

- Prevention cost [P]: the cost of any action taken to investigate, prevent or reduce the risk of non-conformity.

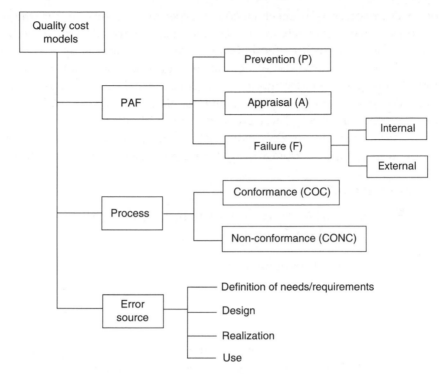

Figure 2.3 The three quality cost models

- Appraisal cost [A]: the cost of evaluating the achievement of quality requirements, for example, inspection and test.
- Failure costs [F] however caused, reduce profits. Failure cost is usually split into two components – internal failure and external failure:
  - *internal failure cost*: the cost arising within the organization due to non-conformities;
  - *external failure cost*: the cost arising after delivery of the product or service due to non-conformities.

Prevention costs, and to a large extent, appraisal costs are *discretionary*. They cost money to deploy. Here, we are looking for justification and cost-effectiveness. It can be argued that failure costs are *avoidable* by getting the right things done right the first time.

Process model

In the more modern process model the costs are made up of two components, both of which offer Six Sigma opportunities for improvement:

- *Cost of conformance* [COC]: the intrinsic cost of providing products or services to defined standards. This does not imply that the process is efficient in terms of, or even necessary to meet, customer expectations. For example, the cost of 'over design' is rarely measured let alone analysed with a view to improvement. When it is, the indications are that it makes up a very substantial part of total costs. A significant proportion of avoidable costs is found to lie upstream. Design for Six Sigma methods such as quality function deployment and value analysis methodology can be very useful here to the Six Sigma black belt. These are discussed in Chapter 4.

● *Cost of non-conformance* [CONC]: the cost of waste, for example, arising from unsatisfactory inputs, errors arising during processing and rejected outputs.

Error source model

The error source model relates errors back to their various sources. The various sources typically are along the lines:

● S1: definition of needs/requirements;
● S2: design;
● S3: realization;
● S4: use.

The error source model focuses on identifying the cost (in £, $, person-days, etc.) of errors associated with its stage or a preceding stage; thus

● a figure in the box S4:S4 indicates the cost in £ (or other unit of measure) related to an error detected at S4 due to an error committed at S4;
● similarly S1:S4 indicates the cost of an error at S4 (use) attributed to S1 (definition of needs/requirements).

Example

Some results are given in Table 2.3 for the application of the error source model in an IT area. Establish priorities for a Six Sigma project.

Table 2.3 Results matrix for error source model in information technology area

	S1	*S2*	*S3*	*S4*	*Total*
S1	1	4	3	14	22
S2		3	2	7	12
S3			1	6	7
S4				1	1
Total	1	7	6	28	42

Conclusions drawn from the matrix (Table 2.3) are:

1 Fifty-two per cent of the person-day reworking was traced to errors in S1 (definition of needs/requirements).
2 Sixty-four per cent of the man-days rework did not manifest itself until after implementation (at S4). Hence, the error detection processes at stages S1–S3 are deemed inefficient.

These two matters could well form the basis for a Six Sigma project.

Concerns that sometimes needs to be addressed are the multiple-ownership issue; behavioural factors such as people 'defend their own corner'; and that the identification of the primary source of an error is often a matter of judgement. Consequently, this model works better in an 'error friendly' culture. Note the difference between being error friendly and error tolerant.

What impact does quality costs have on business performance?

Surveys indicate that the cost of quality, as measured, very frequently far exceeds profit margins on sales. This is so even when it is appreciated that the measurements are revealing just the 'tip of the iceberg'. As such, quality costs usually represent a 'gold mine' for improvement activities. We have seen that for organizations operating at a three Sigma level of performance quality costs can reach 25–40% of turnover and even some 15–25% of sales at the four Sigma level, the industry average level. In most organizations these costs are buried under a variety of uninformative overheads, grossly underestimated and debits in one area are hidden by credits in another. Bringing them out in the open will clearly indicate the order of priority of Six Sigma projects to reduce losses and provide a control to ensure that gains are permanently held.

Is there an economics of quality or is quality free?

Phil Crosby, on the one hand, contends that quality is not a gift but it is free. What costs money are the non-quality things – all the actions that involve not doing jobs 'right the first time'. He asserts that every penny you do not spend on doing things wrong goes right to the 'bottom line'. If we concentrate on achieving 'first-time quality' it will probably double the profits of our organization. He says that is a lot of money for free. He further claims that people throughout any organization can take practical, non-technical steps to prevent those 'miscalculated invoices', 'computer programming errors', 'lost mail', 'dirty crockery', and the like. Crosby's perception is that there is no such thing as the economics of quality. It is always cheaper to do the job right the first time. Joseph Juran (Juran, J. and Gryna, F., 1980) takes quite a different

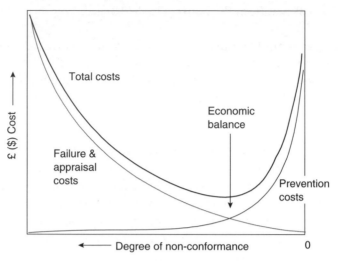

Figure 2.4 Economic model shows that there is an optimum to the cost of conformance

view. His view is expressed in the well-known model of the 'economics of conformance', on which Figure 2.4 is based.

To the right of the optimum, or economic balance point, it is suggested that improvement projects tend to be uneconomic due to perfectionism. To the left of the optimum we have the zone for improvement projects. Around the optimum is the zone of indifference, here we should control not improve.

Frank Price (Price, F., 1985), on the other hand, calls this type of economic model: 'the mathematics of mediocrity; the doctrine of the second rate'.

What should be done about these seemingly opposing schools of thought? In reality, there is little need to take sides or make a decision on the 'perfectionist approach versus the economic approach'. The reason is that, in practice, these two schools of thought merge together as all organizations have a significant number of processes that are well to the left of the economic balance point. Even these have to be prioritized. In real life we need to heed two fundamentals.

First, we should bear in mind that there are 'horses for courses'. What is appropriate in one situation is not in another. In some circumstances, for example, in risk-taking environments such as innovation, research and development, it is vital for people to be free to make mistakes along the way, otherwise creativity is stifled. Take Thomas Eddison the famous inventor who invented the incandescent lamp amongst other things. He responded thus to the remark that he had failed 25 000 times while experimenting with the electric storage battery. 'No, I didn't fail', he replied, 'I discovered 24 999 ways that the storage battery doesn't work'.

There are many other well-known sayings on this subject. An apt one, by Samuel Smiles is: 'We often discover what will do, by finding out what will not do; and probably he who never made a mistake never made a discovery'.

On the other hand, there is the tongue in cheek maxim: 'Lord deliver me from the man who never makes a mistake, and also from the man who makes the same mistake twice' (William Mayo). This freedom, however, is not intended to relieve personnel of their responsibilities to act in a professionally responsible manner.

Of course, in routine tasks, error-free performance is vitally important. Frequently, it is necessary to lower the tolerance level of people to the acceptance that a certain amount of error is acceptable, that 'it is a way of life here', that it is budgeted for anyhow. The acceptance that the current level of mistakes is inevitable is not an acceptable operating philosophy if we are just to survive in today's economic climate. However, in this respect, one should bear in mind that there are many reasons for making errors not just those due to want of attention or lack of appropriate attitude. These different reasons for error need to be responded to, by Six Sigma personnel, by taking countermeasures appropriate to the particular cause. This is discussed later.

Second, in practice, Six Sigma projects aimed at the reduction of quality costs should always be selected and prioritized on the basis of feasibility in terms of technical tractability and a reasonable return on investment.

Case study 1

Surveys conducted in the United States of America concluded that costs of product faults alone far exceeded the profit margin on sales over a cross-section of industries. Summary results are given in Table 2.4.

Table 2.4 indicates that known failure costs, which can be expected to represent only the tip of the iceberg, can reach up to nearly five times the profit margins. This indicates considerable scope for continual-improvement processes.

Table 2.4 Failure costs in relation to profit margin over a range of industry

Industry	Median failure costs (% of sales)	Median profit (% of sales)
Aluminium die casting	5.7	2.3
Confectionery	6.9	4.7
Commercial printing	6.5	4.2
Electronic components	7.3	4.1
Household appliances	6.9	2.5
Industrial machinery	7.6	3.5
Garden equipment	6.8	2.2
Plastic products	7.4	1.5
Sport goods	6.9	4.0

Case study 2

A similar situation prevails in Europe. In one organization quality costs are reported by the Comptroller of the organization in standard format. The organization is split into a number of operating divisions dealing with different product ranges. Typical such costs are shown in Table 2.5, which shows a wide variation both in the extent of the reported costs and their nature. It should be noted that Table 2.5 ignores over-design and the lack of effectiveness and efficiency or otherwise of processes throughout the organization, giving rise to conformity costs. Obviously, any Six Sigma initiative, aimed at the 'bottom line', would have a different focus from division to division. Hence, we need to be very careful about stereotyping the approach to Six Sigma: this even within a single organization.

Case study 3

Let us turn now to quite a different sector, that of a well-known European clothing retailer noted for its high-quality merchandise. Typical annual drainage due to quality losses in part of the supply chain are shown in Table 2.6. It is seen that these selected quality losses alone extend to over 11% of turnover. Other types of

Table 2.5 Range of extent and nature of visible quality costs within one organization

Type of product	*% of output**		
	Inspection & test (appraisal)	*Failures*	
		In works	*Ex works*
Small transformers	6.3	1.2	1.1
Rectifier	1.7	1.1	4.0
Small industrial motors	0.9	1.9	0.6
Foundry	?	75.8	?
Commercial diesel	4.1	1.9	0.8
Professional diesel	12.5	5.4	5.2
Steam turbines	30.6	24.2	109.6
Traction	3.5	1.6	2.0
Switch-gear	2.1	0.3	0.8
Instruments	13.8	4.0	1.0
Power generators	38.3	56.9	5.5
Aircraft equipment	6.0	5.3	3.0

*Based on estimate analysis of costs prior to margins.

Table 2.6 Selected quality losses sustained on one generic range in the supply chain of a major retail organization

Wastage	*£m per year*
Returns to manufacturers	6
Seconds	14
Rework	8
Inspection	50
Total	£78 m

Note: sales output = £706 million per year.

quality losses and the losses sustained by other than first-tier suppliers (e.g. those who supply cloth, buttons, threads and the like to first-tier suppliers) are not included. The picture presented by this evidence illustrates the opportunities for continual improvement in a supply chain offered by initiatives such as Six Sigma.

Case study 4

Take the case of a particular detergent supplier. An example of the quality lever effect is evidenced by the adverse impact on business performance caused by a single marketing/research blunder. Rotting of clothes was attributed to a manganese component in a particular washing powder:

- £57 million write off of stocks of discredited product;
- £200 million cost of development at launch;
- reduced European profits by 16%;
- unknown cost of damage limitation programme.

Our quality costs are nowhere near as high as those quoted

The typical reaction of a 'captain of industry or commerce' to the order of quality costs mentioned might well be 'No way! I don't have one process approaching a yield as low as that quoted. Go bug someone else with your half baked notions'. How does one respond to such a reaction? Try this. 'We are not talking the same language! The actual fault rate on product-related processes can lead one sadly astray'. Take a few examples in three different types of companies:

- In one engineering company only some 2.7% of invoices are queried by their customers, yet over 50% of the time of the sales force is taken up in placating irate customers.

- In a clothing factory, rework and seconds were running at under 5%, yet over 80% of the time of the supervisors was spent in dealing with matters arising from that 5%.
- In a bank, only 0.8% of the cheques failed to be processed successfully by the automated equipment, yet much more manual time was taken to process the 0.8% faulty than to process the 99.2% dealt with automatically.

Remember also that the cost of quality is not just about enduring excessive costs due to chronic quality/reliability wastage. Let us now reflect on another aspect. What do you think caused the demise of such UK industries as the motor cycle, shipbuilding, machine tool and consumer electronics? Could the answer be: lack of appreciation of the market, lack of strategic quality planning, not listening to the 'voice of the customer'?

Recognition that other improvement initiatives have been fragmented or short-lived

A number of continuous-improvement initiatives have been very successful over the years. Most, however, have been short-lived or fragmented in their approach. The short-life effect has persisted even with extremely well-conceived initiatives. This is likened to a space probe that has failed to achieve lift-off velocity to escape the pull of the earth. Organizations also behave in this way. It is termed resistance to cultural change. Other initiatives have been, and are, highly fragmented in their application. The Six Sigma initiative does not try to reinvent the wheel in the use of tools. What is does is to integrate the best available problem-solving and process-improvement tools into best practice teamwork and management targeted on achieving world-class benchmark standards. The result is to provide an 'effective and efficient'[1] business improvement initiative involving a well-trained critical mass of focused people.

It has to be appreciated that technical merit is, in itself, not sufficient to achieve continuing success in this area. This is illustrated in the quadrant of Figure 2.5.

If an organization lying in the lower left quadrant in Figure 2.5 does not initiate a transformation such as Six Sigma, all one can say is 'rest in peace'. In the lower right-hand quadrant lies the organization that is technically able but lacks the willingness, or ability, to motivate and harness its workforce. It can be extremely successful in conducting isolated technically manned projects aimed at continual improvement. However, it is likely that a fair proportion of the workforce just put enough effort into their work to hold their job. In the top

---

[1]Effective implies 'doing the right things'. Efficient refers to 'doing things well'. Effective and efficient relates to 'doing the right things well'.

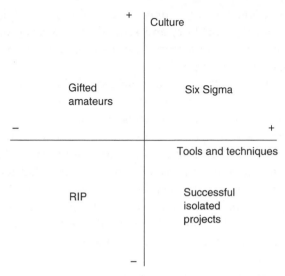

Figure 2.5 Quadrant of organization in terms of culture and techniques

left-hand quadrant is the gifted amateur, the organization that lacks the technical expertise but operates a friendly workplace environment.

All such organizations will benefit from migrating to the top right-hand quadrant where a critical mass of the workforce are motivated, trained and focused on the needs of the business. Experience shows that it is normally harder to move upwards than across the quadrant. This indicates that considerable emphasis need to be placed on the cultural side of Six Sigma, as well as the technical side, if it is to be a continuing force for improvement.

Any initiative may need little more than a spark, a marketing or motivational edge to start it off, but something to sustain the effort in the longer term in the face of the existing 'culture' of an organization is quite another issue. Every organization has its own collection of habits, beliefs and practices. These represent its culture. Resistance to change of this culture is extremely strong from many different sources.

Management and supervision may see any initiative as a new 'ball-game', one that they have not played before. They may well feel that their existing skills, knowledge, expertise and abilities that give them mastery over their present job will disappear. This could all be jeopardized. They will have to go back to square one and learn quite a new 'ball-game' where they may not come out on top.

Technical people who live within a vertical hierarchical organizational structure based on functions could well baulk at being caught up in any initiative that focuses on any cross-functional approach that cuts across existing boundaries. Their perceived unalienable right to make technical decisions without question could well be violated. The acquisition of the tools of their trade by the development of hither-to up-stream competencies in non-upstream personnel could be looked upon as a two-edged sword. First, as a degradation of the status of the up-stream function, and second, the expectation of a resulting intervention in, and even interference with up-stream decision-making brought about by any participative approach.

Staff or personnel generally may be so accustomed to purely doing a routine job that they have become so conditioned to their impotence in changing things that they largely switch off mentally whilst at work.

Obviously, a marked change in culture is required to sustain any continuous-improvement initiative. This change is perhaps more readily brought about in a 'life or death' situation even if the options are somewhat more limited. It is much more difficult in an organization that feels reasonably comfortable in how it is doing at the moment. Being easier does not make it right. The secret is to make the change before one is forced to. Being proactive, rather than reactive, opens up the possibilities and options considerably. We would not attempt to sow flower seeds on concrete. Neither can we expect to establish, nurture and sustain a continuous-improvement initiative in an organization that has a culture that inhibits innovation in the way it operates. The Six Sigma initiative recognizes these facts of life. It weaves changes into the present way of working in an organization in a multi-pronged manner. It:

- creates a vision, a gleam in the eye, by benchmarking against world-class standards: this to inspire and guide;
- develops competencies in appropriate improvement methods in a critical mass of people;
- builds and activates teams focused on improving business performance and customer satisfaction;
- creates a novel supportive and sustaining infrastructure in the form of 'Judo' belts that is intended also to enthuse, motivate and energize participants.

Other reasons for implementing Six Sigma are the expectation that it will stimulate and revitalize a critical mass of people in the organization to seek out and exploit improvement activities aimed at improving organizational performance and to sustain this activity into the future.

Chapter highlights

There are a number of sound reasons why consideration should be given to deploying Six Sigma in an organization. These include:

- the need to continually improve organizational effectiveness and efficiency just even to hold station in a rapidly changing world and with the increasing demands of the marketplace,

- the extent of waste in non-world-class organizations and the opportunities this provides,
- to turn an organization that faces deep-seated problems,
- the results achieved by organizations already committed to Six Sigma,
- to increase the rate of improvement over that of competition and to progressively meet more exacting customer needs and expectations,
- vastly improve employee involvement and engagement over current levels through competency development and active participation in Six Sigma projects,
- distinguish between and exploit the different types of cost of quality models,
- quantify and segregate these costs of quality to confirm the need for improvements and to establish monetary benchmarks and priorities for action for Six Sigma project teams,
- recognize that most previous improvement initiatives have been fragmented or relatively short-lived and hence perceive the need to embed the Six Sigma initiative into the 'blood stream' of the business.

Bibliography

Howell, D. (2001). At sixes and sevens, *Professional Engineering*, May, pp. 27–28.
Juran, J. and Gryna, F. (1980). *Quality planning and analysis*, New York: McGraw-Hill, pp. 26–28.
Price, F. (1985). *Right first time*, London: Gower.

Chapter 3
How does Six Sigma compare with other improvement initiatives?

Resolve to perform what you ought; perform without fail what you resolve

Stonewall Jackson

Overview

A number of improvement initiatives are, or have been at some time, in common currency. These are described at the appreciation level and compared with the Six Sigma process. It will be noted that Six Sigma adopts, and builds upon, many of the best-practice methods and practices applied in other initiatives. It is unique, however, in respect of its enabling and perpetuating infrastructure of 'Judo' belts. It also aims to combine and refocus a whole range of improvement tools that, hitherto, have been largely deployed in a fragmented manner. This fragmentation of deployment of various tools and techniques in a number of organizations is illustrated in Figure 3.1. Such organizations do not deploy these very useful methods in a cohesive manner.

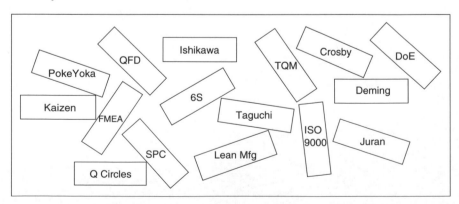

Figure 3.1   Fragmented deployment of improvement tools prior to Six Sigma

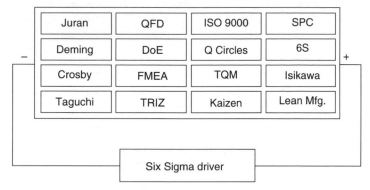

Figure 3.2 Six Sigma as an orientating mechanism for selected elements of various approaches

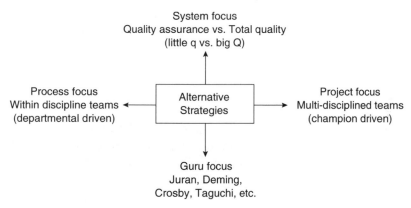

Figure 3.3 Selection of alternative strategic approaches to improvement

Figure 3.2 portrays the Six Sigma process as one that orientates a number of existing, seemingly disparate, practices towards a common goal. The result is seen as a cohesive set of existing practices, focused, marshalled, driven and managed by a unique Six Sigma infrastructure.

Which strategy to deploy?

A number of different strategies can be deployed in quality-improvement processes. A selection of the principal ones is shown in Figure 3.3. It will be seen that Six Sigma embodies all four approaches to a greater or lesser degree.

Table 3.1   Any system approach to Six Sigma should be a Big Q rather than a little q one

Quality focus	Little q	Big Q
Applicability	Manufacturing only	All products, processes and services
Scope	Technical concern related to ultimate customer	Business concern related to all customers; internal and external
Attitude	Reactive after the event control Preservation of the status quo	Proactive preventive approach Continual improvement
Evaluation	Conformance to requirement	Satisfaction of customer needs and expectations
Responsibility	Rely on quality department	Company wide contribution
Competency	Quality people experts in quality	Company wide expertise in quality
What is waste?	Costs associated with deficient manufacture	All costs that would disappear if the right things happen right first time

System focus

Six Sigma takes the 'total quality' as opposed to the more restricted 'quality assurance' system focus route. Juran (Juran, J., 1992), very aptly, terms this 'big Q' as opposed to 'little q'. Big Q and little q are compared in Table 3.1.

Process and project focus

The process and project focus strategies shown in Figure 3.3 relate to team-driven quality-improvement initiatives. In the process or workplace focus, quality-improvement teams are usually made up of people, often of similar disciplines, who work in a particular area. The majority of 'quality circles' and 'kaizen teams' are constituted in this way. Once set up, a team will continue in existence taking on quality-improvement tasks as a daily routine. On the other hand, the project focus approach involves the setting up of project-specific teams, usually multi-disciplined. Each team is established uniquely for each project.

In Six Sigma, both process and project strategies are deployed. These are most effective when the organization already has a good housekeeping system (e.g. ISO 9001 or its sector prescriptive equivalents) and its culture has been shaped and methods previously honed by a commitment to one, or other, of the Gurus (or other form of continual improvement initiative).

Guru focus

A number of well-known and respected gurus have developed their own approaches to continual improvement.

Which Guru, if any, do we follow in applying Six Sigma? A number of issues need addressing before attempting to deal with this question. Probably, the best-known US quality gurus are Deming, Juran and Crosby. All three are concerned with business-performance improvement. They have the same destination in mind but take different routes. If we were to consider adopting the approach of a particular guru it would be well to bear in mind that no one individual has a monopoly of wisdom. We should study them all. Select what is relevant; discard what is not appropriate. Adapt as is necessary. This is the view taken in this book in the proposed method of deployment of Six Sigma. Probably, the most important thing to be said here is:

> build on what you already have.

This statement may appear so simplistic to the point of being quite naive. However, it is said for a particular reason. Even large multinational organizations ignore this quite basic fundamental issue. Take one such organization, recently committed to Six Sigma, as a case in point. This organization has been a pioneer in the development of continual-improvement methodology in their own divisions and in their supply bases world-wide. They have now turned to Six Sigma. In their training of Six Sigma belts they:

- focus almost exclusively on reactive problem-solving at the expense of proactive process improvement;
- they dismiss Cps and Cpks for measured data and per cent non-conforming for attribute data and the importance, diagnostically, of establishing patterns of variation, by taking the retrograde step of using the ubiquitous *Sigma* as the sole means of performance measurement;
- instead of using the term concerns they now unthinkingly talk in terms of defects when, for years, this has been a proscribed word in the organization in view of its product liability implications (of which the organization has had considerable adverse experience).

Think of the adverse effect of this U-turn in both a technical sense and in a personal one. This apparently mindless prescription of what is perceived to be Six Sigma medicine progressively undermines that which has taken many years to build. It is vitally important that Six Sigma implementers and trainers do not get totally taken in with the commercial hype associated with the Six Sigma measure. One needs to keep switched on mentally. Recognize the marketing and motivational reasons for the term Six Sigma, whilst at the same time recognizing that this gives one a wonderful opportunity to further develop, weave in, deploy and exploit best practice: not to degrade existing practice.

Think also of the adverse effect of this U-turn on business performance of both the organization and its world-wide supply base.

Surveys in the United States of America indicate that top management there has tended to adopt, or adapt, Crosby's 14-step improvement process, as the basis of their overall corporate quality management system, more frequently than that of other Gurus. Why is this? Is there a lesson to be learned here in respect to Six Sigma? The prime reason for this was considered to be because his system fitted in well with the existing US management culture. Other reasons, too, probably come into play. Perhaps US management is taken by Crosby's simple, non-technical, inspirational message.

Juran, the professional's professional, is stated to have said of Crosby, 'I do not regard Crosby as an expert on quality. He is an expert in PR. He is a combination of P.T. Barnum and the Pied Piper.' Perchance the content of this derogatory remark may indeed reveal the secret of success in promoting novel concepts such as Six Sigma. The Crosby approach has had considerable influence in the development of continual-improvement processes. However, it is now generally accepted that it serves as just one possible platform on which to build a more mature quality system. Principal views of selected Gurus, of particular relevance to Six Sigma, are outlined in Table 3.2. They contain many 'pearls of wisdom'. As such they should be considered for inclusion in any Six Sigma training and development programme and initiative as contenders for 'best practice'.

The prime differences in the ideologies of Crosby, Juran and Deming can be summarized thus:

- Crosby uses a top-down approach based on quality costs with the aim of zero defects. He provides a well-defined road-map for implementation of his continual-improvement initiative.
- Deming uses a top-down (14 obligations), bottom-up (SPC) approach that provides pressure on the middle. He demands a total commitment that takes years to implement fully.

Table 3.2 Summary of principal concepts of selected gurus in relation to Six Sigma

Guru	Principal ideas/concepts of relevance to Six Sigma
Deming	14 points; PDCA circle; 8 obstacles to transformation; 5 deadly sins
Juran	Quality trilogy; 6-stage planning; 7-stage control; 8-stage improvement
Crosby	4 absolutes; 6 C's of improvement; 14-step improvement process
Feigenbaum	3 management commitments; 4 forces
Taguchi	Design improvement and problem-solving using experimentation projects

- Juran focuses on 'return on investment' rather than zero defects. His approach is appealing to middle and technical management.

In the Six Sigma improvement process, these ideologies should be looked upon as valuable 'navigational aids', as exemplars of world-class practice, rather than a particular 'boat to board'.

ISO 9000:2000 family of quality systems standards

General

The re-jigged International Standards Organization's ISO 9000 family of quality management systems standards is vying for 'No. 1 spot', at least in terms of information load, with the USA-originated Six Sigma initiative. The intent of this ISO 9000 family of standards is to assist organizations, of all types and sizes, to implement and operate effective quality-management systems.

ISO 9000:2000 (ISO TC 176, 2000) describes fundamentals of quality management systems and specifies the coherent and harmonized vocabulary that is essential for a correct interpretation of the terms used in its sister standards.

- ISO 9001:2000 (ISO TC 176, 2000) specifies requirements for a process-based quality-management system where an organization needs to demonstrate its ability to provide products that fulfil customer and applicable regulatory requirements. The term product is used throughout in its broadest sense and encompasses services as well as software, hardware and processed materials. The quality system requirements stated are generic and are intended to be applicable in any industry or economic sector. ISO 9001:2000, itself, does not establish requirements for products.

ISO 9004:2000 (ISO TC 176, 2000) provides guidelines that consider both the effectiveness and efficiency of the quality-management system. The aim of this standard is improvement of the performance of the organization and satisfaction of customers and interested parties who have an interest in the success of the organization.

ISO 19011:2002 (ISO TC 176 and TC 207, 2002) provides appropriate information on the auditing of quality- and environmental-management systems.

Together they are intended to form a coherent set of quality-management system standards facilitating mutual understanding in national and international trade. The widespread acceptance of this family of standards is shown by the fact that over 300 000 certificates have been issued to organizations in over 150 countries by various accreditation and registration bodies.

Quality-management principles

The ISO 9000:2000 family of standards is based on eight quality-management principles. These principles are seen to be fully compatible with the objectives and approach deployed in the Six Sigma process.

The eight principles, shown in Table 3.3, are:

1 *Customer focus*: organizations depend on their customers and, therefore, should understand current and future customer needs, meet customer requirements and strive to exceed customer expectations.
2 *Leadership*: leaders establish unity of purpose and the direction of the organization. They should create and maintain an internal environment in which people can become fully involved in achieving the organization's objectives.
3 *Involvement of people*: people at all levels are the essence of an organization, and their full involvement enables their abilities to be used for the organization's benefit.
4 *Process approach*: a desired result is achieved more efficiently when related resources and activities are managed as a process.
5 *System approach to management*: identifying, understanding and managing a system of inter-related processes for a given objective improves the organization's effectiveness and efficiency.
6 *Continual improvement*: continual improvement should be a permanent objective of the organization.
7 *Factual approach to decision-making*: effective decisions are based on the analysis of data and information.
8 *Mutually beneficial supplier relationships*: an organization and its suppliers are interdependent, and a mutually beneficial relationship enhances the ability of both to create value.

Table 3.3 The eight quality management principles that provide the basis of the ISO 9000 series

1. Customer focus

2. Leadership

3. Involvement of people

4. Process approach

5. System approach to management

6. Continual improvement

7. Factual approach to decision-making

8. Mutually beneficial supplier relationships

Table 3.4 Comparison of ISO 9001 and ISO 9004

ISO 9001:2000 *(prescribes quality system requirements)*	*ISO 9004:2000* *(provides performance-improvement guidelines)*
Minimum requirements	Best practice
Customer satisfaction	Competitive advantage
Reduce risks and preventing failure	Superior performance
Conformance to requirement	Degrees of excellence
Effectiveness	Efficiency

ISO 9004 provides a bridge between ISO 9001 and the Six Sigma performance improvement process. Whilst ISO 9001 states minimum system requirements to meet a standard, ISO 9004 gives guidelines for performance improvement. Table 3.4 shows the principal significant differences between ISO 9001 and ISO 9004.

As the titles indicate, the set of ISO 9000:2000 standards relates to quality systems. An organization on the ISO 9001 register of firms of assessed capability is said to have management system certification. This is quite different from product certification. This distinction should be clearly recognized. As with Six Sigma, the ISO 9000 family is applicable to any type of organization. However, more prescriptive derivatives, of the generic ISO 9000 series, relating to specific sectors (e.g. automotive, medical, information technology) are becoming available. Supporting ISO (International Standards Organization) standards of interest to Six Sigma personnel are:

- ISO 10006: guidelines to quality in project management;
- ISO/TR 10012: quality-assurance requirements for measuring equipment;
- ISO/TR 10014: guidelines for managing economics of quality;
- ISO/TR 10017: guidance on statistical techniques for ISO 9001.

ISO/TR 10017 (ISO TC 176, 1994) is of particular interest to Six Sigma personnel. It outlines the usefulness of statistical techniques in dealing with the variability that may be observed in the behaviour and outcome of practically all processes, even under conditions of apparent stability. Such variability can be observed in the quantifiable characteristics of products and processes, and may be seen to exist at various stages over the total life-cycle of products from market research to customer service and final disposal.

It describes how statistical techniques can help measure, describe, analyse, interpret and model such variability, even with a relatively limited amount of data. Statistical analysis of such data can help provide a better understanding of the nature, extent and causes of variability. This could help to solve and even prevent problems that may result from such variability.

It relates how statistical techniques can thus permit better use of available data to assist in decision-making, and thereby help to continually improve the quality of products and processes to achieve customer satisfaction. These techniques are applicable to a wide spectrum of activities, such as market research, design, development, production, verification, installation and servicing. The techniques covered are: descriptive statistics; design of experiments; hypotheses testing; measurement analysis; process capability analysis; regression analysis; reliability analysis; sampling; simulation and statistical process control charts. Each technique is dealt with under the headings: what it is; what it is used for; benefits; limitations and cautions and examples of applications.

As such it provides a useful reference for those engaged in Six Sigma activities. Summarizing, ISO 9001, its supporting standards and more prescriptive sector derivatives, provides a useful backdrop, in terms of good housekeeping and technical support, for Six Sigma activities. Although ISO 9004 gives factual guidelines for quality improvement there is much less take-up on this standard than the ISO 9001, which is in widespread use throughout the world. Whilst technically sound, ISO 9004, unlike Six Sigma, is not considered to be supported by sufficient promotional drive to convince organizations as to why they should implement ISO 9004. Organizations, generally, do not seem to be 'turned on' as much by ISO 9004 as ISO 9001. The primary reason for this is surely that ISO 9001 is a real money spinner for certification bodies and hence has been, and continues to be, strongly promoted by them for sound commercial reasons. This should send a very clear message to those who take issue with the near messianic zeal, and statistical hyperbole, associated with the promotion of Six Sigma; and who dismiss the Six Sigma continual-improvement initiative purely on these grounds.

The more prescriptive sector derivatives of ISO 9001, such as the automotive sector ISO Technical Report 16949, do not explicitly invoke a Six Sigma initiative. However, ISO TR 16949 invokes all the requirements of ISO 9001 together with a number of more prescriptive demands. In terms of continual improvement, for example, it states the organization *shall*:

- Have a process to motivate and empower employees to achieve quality objectives, to make continual improvements and to create an environment to promote innovation. The process shall include the promotion of quality and technological awareness throughout the whole organization.
- Define a process for continual improvement [re ISO 9004 Annex B].
- Define processes for problem-solving, leading to root cause identification and elimination. (If a customer prescribed problem-solving format exists, the organization shall use the prescribed format.)
- Use error-proofing methods in their corrective action process.

- Determine and use the appropriate statistical tools for each process.
- Understand and utilize basic statistical concepts, such as variation, control (stability), process capability and over-adjustment throughout the organization.
- Conduct statistical studies to analyse the variation present in the results of each type of measuring and test equipment system.
- Use a multidisciplinary approach to prepare for product realization, including the use of potential failure mode and effects analysis and the identification, development and monitoring of special characteristics.

Note. In ISO language, *shall* refers to 'requirements'.

All these features fall within the scope of Six Sigma activities as expounded in this book. To meet the true goals of continual improvement, quality systems standards such as ISO 9001 and its derivatives need to be coupled with 'customer-specific product, process and service requirements', and a 'dedicated organization-wide initiative for continual improvement'. This is borne out by feedback to the effect that 'there are too many problem suppliers with certificates' and that 'supplier parts per million performance has not shown much improvement, if any, over the last 18 months'. Hence, the need for a new continual-improvement initiative such as Six Sigma.

QS 9000 is the forerunner to ISO TS 16949. More than 20 000 automotive-related organizations already hold QS 9000 certificates. It is expected that they will migrate to ISO TS 16949. It should be noted here, too, that Ford, for example, is committed, in a big way to Six Sigma. An example is at their new diesel engine plant at Dagenham that is scheduled to produce 900 000 units a year in 2004. Ford Dagenham states that its suppliers will also have to deploy Six Sigma.

Quality excellence models: total quality management

Total quality management (TQM) is a rather nebulous term. Surveys confirm that it means different things to different people.

In practice, organization-wide deployment of TQM is most commonly associated with senior management involvement, widespread training and the activation of various kinds of project teams. This is frequently coupled with the adoption of the particular phenomenon of the day, for example, JIT (just in time).

The rolling-out of TQM, throughout an organization, is usually preceded by a period of considerable consultation, discussion and fact-finding. During this time, gurus are consulted, ideas are fostered and views and perspectives aligned. Many attempts founder at this stage. Surveys also indicate that many organizations that claim to have a well-developed TQM approach do not. TQM is defined in ISO 8402:1994 as: 'management approach of an organization, centred on quality, based on the participation of all its members and aiming at long-term success through customer satisfaction, and benefits to all members of the organization and to society.'

Notes of further explanation are given.

Note 1. The expression 'all its members' designates personnel in all departments and at all levels of the organizational structure.

Note 2. The strong and persistent leadership of top management and the education and training of all members of the organization are essential for the success of this approach.

Note 3. In TQM, the concept of quality relates to the achievement of all managerial objectives.

The term 'total quality management' has not been thought necessary to define in ISO 9000:2000, the ISO standard that has replaced ISO 8402. The principal reasons for this are, first, that it is not now a term used in the latest ISO 9000 family of standards. Second, although more and more people tend not to use the specific term they do focus on the underlying principles involved. These principles are enunciated in the quality excellence models developed within Europe and the United States of America.

Organizational excellence models and Six Sigma

Those contemplating the deployment of the Six Sigma initiative have ready-made models of organizational excellence models freely available to them in the form of the European and USA criteria for self-assessment purposes. It is recommended that any of these models be used for determining where a particular organization currently stands in relation to established excellence criteria and for subsequent 'gap' analysis to facilitate the prioritizing of improvement actions. Both models are non-prescriptive in the sense that the focus is on results orientated requirements. The means (enablers) criteria are deliberately non-prescriptive and adaptable. An organization is encouraged to innovate and to tailor and adapt its approach based on its singular business strategy, set-up and resources. No particular organizational structure, tools, techniques or systems is mandated. In a Six Sigma context, the European Foundation for Quality Management (EFQM) and USA Baldrige criteria form an excellent tool for, amongst other things, establishing and prioritizing opportunities for improvement and for establishing measures for, and values of, results. The Six Sigma initiative is entirely compatible with both the USA and European excellence models. It is encouraged that these criteria be used from a Six Sigma diagnostic perspective and for potential project selection across the organization. Self-assessment responses to the criteria and answers to the key questions posed are best based on three dimensions:

1 *Approach*: appropriateness, effectiveness, evidence of benefits achieved.
2 *Deployment*: breadth and degree of application of the approach.
3 *Results*: current performance in relation to Six Sigma benchmarks.

These models are practical expositions of the so-called 'Moses premise', namely that there exists a 'promised land' where total organizational excellence or perfection prevails: one that can be reached through sustained directed effort.

The European Foundation for Quality Management (EFQM) excellence model

The European Foundation for Quality Management's (EFQM's) mission is 'to be the driving force for sustainable excellence in Europe'. Its excellence model was first introduced in 1992 as the framework for assessing applications for The European Quality Award. It is estimated that over 20 000 organizations across Europe are currently using the model. The EFQM model recognizes that to succeed, organizations need to establish an appropriate management system regardless of their sector, size, structure, or maturity.

The EFQM excellence model is intended as a practical tool to help an organization to achieve this by measuring where it is on their path to excellence. As a precursor to a Six Sigma initiative, it helps an organization to understand the gaps, and stimulates it to provide solutions.

The EFQM model is a non-prescriptive framework that recognizes that there are many approaches to achieving sustainable excellence. The model is based on nine criteria. Five of these are 'Enablers' and four are 'Results'. The 'Enabler' criteria cover what an organization does. The 'Results' criteria cover what an organization achieves. 'Results' are caused by 'Enablers'. The five enablers are: Leadership, Policy and Strategy, People, Partnerships and Resources and Processes. The four results are: Customer Results, People Results, Society Results and Key Performance Results. These are shown pictorially in Figure 3.4.

The USA Baldrige criteria for performance excellence

The Baldrige criteria for performance excellence relates to the USA National Quality Award created by Public Law. The primary reasons for the Act was the acknowledgement that the United States of America was being challenged strongly by foreign competition, poor quality was costing businesses as much as 20% of sales revenue nationally, that improvements in quality go hand in hand with lower costs, improved productivity and increased profitability. It also recognized that a commitment to excellence was essential to the well-being

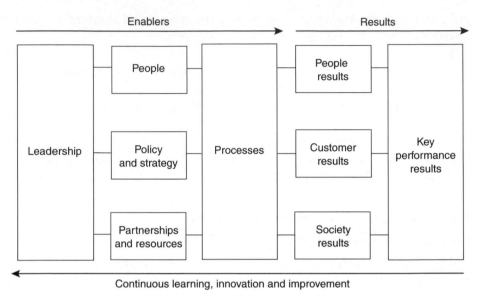

Figure 3.4   Outline of the European Foundation for quality excellence model

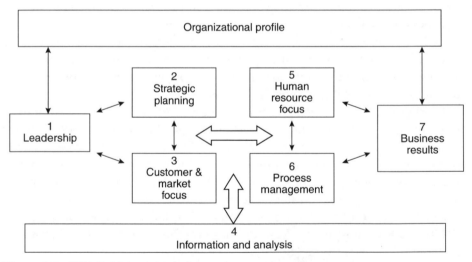

Figure 3.5   USA Baldrige criteria for performance excellence

of the Nation's economy and ability to compete in the global marketplace. There was an appreciation that this concept of quality improvement must be management led and customer focused and was applicable to all types and sizes of organization in both the public and private sector. The Baldrige USA National Quality Program (BNQP) at the National Institute of Standards and Technology (NIST) is a customer-focused federal-change agent that enhances the competitiveness, quality and productivity of US organizations. The American Society for Quality (ASQ) administers the National Quality Award under contract to NIST. The Baldrige criteria for business excellence is made up of seven key core values and concepts. These are shown in Figure 3.5.

The role of the US gurus

The Juran way

Control versus improvement

Joseph Juran (Juran, J. and Blanton Godfrey, A., 1998) has been looked upon for many years as *the* world authority on quality. He is the professional's professional. Juran starts off with the simple direct premise that management activity is directed either at:

- *control*: preventing change;
- *improvement*:creating change.

He puts the view that there is one universal sequence of events for control and another for achievement of improvement. In certain situations control is desirable, even essential, to ensure that budgets, quotas, specifications and the like are met. But holding rejects, say, at a budgeted level of 7%, particularly if the value of this loss exceeds the profits, does not make good business sense. A preoccupation with budgets and control should not blind one to the opportunity for improvement. This may seem obvious but dwell, for a moment, at the reality in your area of management.

> *Case study.* Take the sock manufacturer with 68 machines on three-shift operation with a cycle time of 3 min and who has lived with a seconds rate of some 7% for the last 30 years. When the author proposed a breakthrough project, which, on the basis of pilot studies, was likely to reduce the seconds rate to some 1–2% – the manufacturer accused the author of being a pedlar of unemployment. Why? It would put a number of market traders, who paid cash for their cast-offs, out of business!

This would seem to be a blinding glimpse of the obvious (BGO). Why was it not done years ago? Juran suggests that managers:

- are blinkered by their axiomatic beliefs;
- lack the time and the skills;
- are afraid the answer might conflict with what they have said and done for years.

Juran is a strong believer in defining and estimating the costs of not getting things right the first time. He argues that we need quality costs both in break-through and control:

- *Breakthrough*: to identify principal opportunities for cost reduction. To monitor and stimulate progress.
- *Control*: to hold gains and provide data for ongoing control of quality costs.

Quality improvement, he claims, is concerned with tackling both sporadic and chronic quality problems. However, the treatment is different for each. A sporadic problem is a sudden adverse change in the status quo, requiring remedy through changing the status quo, by adopting the control sequence. A chronic problem is a long-standing adverse situation requiring remedy through chang-ing the status quo, by adopting the breakthrough sequence. A graphical illus-tration of this is shown in Figure 3.6. Figure 3.6 also contrasts a simple run chart with a type of Shewhart control chart, as recommended by Deming, and associated with statistical process control (SPC).

In this area, the management initially went blue with rage when they learnt that one machinist had worked through a shift with a broken needle causing perforations in the crotch area of dozens of briefs. This anger was accentuated by the fact they she did this on over-time. It was pointed out to the manage-ment that their principal focus should be on reducing common cause variation as it was this that gave rise to the recurring losses. They quickly responded in a very positive sense as is evidenced by the marked improvement in perform-ance in the control chart of Figure 3.7.

In the selection of improvement projects Six Sigma personnel can learn two lessons from this:

- One, by venting their fury the management frightened the girl so much that she was too scared to return to work. Thence the reason for this momentary lapse of control was never discovered.
- Two, management had budgeted for, and continued to be unconcerned with, the endemic, or chronic, situation causing an ongoing loss that was higher

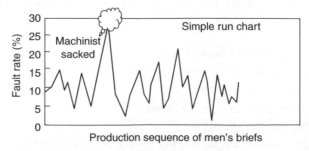

Figure 3.6   Simple run chart for assembly of men's briefs

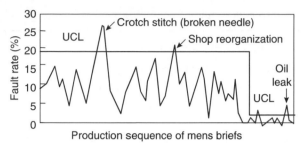

Production sequence of mens briefs

Figure 3.7 Illustration of the role of a simple control chart to distinguish between sporadic and chronic situations (UCL, upper control limit)

than the profit margin on the product. Once the situation was made so plainly transparent with the use of a control chart it became too obvious to be ignored and common sense prevailed. The problem with common sense is it not all that 'common'.

These sporadic and chronic definitions correspond with Deming's special and common causes as used in statistical process control. In Figure 3.7, it is seen that three sporadic events (special cause variation) are indicated by points above the upper control limit (UCL). Figure 3.7 also shows the effect of improving the process by reducing the chronic level (common cause variation) from some 9% to less than 1%. The change in level of the UCL resulted from this significant improvement. All too frequently, priority is given to expending energy on fire-fighting sporadic problems when larger savings are possible with chronic ones.

The Six Sigma practitioner is expected to make considerable use of such a high-value tool, as the control chart, in both attribute and measured data situations. This is dealt with later in the book.

Juran's six stages of quality planning

Juran starts off with the premise that most quality problems are pre-planned in. Hence, the greatest leverage in business improvement can be obtained by focusing, at the up-stream design stage, on the planning process itself. He identifies six stages of quality planning. These are shown in Table 3.5.

Six Sigma personnel should note that Juran is referring here to the myriad of internal customers within an organization as well as the ultimate customer(s) of the product or service. This is the essence of the process-based approach. Juran's six-point planning strategy provides a convenient check-list for the Six Sigma 'belt', particularly at the project definition stage. For example, who is the customer of the process under consideration? What are the customer needs and expectations? Are product/service features aligned with customer needs and expectations? And so on.

Table 3.5 Juran's six stages of quality planning

1. Identify the customers at each stage of the process
2. Determine customer needs and expectations
3. Develop product/service features in line with customer needs and expectations
4. Establish quality goals to meet customer and supplier needs at minimum combined cost
5. Develop resources to provide the needed product/service features
6. Ensure resources are capable of meeting quality goals under operating conditions – right first time

Table 3.6 Juran's seven stages of control

1. Choose control parameters – what to control
2. Define units of measure
3. Establish standards of performance
4. Create methods of measurement
5. Measure performance
6. Interpret the results: actual vs. standard
7. Take action – on the difference

Juran's seven stages of control

Jurans' seven stages of control align largely with the measure phase of a standard Six Sigma project. These are shown in Table 3.6.

Juran's eight steps for breakthrough

Juran considers his eight steps for breakthrough to new levels of performance as a 'universal sequence of events' applicable to any situation. These are shown in Table 3.7.

Juran stresses the need to be very sensitive to the culture of the organization in his first point. Simply expressing the expected benefits of a project in monetary terms may not be sufficient in itself. The Six Sigma belt needs to be aware of, and take into account, the habits and attitudes of people in the organization. These will have been formed in the light of management style and experience of previous attempts at sustained business-performance improvement. Juran also recognizes the need, in points three and four, for some form of infrastructure to guide and direct projects, and to appropriate the necessary resources and ensure the availability of appropriate information and assistance. Juran also appreciates the necessity to take into account the feelings of people when

Table 3.7   Juran's eight steps for breakthrough

1. Identify need secure breakthrough in attitude
2. Identify project(s)
3. Organize to guide projects
4. Organize for diagnosis
5. Discover causes
6. Ensure acceptance of remedy
7. Implement change
8. Hold gains

change is involved in point six. This is achieved by explaining the need for change to those most affected and by gaining their active involvement in, and acceptance of, the change.

Summarizing, the Juran project approach is eminently suited to, and provides a sound alternative basis for, the deployment of Six Sigma projects. There is just one subtle difference between the Juran approach and that normally taken in many Six Sigma project activities. Juran feels that project team training should be limited to that required for a specific task. In that way the training experience is immediately productive and highly motivational. The reason for this is that he strongly believes that behaviour transformation is a key element in sustaining improvement projects. In this respect, he rates behavioural science as being as important a tool as either a technical or statistical one. This transformation is best achieved, in his view, by getting early and positive results from projects. Perhaps there is a Six Sigma lesson to be learned here. Lengthy off-the-peg training programmes for Six Sigma 'belts' whilst being very beneficial for consultants and trainers may not be so nearly efficient or effective for the organization deploying Six Sigma as short pre-project task-orientated training.

The Deming way

Top-down + bottom-up approach

Edwards Deming (Deming, W.E., 1982) uses both a top-down and bottom-up approach to quality management. The top-down aspect is brought out in his 14 obligations for top management. The bottom-up aspect arises from his process focus in terms of statistical process control (SPC). With SPC, Deming provides the people who work in the system (which is usually not of their making) with the means to monitor their task/work/process in a standard 'common language' format termed control charts the world over. And, after all, is not 'feedback the breakfast of champions?'

Bottom-up approach: statistical process control

The term SPC does not relate to some esoteric discipline but rather to a simple pictorial method, which recognizes that there are two types of people and two types of variation. First, the people. There are operational people who work IN the system and there are technical and managerial people who are responsible FOR the system. Deming recognizes that the bulk of our quality problems arise from 'the system itself' rather than from those who 'work in the system'. This is contrary to the oft-accepted view. Second, the types of variation. Like Juran, Deming recognizes two types of variation:

Special cause variation: those sources of variation that are NOT inherent in the system, for example, an irregular event such as a power surge or an isolated road delay due to an accident. Special cause variation is usually dealt with by *people who work in the system*.

Common cause variation: those sources of natural variation in the process itself. For example, a turret capstan may produce to 0.25 mm and a grinder to 0.025 mm. The average delay on a particular journey is 15 min, or average absenteeism is 7%. Common cause variation can often only be reduced by *people responsible for the system*, not those who work in the system.

Hence, it is imperative that we so set up our organization that we provide the means for people who work in the system:

- to continually monitor performance and to solve the problems they are able to solve at operational level;
- feedback information on problems they cannot solve to those who can, with the expectation of a positive response in a reasonable time frame.

This provides the link between the Deming methodology (SPC) and the Deming philosophy (14 Obligations of Management).

Top-down approach: 14 obligations of management

Dr Deming's 14 (see Table 3.8) obligations take a lot of time to understand, much less institutionalize. It is necessary, but not sufficient, that top management understand and support them. The sufficient condition for institutionalization must include the understanding and support of ALL middle managers and supervision to whom the day-to-day management of the company is delegated. This may take a fair time to accomplish. However, if we are to compete in this new economic era, we do not really have a choice. But, as Deming says

You do not HAVE to do any of these things.

For, after all,

survival is NOT compulsory!

Table 3.8 Deming's 14 obligations

1. Create constancy of purpose for continual improvement
2. Adopt the new philosophy
3. Cease dependence on mass inspection to achieve quality
4. End practice of awarding business on the basis of price tag alone
5. Improve constantly and forever every activity in the company
6. Institute modern methods of training
7. Institute positive approach in supervision
8. Drive out fear
9. Break down barriers
10. Stop exhortation: provide road-map
11. Eliminate work standards that prescribe quotas alone
12. Remove barriers that impede pride of workmanship
13. Institute a vigorous programme of self-improvement
14. Create a structure; to push the above points relentlessly

Deming's first obligation states the need for 'constancy of purpose'. This is where most organizations appear to have failed over the years in their pursuit of never-ending improvement. They try one thing after another, a little of this and a little of that. Even when a particular initiative is up and running successfully it ultimately peters out through lack of constancy of purpose. How many such shooting stars have you experienced in your organization? How many rainbows have been chased? How many promised lands have turned out to be mirages?

Various 'right first time' programmes, 'zero D', 'quality circles' and many others may spring to mind. Where are they now? What is the secret to this elusiveness of 'constancy of purpose'? The secret surely lies with the top management. One cannot expect to deploy any such initiative as one would install a machine, simply on a step-by-step basis reading from the instruction manual. Before deploying any initiative that involves change it is important to face up to two primary issues:

- recognizing and dealing with the cultural change required in the organization, and
- ensuring that a sustaining infrastructure is created.

This is the core message of Deming's first obligation that has to be taken on board for a successful and sustained deployment of Six Sigma.

Six Sigma training, is aligned to some extent with Deming's sixth and seventh obligations. Deming even goes further and says that *all employees* (or at least a critical mass) should be trained in tools such as:

- *Pareto analysis*: to focus problem-solving on the vital few rather than the trivial many.
- *Flow charting*: to focus on the task/process in terms of supplier > task > customer inter-relationships.
- *Problem-solving methodology*: six steps: select > record > examine > develop > install > maintain.
- *Ishikawa diagrams*: cause-and-effect diagrams for group problem-solving.
- *Inter-personal skills*: team working.
- *Control charting*: to monitor tasks and processes; to isolate special from common causes.

Deming proposes, in obligation seven, that *supervision* need to develop a more participative style of management. They must be taught to help people on the job. They will probably need training/development in basic statistical skills, inter-personal skills and the varying styles of management; directing, coaching, supporting and delegating. Obligation eight refers to the driving out of fear. Juran disagrees with Deming on this point in the sense that Juran states that fear can bring the best out of people. Deming feels very strongly, however, on this point. If this obligation is not one of the first to be implemented all else is likely to be of little avail. He says that it is essential to drive out fear across the organization by encouraging two-way non-punitive communication. The economic loss resulting from fear to ask questions, express ideas or report trouble is appalling. This is of vital importance to ensure validity of results in process monitoring. Obligation nine is also of particular relevance to Six Sigma activities. It refers to the need for cross-functional teamwork. All functions within an organization are dependent on one another, they have supplier ↔ customer relationships. Create a common language (e.g. SPC) that can be used not only inter-departmentally but also with outside suppliers and customers.

Whilst Deming is concerned rather more with on-the-job responsibilities and activities as opposed to project work, his obligations, philosophy and methods form a sound basis for Six Sigma deployment.

The Deming PDCA circle

The Deming PDCA circle (Figure 3.8) forms the basis for many quality-improvement initiatives including Six Sigma.

Obstacles to transformation

Deming states a number of obstacles that one can expect to meet in pursuing a business transformation. These include:

- *Hope for instant pudding*: the supposition that improvement of quality and productivity can be suddenly accomplished by affirmation of faith. Is not quality free?

Figure 3.8 The Deming PDCA circle

- *Our problems are different*: they are different to be sure but the principles that will solve them are universal in nature.
- *Show me an example in my industry*: quality control/improvement is a method transferable to different problems and circumstances.
- *Insulation surrounding top management*: inability of staff to reach their management. If you cannot argue with your boss he/she is not worth working for.
- *We prefer not to make any change*: do not want to tamper with the existing system: hoping the big problems will go away. They will not!
- *Much data, little information*: quality control to some people means statistics on defects and failures. They tell us all about faults but not how to reduce their frequency and severity.
- *Our troubles lie wholly with the workforce*: They do not. The workforce work in the system, management are responsible for the system. Most problems are system ones.
- *We installed quality control*: No! You can install a new machine but not quality control. Quality control is a learning process led by management. (By 'quality control', Deming's intention is also to include quality-performance measurement and quality improvement.)

The five deadly sins (of western management)

Deming lists what he calls the five deadly sins of western management. These are:

1 Lack of constancy of purpose to plan product and service that will have a market, keep the company in business and provide jobs.
2 Emphasis on short-term profits; short-term thinking, fed by fear of unfriendly take-over and by push from bankers and owners for dividends.

3 Personal review system, merit rating, annual review or annual appraisal, by whatever name, for people in management, the effects of which are devastating.
4 Mobility of management; job-hopping from one company to another.
5 Use of visible figures only for management, with little or no consideration of figures that are unknown or unknowable.

Deming's simple overall philosophy

Deming's simple overall philosophy is encapsulated in his chain reaction diagram shown in Figure 3.9. Who can argue with this axiom?

The Crosby way

Overview

Philip Crosby (Crosby, P.B., 1979, 1981) is probably best known for his emphasis on Zero Defects and the somewhat contentious statement that: 'quality is free'.

He acknowledges the tremendous growth of interest in quality. Upwards of 70 000 executives have already been through his quality college in Florida. However, he feels much of the new-found interest of management in quality is superficial. Management people still do not understand quality – they choose to delegate quality responsibilities to a specialist department – labelled 'quality'. And many quality people do not understand business. Consequently, the bulk of the workforce take the view that quality is not their individual concern – it is that of the quality department – and, it is a 'pain in the neck' anyhow in that it holds back production. This is the dilemma.

He repeatedly emphasizes the need to 'do it right the first time'. He argues that the price of nonconformance is typically some 20–40% of company revenue. He looks on the phrase 'to err is human' as a facile excuse rather than a feasible explanation. Errors are often related to levels of human tolerance. He asks, 'why do you think it is that we get very few errors in a payroll department?' Like Deming, he recognizes, that up to 80% of the potential for

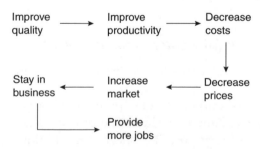

Figure 3.9 Deming's chain reaction

improved quality is related to the activities of, so called, white collar workers. He also makes the point that the opportunity for improvement in quality is far greater in 'service' areas than in that traditional hunting ground of 'manufacturing'. The price of non-conformance (PONC) is considered to be typically 25% in manufacturing and 40% in service industries.

Crosby's 14-step quality improvement process (QIP)

Crosby provides an explicit structural approach to cultural change and quality improvement in his '14 Steps' (Table 3.9). It provides an alternative continual-improvement approach to the Six Sigma method as far as team reactive approaches to existing activities and events are concerned.

Table 3.9 Crosby's 14-step quality-improvement process

1. Management commitment	Make this crystal clear to all (in deeds as well as words)
2. Quality improvement teams (QITs)	Set up QITs with people from each department. Focus them on their QIP role
3. Quality measurement	Determine status of non-conformance through-out company
4. Cost of quality	Estimate COQ [cost of conformance (COC) + cost of non-conformance (CONC)] to pinpoint areas of business
5. Quality awareness	Provide means of raising personal concern for quality in ALL employees
6. Corrective action	Develop systematic means of resolving, forever, concerns found in previous steps
7. Right first time planning	Plan for company-wide first-time quality (Crosby's Zero Defects)
8. Quality education and training	Train everyone in QIP
9. Launch right first time	As the Company performance standard
10. Goal setting	Encourage self-setting of QI goals
11. Error cause removal (ECR)	Ensure reporting of inhibitors to error-free work and timely response
12. Recognition	Show appreciation of those participating
13. Quality council participation	Form liaison body
14. Do it all over again	It is a never-ending process

Crosby's four absolutes of quality management

Crosby proposes four absolutes for the management of quality. These are shown in Table 3.10.

Crosby suggests that these four absolutes need internalizing and institutionalizing. The four absolutes are compatible to a degree with the Six Sigma process. His first absolute 'conformance to requirement' can be taken to be somewhat restricted in outlook. Requirement is best interpreted in the more general Six Sigma sense to mean 'need or expectation that is stated, generally implied or obligatory'. The Kano model of Figure 4.2 should also be referred to in this respect. His third absolute also should most certainly be extended to include the cost of over-conformance. It is vital, in both cases, to respect the huge impact on costs of upstream activities such as the interpretation of customer needs and expectations in the definition of the design requirement and its subsequent translation into product or service design features.

Crosby's six Cs of quality improvement (QI) (shown in Table 3.11) are fully compatible with the Six Sigma initiative. As such they should be recognized, and taken on board, by everyone concerned with Six Sigma.

The Feigenbaum way

Armand Feigenbaum (Feigenbaum, A., 1961) introduced the concept of 'total quality control'. Feigenbaum goes about his work quietly without hype. Thence, he is not so well known as his three compatriots just discussed. He focuses on 'tailor-made' rather than 'off-the-peg' quality systems. His best known saying probably is:

> Quality is everybody's business. And everybody's business becomes nobody's business.

Table 3.10 Crosby's four absolutes

Aspect	Conventional wisdom	New reality
1. Quality-definition	Goodness, Technical excellence, Grade	Conformance to requirements
2. System	Appraisal and detection of errors	Prevention: process capability in line with requirements and in control
3. Measurement	Product percent and number defective	Company-wide cost of non-conformance
4. Performance standard	Budgeted/planned defective levels	Zero defects

Table 3.11 Crosby's six Cs (with amendments)

Comprehension	What we want of QI Vision > planning > doing > measuring > performance standard What WE are going to commit ourselves to
Commitment	Demonstrate by personal example Deeds required as well as words
Competence	Train across the board Develop technical and inter-personal skills
Communication	Establish a common language Keep it simple Keep it open – high visibility

Correction	Keep your hand on the tiller
	Do not catch people doing things wrong and ZAP them;
	  catch people doing things approximately right and improve
	  their performance

Continuance	Make the cultural change part of the woodwork – the bloodstream of the business

Table 3.12 Feigenbaum's three management commitments

1. Be excellence driven *not* failure driven
2. Make quality improvement a basic habit that is relentlessly pursued within the organization
3. Promote quality and cost as complementary *not* conflicting objectives

Here, he is emphasizing two points. One, there is a need for first-line accountability for quality. Two, there is a need for a strong enabling infrastructure. This is aligned precisely with Six Sigma thinking. His ideology is expressed succinctly in his 'three management commitments' and 'four forces' (see Tables 3.12 and 3.13). These commitments and forces are also fully compatible with the Six Sigma process. Feigenbaum's first management commitment, in particular, should be noted by Six Sigma practitioners. Belts may quite naturally tend to be blinkered somewhat by purely focusing on increasing the value of Sigma. By reacting exclusively to non-conformities, to the exclusion of exploiting improvement opportunities in process, product and system design, particularly upstream, massive high-leverage opportunities may be missed. This is discussed more fully in Chapter 4.

Feigenbaum's reference to programmes would now be taken to mean processes. A programme usually has a beginning and end. Improvement processes are intended to be everlasting.

Table 3.13   Feigenbaum's four forces

1. Quality systems are *not* the responsibility of a single function. They must be applied on a co-ordinated basis by all functions

2. Quality programmes must be continuously coupled with both the customer and the supplier on both a feed-forward and feedback basis

3. Quality concerns transcend and do not respect organizational boundaries. Quality programmes must be organized accordingly

4. Quality-related operations are so extended, intricate and involved today. They thus require integrated high-level control from concept to customer

The role of the Japanese gurus in Six Sigma

The Ishikawa way

Cause-and-effect diagram: the seven basic tools

Kaoru Ishikawa (Ishikawa, K., 1985) is probably best known for the 'Ishikawa diagram', the original name for the 'cause-and-effect' or 'fishbone' diagram that is now in general use. Ishikawa is also closely associated with the use of the 'seven basic tools' by the many rather than the few. He pioneered the widespread application of these tools (Pareto analysis, cause-and-effect diagrams, tally charts, histograms, scatter diagrams, process flow charts and run charts). He was also instrumental in creating the 'quality circle' movement in Japan. He recognized, as early as 1949, that quality was too important to rest in the hands of specialists and conceived the concept of company-wide quality control (CWQC). The Ishikawa diagram and the other six tools should be part of the tool-kit of all Six Sigma participants. They should also recognize, as Ishikawa did, that quality is a direct concern of everyone in the organization.

Quality circles

Concept

Typically, a Quality Circle is a small group of people usually from the same area of work who voluntarily meet together on a regular basis to identify, analyse and solve quality problems in their area. The circle size is usually between six and eight so that every member can participate fully on an equal basis. The length of each meeting is usually not more than 1 h and usually takes place at a frequency of not less than once a month. Each circle has a leader who has received training in group dynamics, communication and problem-solving techniques. Each circle leader is guided and helped by a facilitator who is a member of the Quality Circle Steering Committee that establishes policy and procedures and also reviews progress. A problem for resolution is selected by the circle from their area of work and is then discussed, analysed and finally solved. The solution is communicated to the top management by face-to-face presentation supported by visual aids.

Circle objectives include: problem-solving and problem prevention; enhancing quality; personal development and involvement These objectives are often extended to include topics such as safety, productivity, housekeeping and cost reduction.

Management commitment

A top-level management commitment is the first prerequisite to a successful quality circle programme. The management needs to:

- *Understand circle philosophy and operation.*
- *Assess company human relationships*: is the present climate one of conflict or participation? What sort of management style operates within the company? If people are to discuss freely there must be an environment that encourages participation.
- *Appreciate organizational factors*: consider how the circle set-up fits in to the existing company organizational chart and the general pattern of working. Although there is no change in the structure (apart from the facilitator), it does mean giving the supervisor a greater leadership role and using specialist functions more for consultation.
- *Accept the implications of management support*: a supportive attitude from the top management is essential. This is evidenced in the initial promotion to sell the idea to middle management and workers and by a continuing active interest. There should, however, be no domination or interference on the part of the management once the programme is set up.
- *Ensure union involvement*: full discussions with union representatives at an early stage so that they will be fully in the picture. This will allay suspicion and fears that their position is being threatened. Unions who are brought in at this stage are usually prepared to back the idea – if left out their response may be to black it!
- *Provide financial backing*: this is an investment in people with the aim of giving them the opportunity and training to develop their own potential. The costs include training, facilitators' salary, pay for circle members and general promotional activities. By-products should be a saving in failure costs and improved quality.
- *Authorize the changes required*: the set-up of the Steering Committee, appointment of the facilitator and operation of the circles should be laid down in a policy document that has the seal of management approval.

- *Give due consideration to circle presentations*: this provides a means of recognition of the circle's activities and as such is important to the ongoing success of the programme. It is a management responsibility to make the decision on whether the plan should be implemented or rejected. In the latter case care should be taken to explain the reasons for rejection.

How to run problem-solving sessions

Most problem-solving sessions in quality circles follow strict protocol. This protocol is described in Chapter 6.

Six Sigma and quality circles

There is much in common between Six Sigma and quality circles. Significant differences are:

- *Choice of project*: in quality circles members often identify and choose projects in their own area of work while in Six Sigma the projects are chosen by managers and may cross functional boundaries.
- *Extent of training*: in quality circles pre-project training of circle members is kept to a bare minimum. Members are further trained appropriately, on the job, as a project proceeds. There is no training for training sake. With Six Sigma there is quite lengthy pre-project training.
- *Outcome expectations*: unlike quality circles, with Six Sigma significant 'bottom line' savings are the principal, if not sole, focus.

An actual case study illustrated these features.

Case study

Visualize a chicken-processing unit in a village in East Anglia where chickens are cut into portions to be sold in supermarkets. The author was concerned with the initiation of quality circles in the plant. Involvement was planned to take place initially on six successive Friday afternoons with two circles – with 1h sessions for each. In the event one Friday was snowed out with the roads impassable.

On the fifth Friday, a room in the local pub was hired for presentations to the management. Mainly housewives, with no previous training in industrial problem-solving or public speaking, presented their projects to the management. Each team made it a team effort as pre-planned. They set up the room ahead of time; they had their exhibits in place and flip charts prepared beforehand. They were very careful that they could be read from the back. They placed a name card in front of everyone present. They started on time and introduced each member at the beginning. They had prepared themselves for any penetrating questions from the management. For each project that they had been concerned they made an impressive and logical presentation according to a pre-arranged schedule, for instance:

- Introduction   2 min   Leader (Betty)
- The problem as found and its effect   4 min   Joan
- Causes of the problem   6 min   Sandra
- Recommendation   3 min   Cassandra
- Likely effect of implementing solution   2 min   Meera
- Discussion and management response: Thanks   13 min
- Thanks

The girls ran a tight ship and kept to the time schedule. It was only the management response that overran. Typical of the projects conducted, presented and agreed by management were:

1 One girl worked with a continual fear and dread of a frozen chicken leg or thigh falling off an overhead conveyor line. Sometime it struck her on the shoulder and occasionally on the back of the head and neck. This was happening only at the rate of some three per week. But when she was not hit for some time this raised her concerns even further as she felt that the next one was more imminent. The solution here was to remove every other slat from the conveyor.

2 All the girls had expressed a concern about the tardiness of the knife sharpening procedures in place and the hassle in getting it done. The one mechanic on the plant was responsible for knife sharpening. He had to fit this in with his other onerous and time-consuming duties. The solution recommended and adopted was a two-stage knife sharpening procedure: stage 1 to be done by the girls themselves, at a sharpening station as and when required; stage 2 to be done by the mechanic at specified intervals. There was an added bonus on this project as one of the girls had previously worked at a competitor's plant where better knives were used. They recommended that a few of these type of knives be bought for trials. This proposal was agreed by the management. Ultimately the new, better, knives were adopted across the plant as standard.

3 Only one set of project recommendations was rejected by the management. One of the jobs was to place chicken legs and thighs into polystyrene trays. The girls disliked the occasional sound of breaking bones as they compressed the chicken parts into the tray. They experimented with, and proposed a larger tray. Management explained just why this idea would not be viable. First, customers would feel that they are getting short measure. Second, non-standard larger trays would take up unacceptably larger space on the supermarket shelves. The girls understood the reasoning and fully accepted the commercial implications involved. They learnt a lot from this

project in terms of taking into account a broader view of situations. The problem was overcome by a method proposed by the management of how to compress the joints without the sound of cracking.

The management were thoroughly convinced of the value of quality circles and they became a new way of life in the plant – until – a few months later when the management changed. Quality circles were thrown out and completely forgotten by the management – but not by the workforce!

Another lesson is to be learned from this by those contemplating setting up, and sustaining, a Six Sigma organization.

Imia's *kaizen* process

Overview

Kaizen is a Japanese word that means *improvement*. Masaaki Imai (Imia, M., 1986) conceived the kaizen process to promote continual improvement by the workforce at the point of work (*gemba*) as a matter of daily habit. Success is achieved when this becomes common standard practice throughout an organization. This is accomplished through the unleashing of existing know-how and common sense supported by basic improvement tools. It demands motivation and empowerment of the workforce and ongoing support and encouragement by the management. The process could, perhaps, be more precisely described by the Japanese term *gemba kaizen*, which means 'at the place of work improvement'. Imai distinguishes between two types of change:

- Large-step change through innovation. Innovation is high cost, investment based. It usually results from the top management introducing new technology, or spending money on specific equipment and the like. This is a discrete breakthrough activity that lacks continuity.
- Gradual change as a never-ending improvement process. This is *kaizen*. Kaizen is low cost, effort based. It results from existing resources. A large number of people make small improvements in work practices on a regular daily basis.

Kaizen is aimed primarily at three objectives:

1 improving the quality of not only products and services but also the processes used to realize them;
2 reducing the cost of development, making and delivery of products and services;
3 ensuring timely delivery.

These objectives are achieved by a three-pronged approach. First, is the elimination of *muda*. Muda is the Japanese term for waste in its most general sense.

Table 3.14 The five Ss

1	*Seiri*	Sort	Remove the unnecessary
2	*Seiton*	Straighten	Put what remains in order so that they can be readily accessed
3	*Seiso*	Scrub	Keep the workplace clean
4	*Seiketsu*	Systemize	Make cleaning and checking a routine practice
5	*Shitsuke*	Standardize	Standardize the previous four steps to perpetuate the process

It relates to every non-value-adding activity. Waste is recognized to come in a number of forms, such as: rejects/repair/rework; waiting/idle time; inventory excess; unnecessary movement and energy to perform tasks; inefficient and unnecessary tasks; timing/failure to synchronize systems; overproduction; and transport/movement of things. Second comes good housekeeping. Here *kaizen* uses the *5S* approach. 5S refers to five Japanese words beginning with S. The meaning and purpose of the 5Ss are shown in Table 3.14.

Third, there is standardization. Standards are a very important element of kaizen. They describe best practice. They preserve knowledge. They measure performance. They facilitate improvement. They establish objectives and provide a basis for training. They ensure that changes are retained and that people do not revert back to the previous way of doing things. *Kaizen* disciples point out the difference between Japan and the West as far as setting, maintaining and improving standards are concerned. In the West, it is suggested that the people who set the standards are the technical people who are normally detached from the actual process.

Go to gemba

In Japan, a much greater influence arises from the *gemba*. *Gemba* is a Japanese term that, in *kaizen*, refers to the place where the real action occurs. It is an all-embracing term that includes such places as bedrooms, bar, restaurant, lobby, reception in hotels, at desks in offices and at workplaces in industrial plants. *Gemba* is where the value-adding activity occurs. In *Kaizen*, management are encouraged to take a deep interest in, and keep in close touch with, *gemba* and to visit it regularly. This is quite different from Western practice. In the West, it is suggested that the management generally have little contact with *gemba*. They are largely desk-bound. They are happy to distance themselves from what actually happens at *gemba*. As such they are frequently out of touch with reality. They give orders based on a perception of *gemba* formed by reports, meetings in offices and information passed to them.

Case study

An example of this is one experienced by the author at an engineering nut manufacturer who had a cracking problem. An investigation into nut cracking took place to determine causal factors. Meetings were convened by the technical director and attended by the chief metallurgist and chief engineer amongst others. The technical director expressed considerable concern when it was suggested that perhaps the setter-operator directly concerned with the forming operation should become involved. After learned technical discussions various proportions of metallurgical elements in the material, variation in coil batch to coil batch, supplier to supplier, operator to operator and machine to machine aspects were taken into account in the design of a series of experiments. A fair amount of time, energy and expense was expended. The operators co-operated fully in conducting the experiment. However, their views were not sought or given. All of this was to no avail.

At long last the people involved 'went to *gemba*'. A quick discussion with the setter/operator revealed that the variation lay within a coil. He said 'When I feed a coil in and it is too hard to work I simply start from the other end and feed in the bar until it again becomes progressively too hard to work. In this way I can very often use up the bulk of each coil'. The quick and simple answer lay in *gemba*; variation in hardness within a coil.

Imai's five golden rules for gemba management

In *Kaizen* management 'go to *gemba*' regularly. They stay in one spot for several minutes and observe reality. In so doing they learn much. They will identify many areas that can be improved with little, or no, cost to the organization. Imai provides five simple but golden rules for *gemba* management, as indicated in Table 3.15.

Table 3.15   Imai's five simple but golden rules for *gemba* management

---

1. When an abnormality arises go to *gemba* first

2. Check the *gembutsu* (the relevant item)

3. Take temporary countermeasures on the spot

4. Find and remove the root cause

5. Standardize to prevent recurrence

Us and them

In Kaizen activities very basic tools are normally used, such as the 5W and 2H approach; Deming PDCA cycle; 5S housekeeping; work study elements; 5M for production and 5P for services. Management style and attitude is important to kaizen. It is suggested, by kaizen disciples, that traditional management frequently view the organization to be made up of two types of people, us and them. There are those who specify and manage work and those who do what they are told. This is tantamount to inviting workers to switch off mentally whilst at work. A case study illustrates the consequences of this culture.

Case study. Take the jig borer operator after spending a lifetime with a major precision engineering organization. On receipt of his gold watch at his farewell ceremony he said a few words to the management for the first and last time in nearly 40 years of service. He said 'I am very proud of what I have achieved here. There is only one other jig borer as technically advanced as mine in the whole world. Therefore I must be either the Number 1 or Number 2 jig borer operator in the world'. He continued 'In spite of that I have never in my whole time here ever been asked for my opinion on any aspect of jig borer operation. I have been treated purely as an attachment to the machine'.

What a damning indictment!

Kaizen will not work in such a culture. *Kaizen* followers such as Professor Kawase[1] also see two classes of people in an organization: those who earn money and those who do not. He considers only people in the frontline, at *gemba*, who develop, produce products and deliver services and sell actually earn money for the company. The people who do not earn money are those who have such titles as chief, head and manager. He refers to these people as dependants. He suggests that the non-money earners often think that they know better than money earners because they are better educated. In so thinking they often make the job of the latter more difficult. What they should be thinking is 'What can we do to help the money earners do their job better?' He goes on to state:

If the customer is 'king' then the people at *gemba* are 'god' [Buddha].

Continuity of deployment

Kaizen promoters such as the Kaizen Institute recognize that other comparable initiatives, such as quality circles, that continue to survive and prosper in Japan

---

[1]*Solving industrial engineering problems* by Takeshi Kawase; Nikkan Kogyo Shinbun (in Japanese).

have long since been discarded in the West. This is attributed to a difference in business cultures. They recognize that it is necessary to build in the necessary infrastructure, systems and procedures to ensure continuity of deployment of initiatives, such as *kaizen*, in Western organizations.

Kaizen *and Six Sigma*

Kaizen and Six Sigma share a common objective that of continuing improvement in quality, cost and delivery. The kaizen approach to initiating, encouraging, supporting and sustaining workforce engagement in improvement activities, as a daily habit, should be embodied in any Six Sigma initiative. This would counteract a fundamental weakness perceived in the Western approach in this area. In Japan, *kaizen* is complemented by quality circles. In the West, Six Sigma project teams can well take the place of quality circles. Such Six Sigma project teams concern themselves also with higher-level activities that demand innovation, originality and creativity. Quality circles were most often made up of people doing similar jobs. Six Sigma project teams extend this concept and may also be formed by members having mixed disciplines appropriate to the requirements of the project being undertaken.

The lean organization (Taiichi Ohno)

Lean organizations are based on the production system evolved at Toyota largely under the guidance of Taiichi Ohno (Ohno, T., 1988). The aims of a lean organization are to achieve the highest quality, the lowest cost and the shortest lead-time. It is claimed that a lean system can be expected to yield: 50% of the hours of human effort; 50% less defects; 1/3 the hours of technical effort; 50% less space and 1/10 or less of in-process inventories. Three key features on which 'lean' is based are continuous flow, pull system and waste elimination.

Continuous flow is achieved by influences such as:

- *line balancing*: the equalizing of cycle times of small units of product through allocation of operatives and machines;
- *nagara*: smoothing flow through synchronization of production processes and maximum utilization of available time and overlapping of operations where appropriate;
- *smed* (single minute exchange of die) [due to Shigeo Shingo (Shingo, S., 1986)]: literally refers to the ability to changing a set-up in a minute or less. In practice it relates to very rapid set-ups;
- *andon*: system of flashing lights to indicate production status, for example, green – OK; red – not OK, production stopped;
- *takt* time: time to produce one item, for example, a car every 3 min.

Pull systems are those based on actual real-time needs of downstream operations rather than the traditional push system based on a predetermined plan that may not be currently valid. Influences include:

- *JIT* (*just-in-time*): a production scheduling concept for each operation that calls for any item to be produced precisely when needed.
- *Kanban*: a card, sheet or container used to authorize production or movement of an item. The quantity authorized per kanban is minimal, ideally one.

Waste elimination involves tools such as:

- cellular and flexible manufacturing;
- *kaizen*: continuous improvement as a routine;
- 5S housekeeping disciplines;
- *jidoka*: process whereby the operation stops if a defect is found;
- *poka-yoke*: error proofing;
- *shojinka*: the capability to vary the process to fit the demand profile; this involves flexibility in manning and work-centre layout.

Seven types of waste are identified (as with *kaizen*). These are excess (or early) production or delivery, delays, transportation (to and from processes), movement (within processes), inventory, inspection and errors.

Six Sigma personnel should be aware of the concepts involved with lean organizations as these are aligned to a great extent with those of Six Sigma. It is also advisable that they become familiar with the methods used as it is inevitable that their projects will involve waste elimination and possibly also continuous flow pull systems.

The Taguchi way

Most people associate Genichi Taguchi (Taguchi, G., 1986) purely with certain types of experimental designs for problem-solving. This aspect can be extremely beneficial as will be shown later in the book. However, his greatest technical contribution is to the various stages of product/process/service development: system design, parameter design and tolerance design. Eight concepts make up the key elements of Taguchi's design quality strategy. These are shown in Table 3.16 and discussed in detail in Chapter 4.

It is highly unlikely that Six Sigma personnel will conduct many improvement projects before coming into contact with both Taguchi design concepts and the methods of Taguchi style designed experimentation.

Valid criticisms have been made, by statisticians, on a few aspects of Taguchi methods of experimental analysis such as his use of generic signal/noise metrics and accumulation theories. These criticisms pale into insignificance,

Table 3.16   Eight key concepts of the Taguchi quality engineering philosophy

1. Minimize loss by ensuring uniformity around the preferred value
2. Design processes/products that produce uniform products economically
3. Exploit non-linear effects of process parameters on performance characteristics
4. Cure the effect not the cause
5. A zero defect standard is an inadequate goal
6. Design products/processes robust against operating conditions/use
7. Taguchi method is not essentially a problem-solving technique
8. Exploit the three types of product/process parameters

however, compared with their usefulness and his achievements. He has succeeded in:

- Drawing attention to fundamental aspects of high-quality, low-cost, product, process and service design.
- Introducing designed experimentation to many. Prior to Taguchi experimentation was confined, mainly, to a few specific projects designed and analysed by statistical experts.

Taguchi design concepts and experimental methodology are a must for the toolbox of the Six Sigma black belt. These subjects are dealt with in more detail later in the book.

Chapter highlights

- A number of different strategies and models for continual improvement of business performance are in common currency. These include those with a system focus, a process focus, project focus and a Guru focus. Many are being deployed in a fragmented manner.
- The Six Sigma initiative provides an orientating and integrating mechanism for selected approaches.
- Six Sigma embodies best-practice elements of all four focuses.
- With respect to the system focus Six Sigma is based on the total quality as opposed to the more restricted quality assurance route.
- In Six Sigma, both process and project focuses are deployed as projects are undertaken locally in workplaces by green belts and across functional and departmental interfaces by black belts.

- Which Guru should the Six Sigma practitioner follow? Six Sigma implementers need to be aware of the principal ideas and concepts and views of the more prominent Gurus. They will probably end up with features from each to varying degrees depending on the existing culture and practices within, and the vision for, their organization. The important thing is to standardize on the chosen approach and so establish a common language throughout the organization. Probably the best advice is 'build on what you already have'.

- From a systems viewpoint, the most widely applied system applied throughout the world is based on ISO 9001 and its more prescriptive sector derivatives. The year 2000 version is based on eight management principles. These underpin the Six Sigma approach. These are customer focus, leadership, involvement of people, process approach, system approach, factual approach to decision-making and mutually beneficial supplier relationships. As ISO 9001 is used for conformity assessment it prescribes minimum acceptable quality system requirements. It is not intended to be a 'best in class' standard. However, its sister standard, ISO 9004, provides generic guidelines for best practice, competitive advantage and superior performance. Both provide a sound backdrop for the deployment of the more prescriptive Six Sigma world-class initiative.

- The European Foundation for Quality Management and the USA Malcolm Baldrige are the best known quality-excellence models. Both are generic and recognize that there are many paths to achieving sustainable excellence. Both are suitable precursors to a Six Sigma initiative by providing a self-assessment mechanism for a rigorous gap analysis and a stimulant to arriving at focused solutions.

Bibliography

Crosby, P.B. (1979). *Quality is free: the art of making certain*, New York: McGraw-Hill.
Crosby, P.B. (1981). *Quality withour tears: the art of hassle-free management*, New York: McGraw-Hill.
Deming, W.E. (1982). *Out of the crisis*, Cambridge: Cambridge University Press.
Feigenbaum, A. (1961). *Total quality control*, New York: McGraw-Hill.
Imia, M. (1986). *Kaizen: the key to Japan's competitive success*, New York: McGraw-Hill.
Ishikawa, K. (1985). *What is total quality control? The Japanese way*, NJ: Prentice-Hall.
ISO TC 176 (1994). *Technical Report 10017*, Geneva: ISO.
ISO TC 176 (2000). *ISO 9001:2000 Quality management systems – requirements*, Geneva: ISO.
ISO TC 176 (2000). *ISO 9000:2000 Quality management systems – fundamental and vocabulary*, Geneva: ISO.
ISO TC 176 (2000). *ISO 9004:2000 Quality management systems – guidelines for performance improvements*, Geneva: ISO.
ISO TC 176 and TC207 (2002). *ISO 19011:2002: Guidelines for quality and/or environmental management systems auditing*, Geneva: ISO.

Juran, J. (1992). *Juran on quality by design*, New York: McMillan, pp. 11–12.

Juran, J. and Blanton, Godfrey, A. (1998). *Juran's quality handbook*, New York: McGraw-Hill.

Ohno, T. (1988). *Toyota production system*, Stamford, CT: Productivity Press.

Shingo, S. (1986). *Zero quality control: source inspection and the Poka-Yoke system*, Stamford, CT: Productivity Press.

Taguchi, G. (1986). *Introduction to quality engineering*, Tokyo: Asian Productivity Association.

Chapter 4
How can Six Sigma achieve the greatest impact on business performance?

> First, have a definite, clear practical ideal, a goal, an objective.
> Second, have the necessary means to achieve your ends,
> wisdom, money, materials and methods. Third, adjust
> all your means to that end.
>
> *Aristotle*

Common aim of Six Sigma projects

The common aim of the Six Sigma initiative is to improve value. The Six Sigma value-improvement process is based on:

- focus on the establishment of measures of value;
- focus on business objectives and targets against which improvement is assessed;
- focus on processes (the how) and functions (the why).

The Six Sigma initiative described in this book contrasts with many standard Six Sigma initiatives. It recognizes that Six Sigma has moved on since its originators focused almost exclusively on reducing 'defects' to a declared world-class value of Six Sigma (3.4 'defects' per million opportunities). It pursues the wider concept of overall value enhancement rather than the more restricted target of minimizing the number of non-conformities per million opportunities. One can be a Six Sigma organization producing to a standard of 3.4 non-conformities per million opportunities, yet have a product or service that is neither competitive nor meets the value concepts expected by potential customers. Successful deployment of the Six Sigma initiative is dependent on six features as listed in Table 4.1.

Table 4.1   Features inherent in the Six Sigma initiative

1. The three focuses
2. Pursuit of innovation and creativity
3. Positive and proactive teamwork
4. Training to develop competencies
5. Generation of a culture that is receptive to innovation
6. Application of the appropriate methodology

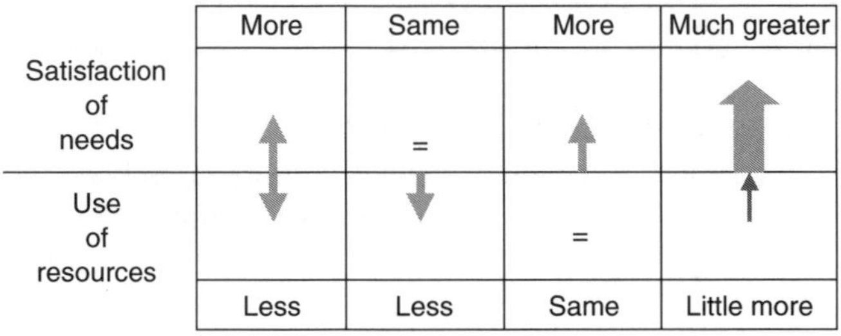

	More	Same	More	Much greater
Satisfaction of needs	↕	=	↑	⬆
Use of resources	↓	↓	=	↑
	Less	Less	Same	Little more

Figure 4.1   Different ways of enhancing value

What is value?

Value is relative, not absolute. External customers might consider something to be of better value if they have to pay less for a product or service that meets their expectations. On the other hand, suppliers may look on better value to be when they have to use less resources to provide a product, or service, that satisfies the external customer, Value (BSI, 2000; CEN/TC 279, 2000) may be expressed by the relationship:

$$\text{Value} \propto \frac{\text{Satisfaction of needs}}{\text{Use of resources}}$$

The ∝ symbol (read the ∝ symbol to mean 'is a function of') indicates that 'satisfaction of needs' and 'use of resources' can be traded off, one against the other, to obtain an optimum balance. Hence, from a Six Sigma viewpoint, optimization of value may be achieved in a number of ways. The better the needs are satisfied and/or the fewer the resources used, the greater is the value. This is illustrated diagrammatically in Figure 4.1.

Types of resources and needs: the Kano model

Resources comprise everything that is required to satisfy a need. They include things such as money, time, hardware, software and people. In some cases, the

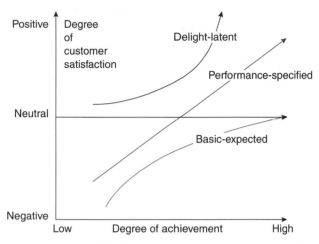

Figure 4.2   Kano's model of customer satisfaction in terms of need fulfilment

availability of a resource may be of more importance than its cost. Two different classes of needs are of particular interest to us in Six Sigma value-improvement projects. First, in applying a particular improvement method to reduce resource cost whilst retaining the original value, termed value analysis, there is a need to distinguish between:

- *Use needs*: which refer to basic tangible function (e.g. a knife as a cutting instrument).
- *Esteem needs*: which are often more subjective, such as:
  - for a service, a salesperson who has inter-personal skills and attributes that encourage people to deal with him/her;
  - for a product, a necktie.

Second, it is particularly important to recognize that satisfaction of needs frequently involves more than just 'avoidance of failure to perform a function' or 'conforming to requirement'. Achieving an improvement of, say, 4 *Sigma* to 6 *Sigma*, namely going from 6210 to 3.4 failures per million opportunities would most certainly significantly decrease customer dissatisfaction with a product, or service. However, even achieving zero failures does not normally, in itself, create customer satisfaction but purely a feeling of neutrality about the product or service.

This distinction is brought out in the Kano[1] model shown in Figure 4.2 and the tree diagram given in Figure 4.3.

---

[1]Due to Dr Noriaki Kano.

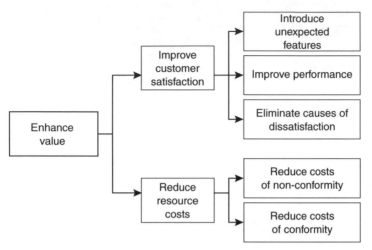

Figure 4.3 Value as a function of resources expended and satisfaction achieved

In the Kano model, three types of needs are recognized:

- basic needs (must have);
- performance needs (more/faster/easier is better);
- excitement needs (unexpected).

Basic needs are those that the customer expects to be met in a product or service. Examples are, clean cutlery or a place setting in a restaurant, clean bed-sheets in a hotel, a motor vehicle that starts easily, a telephone that has a dialing tone when it is picked up and a light that operates when switched on. Basic needs fail to satisfy if achieved, but dissatisfy the customer if they are not. The upside potential is small or non-existent and the downside potential is large. Meeting basic needs is an essential prerequisite to meeting higher needs. If these basic needs are not met the other, upper order, needs become irrelevant. If these are not achieved the customer is dissatisfied. The customer complains and/or does business elsewhere in future. Such a situation may be measured by the loss of market share, fault rate, things-gone-wrong, customer-complaints, warranty claims and product recalls. There will be varying degrees of dissatisfaction depending on the degree of fulfilment. If they are fully achieved the expectation is such that customer will probably not even notice. He or she will not feel satisfied, purely neutral or oblivious to the event.

Performance needs are those that generate increased satisfaction proportionate to the level of achievement. Performance factors are normally already present. The challenge is to select those of most importance to the customer and improve their performance. Service examples are speed of checkout at a hotel and check-in at an airport, the time to take an order and serve food in a restaurant.

Product ones could well be the performance of a motor vehicle in terms of fuel consumption, acceleration and maximum speed and the wattage of a light bulb or microwave oven. Performance features provide considerable scope for improvement in competitive position. They are usually established through market research by heeding and responding to the *voice of the customer* using surveys and techniques such as axiomatic design and quality function deployment.

Excitement needs are latent ones. They are those not in the customer's awareness. If these needs are not met there is no response from the customer. If they are met, the customer gets something unexpected and is delighted. Examples are a bouquet of flowers with a new motor vehicle, a bowl of fruit in a hotel room, and a free aperitif or extra unspecified sorbet course at a restaurant. Excitement features are intended to cause such delight as to attract new customers and retain the loyalty of existing ones. They are not usually identified through market research. Creativity is required in an organization to identify ideas and innovations, based on an appreciation and understanding of the latent needs of customers.

The Kano model is a dynamic rather than static one. With time 'excitement needs' migrate into 'performance needs' and ultimately possibly into 'basic needs'. For example, ABS anti-lock braking on motor vehicles initially created excitement, but are now looked upon as commonplace. It is, thus, essential to recognize, and respond to, the continually changing nature of competitive pressures and customer expectations.

From a Six Sigma perspective, it is crucial that one does not become so set or resolute in the pursuit of the reduction of non-conformities per million opportunities, to minimize customer dissatisfaction, that opportunities are ignored, particularly in upstream activities, to create increasing degrees of satisfaction and even delight. Six Sigma has an important role to play in upstream activities such as the identification, realization and performance improvement of critical to quality characteristics (CTQCs).

How does one differentiate between basic, performance and excitement needs? Two simple questions have been devised to elicit, from a customer, whether or not he/she considers a need to be basic, performance related or excitement. The drill is to ask two kinds of questions about a particular need, characteristic or feature. These are:

> *Question 1.* How do you feel if something (a characteristic or feature) is absent?
> *Question 2.* How do you feel if something (a characteristic or feature) is present?
> Answer Question 1 with either 'bad' or 'neutral'. Answer Question 2 with either 'neutral', 'good' or 'it depends'.
> If the answer to Q1 is 'bad' and to Q2 'neutral', it is a *basic* need.
> If the answer to Q1 is 'neutral' and to Q2 'it depends', it is a *performance* need.
> If the answer to Q1 is 'neutral' and to Q2 'good', it is a *delight* need.

Figure 4.3 emphasizes the point made earlier that Six Sigma aims should extend beyond that of reducing non-conformities to a world-class value of 3.4 non-conformities per million opportunities. Those engaged in Six Sigma continual-improvement activities need to recognize that there are also other, often more fruitful, paths to the enhancement of value in an organization.

How to enhance value throughout the organization

How to enhance product, process and service value upstream

There are a number of focuses available to Six Sigma practitioners to enhance value throughout the organization. Frequently, the most important focus is largely ignored. That is the design process. This activity impacts all subsequent downstream processes, activities and customer reactions. These upstream activities obviously have the greatest leverage but frequently are way down the pecking order in terms of urgency and priority for Six Sigma project activity. This leverage effect is shown in Figure 4.4.

In Figure 4.4, entity can refer, for example, to an organization, a system (e.g. financial, administrative, technical), a product or service. Entity design includes the interpretation and definition of customer (internal as well as external) needs and expectations. Process refers to the means by which the entity is to be realized. For example, the resources to be deployed. Realization refers to the execution, the actual fulfilment activity, for example, manufacture or assembly of a product or delivery of a service.

Upstream design typically leverages the largest value influence on a product, process or service. There is a natural resistance, however, in Six Sigma activities to be proactive and move upstream to plan and prevent problems from arising and use this leverage to advantage. Why? There is a simple and quite under-standable reason for this. The benefits accrued through design enhancement, although very substantial and which influence the whole organization, take some while to work through the system. Hence, the making of quantitative assess-ments of the worth of a particular project may not be possible within the required time scale normally associated with Six Sigma activities. It is, thus, incorrectly, often looked upon as a low-profile activity. Whereas downstream

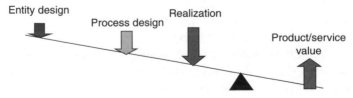

Figure 4.4 The quality lever

Table 4.2 Matrix of typical upstream techniques to enhance value through Six Sigma activities

Type of technique	Type of value				
	Reduce resource costs		Improve customer satisfaction		
	Reduce non-conformity costs	Reduce conformity costs	Eliminate causes of dissatisfaction	Improve performance	Introduce unexpected features
Axiomatic design	×	×	×	×	×
TRIZ	×	×	×	×	
QFD	×	×	×	×	×
VA	×	×			
QE	×	×	×	×	
DoE	×	×	×	×	
PFMEA	×		×		
DFR	×	×	×		
SPC	×		×		

TRIZ, the 'theory of inventive problem-solving'; QFD, 'quality function deployment'; VA, 'value analysis'; QE, 'quality engineering'; DoE, 'design of experiments'; PFMEA, system, design and process 'potential failure mode and effects analysis'; DFR, 'design for realization' (e.g. manufacture, assembly, delivery); SPC, 'statistical process control'.

problem-solving is a high visibility 'fire-fighting' type operation where quantitative gains are quite readily assessed, claimed and validated. Given this we need, in Six Sigma, to advocate, initiate and deploy a disciplined approach and methodology to remove these obstacles and reap the high dividends associated with tackling design upstream.

A number of techniques are now available to designers and Six Sigma practitioners. These are shown in the matrix of Table 4.2 in terms of types of value to which they are primarily relevant.

These techniques comprise a set of principles and practices that constitutes a useful toolkit for Six Sigma practitioners:

– that facilitate improvements in the design of products, processes, systems and services to
  - provide robust configurations that incorporate parts and sub-systems that have been optimized and standardized; this ensures that all critical-to-quality characteristics will reflect best-in-class capability;
  - minimize complexity and hence the potential for non-conformance;
  - have realization, simplicity and cost-effectiveness as cornerstones;

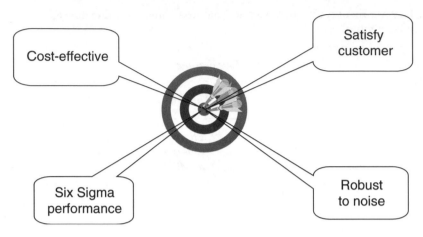

Figure 4.5 Design aims to improve value

– may use the concept of a concurrent design process based on cross-functional teams rather than the traditional design process that involves a number of functional departments working in relative isolation and in series.

The primary aims are to create designs that match customer needs and expectations; are resource efficient; are inherently capable of high yields regardless of complexity and are robust (impervious) to noise due to causes such as, wear, fatigue, deviations from nominal during realization, ambient temperature, humidity and vibration. These aims are portrayed in Figure 4.5.

A number of sources offer opportunities for improvement in the quality of product/process system service design. These include:

Design utility

The utility of the entity as perceived by the customer. This utility is measured in terms of ease and economy of realization, dependability (including reliability, serviceability and availability), functionality, aesthetic appeal and price.

Exploit this opportunity using axiomatic design, TRIZ and quality function deployment (QFD) methodology.

Design integrity

The design is not fundamentally unsound: for example, uses a heat-sensitive adhesive to join components that are subjected to temperature variation.

Exploit this opportunity using Potential Failure Mode and Effects Analysis (PFMEA).

Design parameter optimization

The design is fundamentally sound but certain key product characteristics or process parameters need to be adjusted to improve performance; for example:

- change in pintle sealing cone geometry and tolerances to improve leakage characteristics on a fuel injector valve;
- change in die and pour temperature, tilt speed and melt mix to improve yield of overhead cam manifolds;
- change in proportion of ingredients of a cake mix to improve taste, flavour and texture.

Exploit the opportunity using quality engineering and multi-factor experimentation.

Design robustness

The design performance is vulnerable to noise such as:

- process parameter variation (e.g. teeming temperature, vacuuming time);
- manufacturing, service delivery and material deviations from nominal;
- external factors (e.g. humidity, vibration, supply voltage variation, differences in skill).

Exploit the opportunity using quality engineering and multi-run multiple-factor experimentation with both mean and standard deviation as responses.

Design realization

The design, as specified, facilitates realization and use at minimum cost.

Exploit the opportunity using value analysis, DFR and SPC

These five points are portrayed pictorially in Figure 4.6.
The overall approach and specific techniques are now discussed at appreciation level in sufficient depth to familiarize Six Sigma personnel in the where and when, and an introduction to how, to apply them.

Six Sigma for high-value design

The design process

The design process discussed here not only relates to products that may be sold to external customers but also to the design of services, and the design of internal manufacturing/financial/administrative/information technology systems and

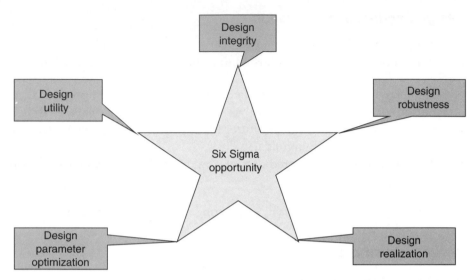

Figure 4.6   Six Sigma opportunities for improvements in value at the design stage

the like. To many not directly concerned with the design process it is often a closed book. It might even represent a Pandora's box, one that people are very reluctant to open for a number of reasons. It may not appear prudent to risk unsettling, a precious, and often scarce, resource, the designer. There could well be some foreboding of what it might reveal. The reluctance might stem from the fear of not understanding the contents or not knowing how to react technically and organizationally to the consequences.

The impact of the design of products, services and functional systems on the success of any business is so great that no one associated with any comprehensive business improvement initiative can afford not to open the key to the box and appreciate the reasoning behind its contents. This is exemplified in the quality lever illustrated in Figure 4.4. The high leverage exerted by entity design and process design in Figure 4.4 indicates that it is essential that the design process and its upstream and downstream interfaces are made transparent and subjected to the same, or even deeper, scrutiny than other processes. Unfortunately, the design process and its interfaces often receive proportionately less attention than downstream processes where much of Six Sigma activity takes place.

Why is this? Improvement in design often lack the immediate direct visibility associated with reactive problem-solving where claims to have reduced fault rates from X to Y% to save £Z per year can quite readily be verified. Also, Six Sigma personnel may not have the necessary knowledge and skills needed to positively influence the contents of the box. The ways to discovering the secrets of the design process and its interfaces, and of utilizing them to secure continual improvement, are dependent on the assimilation of the nature of the design process and the understanding of a number of design methods. As such they form an essential part of the body of knowledge required by a Six Sigma practitioner. This body of knowledge forms the basis of this chapter.

Why is design for Six Sigma so important?

In answering this question do we need to go further than the 'quality lever' and the '10 cash drains' that Clausing has identified in the design/development process? He calls these drains:

1 *Technology push.* Clausing (Clausing, D.P., 1994) suggests three reasons for this cash drain:
   - major resources are spent on new technological concepts without first identifying a customer need;
   - strong customer needs are identified for which technology generation activities are wanting;
   - inadequate transference of technology into system design activities.
2 *Disregard for the voice of the customer.* Here he suggests that many designs reflect the voice of the designer rather than the customer.
3 *The Eureka concept.* Only one design concept is given serious consideration.
4 *Pretend design.* This relates to the situation where the end result is looked upon as a first prototype rather than the best possible competitively priced design.
5 *Pampered product.* This is the product that needs considerable tweaking and tinkering to work.
6 *Hardware swamps.* These arise when experimental hardware requires endless debugging.
7 *Here's the product. Where's the factory?* No, or little, regard is taken of the manufacturing, realization or delivery capabilities.
8 *We've always done it this way.* No attempt is made to improve product parameters or optimize the design process.
9 *Inspection.* Here there is reliance on test and inspection to correct bad designs.
10 *Give me my targets. Let me do my thing.* This is the ivory tower, design in isolation, lack of teamwork, get off my back, approach.

You may recognize some of these in your own organization. To turn these 'cash drains' into 'cash cows', the Six Sigma practitioner obviously needs to have a good understanding of both the design process and modern design practices in the form of the various methods that can be deployed. Effective application of this understanding will result in a significantly reduced time to market, an enhancement of value through higher quality and reduced costs, and improved customer satisfaction. The down side is that it will be rather more difficult to quantify the savings involved in the time scale involved with most Six Sigma projects.

The prescriptive design process

Design as a verb relates to a prescriptive and usually iterative process of creating a design (noun). Designers usually follow a number of generic steps regardless of the object of a customer-driven design or the particular design practices or methods chosen. These are:

1 understand, or anticipate the potential customer's needs and expectations;
2 establish design objectives to satisfy these needs and expectations;
3 generate ideas to create credible solutions;
4 analyse the solution alternatives and select the best option;
5 implement the selected design.

Senge's three levels of thinking

Overview

Senge (Senge, Peter M., 1990) proposes three levels of thinking, *event* level, *pattern* level and *structure* level. Event-level thinking concerns itself with reaction to things that have already occurred. Pattern-level thinking focuses on trends and their implications. Structure-level thinking, the highest level, is directed at the architecture of the overall system, how system elements interact with one another, and the manner in which it influences the behaviour of patterns. Senge's three thinking levels are used as a further backdrop for Figure 4.7. Certain key design practices and methods are also indicated approximately at the level of thinking, and progression of the design process, in which they can most usefully be deployed.

Event-level thinking

The argument is that, historically, event-level thinking has reigned supreme, and continues so to some degree, in many types of organizations. Delivery quality levels are achieved by end-of-line, after-the-event, inspection and test. Significant waste occurs due to the extent of inspection and test required and the consequences of the resultant weeding out of sub-standard product. Warranty claims and customer complaints are used as the main barometer of success. Further upstream, in the physical domain, extensive and prolonged development involves a series of test–modify–retest cycles to achieve correct functioning and to ensure design integrity. In the mid 1990s, for example, the then event-thinking organization, GE (General Electric), identified quality waste of some $10 billion per year.

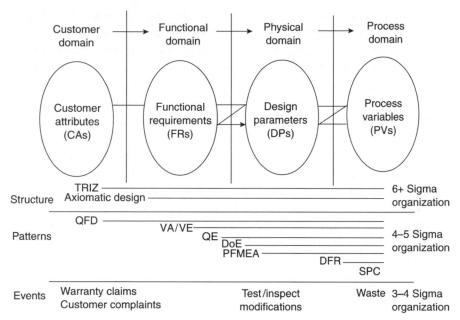

Figure 4.7   Concept to customer mapping

Six Sigma activities directed purely at reacting to events can, on the basis of experience in such organizations committed to Six Sigma, be expected to secure savings per full-time black belt per year of some £150 000. This indicates that considerable benefits can be achieved by application of the simpler reactive problem-solving tools within the framework of a Six Sigma project structure. However, whilst Six Sigma activities are confined to reacting to events that have already occurred it is not expected that the organization will achieve a greater level of achievement than about 4 Sigma overall.

Pattern- and structure-level thinking

Pattern- and structure-level thinking is required to escape from the endless drudgery of 'fire-fighting'. This demands a change in mindset from detection to prevention. This involves going upstream to the hatchery where the various potential problems and hazards are conceived and reared. The tremendous potential for improvement that exists at these higher levels of thinking means that the successful Six Sigma practitioner will need to progressively take on board the body of knowledge and skills associated with modern design practices and methods.

This body of knowledge is often referred to under the umbrella term 'design for Six Sigma' (DFSS). At the pattern level, universally accepted and robust methods that are increasingly being used are indicated in Figure 4.7. These are explored later in this chapter. They include quality function deployment (QFD), which can gainfully be deployed in all domains, value analysis (VA) and value engineering (VE), which straddle a number of domains. Quality engineering (QE) and design of experiments (DoE) include designing for robustness, and parameter and tolerance design. Potential failure mode and effects analysis (PFMEA) and its counterparts, such as fault tree analysis (FTA), hazard analysis and critical control points (HACCP) and key word analysis (KWA) are applicable in some regimes. Design for realization (DFR) includes design for manufacture (DFM) and design for assembly (DFA). Statistical process control (SPC) is intended as an ongoing process monitor downstream so that process disturbances, patterns and trends can be detected and corrected prior to causing problems at the output stage. Performance results can also then be fed upstream to assist in the making of the most appropriate design decisions.

There is little doubt that the application of *structure*-level thinking exerts the greatest leverage for continual improvement. There are two primary reasons for this. First, three very powerful design methods exist at this level. These are 'axiomatic design', quality function deployment and 'TRIZ', a Russian acronym for 'the theory of inventive problem-solving'. Second, when a good basic structure for the design process is adopted, the application of pattern-thinking methods becomes much more effective.

Summarizing, the path of an organization to world-class performance depends, to a large degree, on the extension of Six Sigma activities upstream in the design process. In this way fundamental flaws can be circumvented at source, thus reducing the need for 'after the event' fire-fighting. To achieve this, the Six Sigma practitioner will need to be aware of, and exploit, best-practice design methods as described in this chapter.

Design practice methods

A number of design practice methods or tools to facilitate and systematize the design process are readily available. When applied as standard design practice they help considerably in structuring and making the whole process transparent, thus opening up all stages of the process to independent scrutiny. At the same time, they facilitate the transfer of design knowledge and skills across design projects and interested parties including Six Sigma personnel. Principal design practice methods are described in Figure 4.7 in terms of the three design phases and four design domains shown in Table 4.3.

In Figure 4.7, for each pair of domains, the left domain represents 'what is to be achieved', and the right domain 'how it is to be achieved'. The design process by which this is achieved is termed 'mapping'. For instance, concept design consists of mapping the customer needs (CNs) (the whats) in the customer domain to create functional requirements (FRs) (the hows) in the

Table 4.3 Three design phases and four design domains

Design phase	Design domain	Phase/domain elements	Example
	Customer	Customer needs (CNs) are identified in the language of the customer	Preserve food
Concept	Functional	Mapping of CNs into FRs Functional requirements (FRs) of the design solution that meet customer needs are derived and expressed in the language of the designer	Functional choices: can, dehydrate, cool. Cool chosen
Product	Physical	Mapping of FRs into DPs Design parameters (DPs) that satisfy the functional requirements are defined	Physical choices: cool-box, refrigerator, freezer. Freezer chosen and specified
Process	Process	Mapping of DPs into PVs Process variables (PVs) define how the design is to be realized (e.g. manufactured)	Freezer manufacturing process specified

functional domain. As this is an iterative process it involves zigzagging between the domains.

An example of mapping is shown in the fourth column of Table 4.3. Suppose that in the customer domain the customer wishes to preserve food. The design team will consider the various ways in which this may be accomplished in the functional domain, such as by cooling, dehydrating or canning. The design team then selects, say, a freezer in view of temperature requirements and other constraints. He/she then develops the specification for the freezer in the physical domain. In the process domain a description of the method of manufacture is detailed.

Axiomatic design

Axiomatic design is a process for creating new designs. It can also be very useful in diagnosing and improving existing designs. The axiomatic design approach is based on a fundamental set of principles that determine good design practice. The primary aims of axiomatic design include the enhancement of creativity, the minimization of trial and error iteration, and the facilitation of

Table 4.4   The four key
concepts of axiomatic design

---

1. Four domains
2. Hierarchies
3. Independence axiom
4. Information axiom

---

decision-making on what is the best design among alternatives. A design team that uses the axiomatic design approach will:

1 establish customer needs and expectations (actual and potential) for the object of the design in terms of customer attributes (CAs);
2 evolve a description of the functions required of the object in the form of functional requirements (FRs);
3 develop a specification for the object that will fulfil the functions in the form of design parameters (DPs);
4 describe how the object will be realized in the form of process variables (PVs).

In Figure 4.7, the domains associated with the axiomatic design method is used as a backdrop for indicating other relevant and compatible standard design practices. Axiomatic design, due to Nam Suh (Suh, N. P., 1990; 2001), provides fundamental principles to guide decision-making at the various stages of the design process. The intent is to provide a rational systematic approach to the design process. Four key concepts are involved and are shown in Table 4.4.

The concept of the *four domains*

The customer domain in which the attributes required by the customer (CAs) are expressed. The functional domain where the functional requirements (FRs) that satisfy the required customer attributes are specified (e.g. based on questions using the Kano model). The physical domain where the design parameters (DPs) that fulfil the functional requirement are established. And the process domain where the process variables (PVs) determine how the product, system or service is to be realized. These domains are illustrated in Figure 4.7.

The concept of *hierarchies*

The output from each domain evolves in a hierarchical manner from generic to specific. This enables the mapping of the architecture of the fulfilment domain on the right directly on to the domain to its left. A partial illustration of a typical architecture for the functional and physical domains is shown in Figure 4.8.

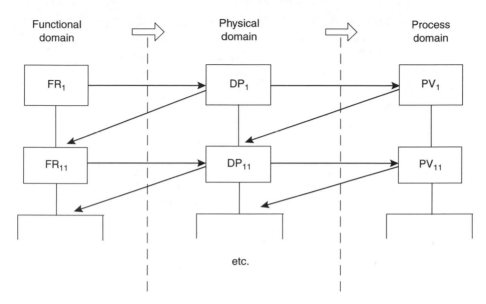

Figure 4.8 Example of zigzagging between domains

This top-down design process is known as decomposition. Decomposition takes place by alternating between pairs of domains. This going back and forth between domains is known as zigzagging. Zigzagging is illustrated in Figure 4.8.

The independence axiom

An axiom is a fundamental truth that cannot be proven or derived. With respect to the function requirements, the intent here is to maximize the independence of the functional requirements. In other words, to fulfil the independence axiom, each functional requirement (FR) should be fulfilled by just one design parameter (DP). A design that is maximally independent is said to be an uncoupled design. A practical example of the difference between an undesirable coupled design and the desirable uncoupled design is the case of two types of cold and hot water taps. Here, the appropriate functional requirements may be expressed as FR_1 = control water flow rate and FR_2 = control water temperature. With a twin-tap design the two design parameters are the hot and cold water tap control knobs. These can be labelled thus: DP_1 = hot tap control knob and DP_2 = cold tap control knob. Adjusting DP_1 affects both flow rate and temperature, namely both FR_1 and FR_2, as does DP_2. This design is known as a coupled one as each DP affects more than one FR. In the axiomatic design process the relationship between FRs and DPs is portrayed in matrix form. For the coupled design described, the matrix shown in Table 4.5 is appropriate. An alternative portrayal is given in Figure 4.9.

Table 4.5 Matrix showing undesirable coupled design

	Hot tap DP_1	*Cold tap* DP_2
Flow rate FR_1	×	×
Temperature FR_2	×	×

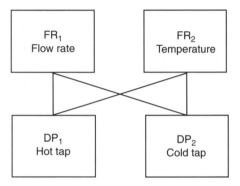

Figure 4.9 Alternative hierarchical portrayal of undesirable coupled design

With such a design getting the correct flow rate and temperature becomes a trial and error process, which normally requires a number of time consuming and tedious iterations. With more complex systems, the problems with coupled designs magnify considerably. For instance, they can only be set up with considerable difficulty over a lengthy period as one small change in one DP can affect several other functions simultaneously. An example was one ground-to-air guided missile that took, on average, some 92 h to set up just in final assembly functional test (this after many, many, hours of extensive pre-assembly nurturing, tweaking and adjustment of modules and sub-assemblies) prior to delivery to the Armed Services. This is not untypical of some complex systems.

An alternative design is the single lever, tilt and turn, mixer tap. This tap conforms to the independence axiom in that each design parameter fulfils only one functional requirement. Flow rate (FR_1), is adjusted by tilting the lever (DP_1), and temperature (FR_2) is adjusted by rotating the handle (DP_2). This uncoupled design is described in Table 4.6 and Figure 4.10.

The information axiom

The intent here is to minimize the information content of a design as this maximizes the probability of success. The term information is used in a somewhat peculiar sense here, as a measure of complexity. The information content of a design (I) is expressed, in a generic sense, somewhat theoretically in terms

Table 4.6 Matrix for desirable uncoupled design

	Tilt DP_1	*Rotate* DP_2
Flow rate FR_1	$\times$	0
Temperature FR_2	0	$\times$

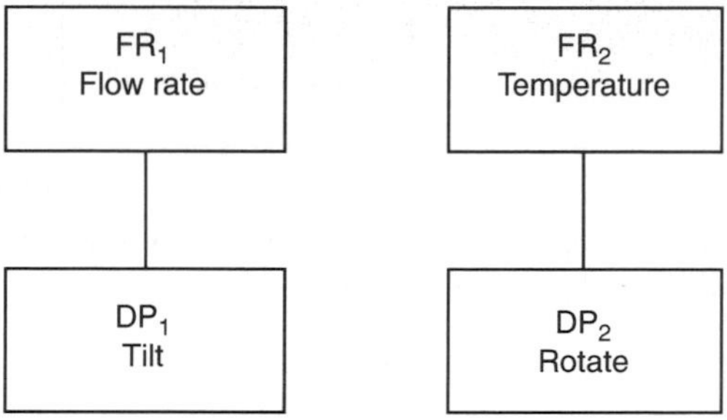

```
┌─────────────┐        ┌─────────────┐
│    FR₁      │        │    FR₂      │
│  Flow rate  │        │ Temperature │
└──────┬──────┘        └──────┬──────┘
       │                      │
┌──────┴──────┐        ┌──────┴──────┐
│    DP₁      │        │    DP₂      │
│    Tilt     │        │   Rotate    │
└─────────────┘        └─────────────┘
```

Figure 4.10 Alternative hierarchical portrayal of desirable uncoupled design

of entropy, as the logarithm of the inverse of the probability of successfully satisfying a functional requirement (FR), p:

$$I = \log_2 \frac{1}{p}$$

At a more practical level, if uniform probability distributions are involved, this equation reduces to:

$$I = \log_2 \left(\frac{\text{system range}}{\text{common range}} \right)$$

where 'system range' is the capability of the current system expressed in terms of specified tolerance, 'common range' is the amount of overlap between the design range and the system capability and 'design range' is the acceptable range specified for the design parameter (DP). These ranges are expressed pictorially in Figure 4.11.

It is seen that when the system capability is wholly within the specified design tolerance the common range is equal to the system range and the information content is minimal. If one is using statistical process control then the higher the Cpk values the lower the information content. Similarly for the Six Sigma practitioner the higher the Sigma value the lower the information content. These features confirm the reasoning that designs that specify target

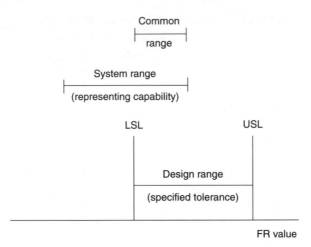

Figure 4.11 Information content of a design is minimum when the system range, representing capability, is wholly within the specified tolerance

values and tolerances that are within system capabilities better meet this information axiom. Also the reduction of the number of functional requirements, the standardization and reduction of number of parts, and the use of symmetry facilitates the reduction of information content of a design.

When there are n functional requirements the total information content becomes:

$$I_{\text{total}} = \sum_{i=1}^{n} I_i$$

Axiomatic design is not only applicable to product design, it is equally relevant to any kind of system design. Take the design of a manufacturing system, for example, where the overall functional requirement (FR) is to maximize return on investment. A partial hierarchical breakdown in the functional and physical domains could take the form as indicated in Figure 4.12.

Quality function deployment

Relevance of QFD to Six Sigma

What is the relevance of QFD to Six Sigma activities? Normally, in Six Sigma we focus on the reduction of non-conformities to 3.4 per million opportunities through: corrective action, action to eliminate the *cause* of a *detected* non-conformity, and preventive action, action to eliminate the *cause* of a *potential* non-conformity. So, when we arrive at our destination of (near) failure-free products, processes and services, we may appear to have reached the ultimate in achievement. But perhaps not.

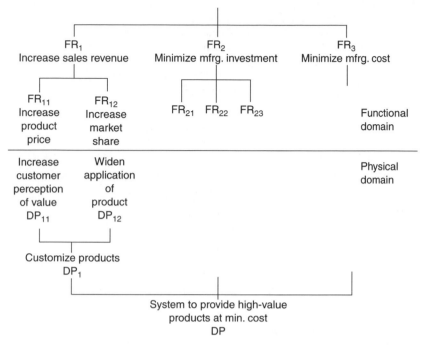

Figure 4.12 Example of partial hierarchical axiomatic design structure for manufacturing system (*Source*: Wally Towner and Chris Brown, Axiomatic design as the basis for designing a lean manufacturing system; unpublished paper)

Quality is more than making things failure-free. It is about fitting our product/service to the customers' perception of quality/value. And this perception is continually changing. In one company, whilst a plot of TGW (things gone wrong) has progressively decreased over the years, surveys have shown that the company is only just keeping up with the expectations of the marketplace. So, in Six Sigma, we need to be concerned not only with 'doing things right' but also about 'doing the right things right'.

QFD is very relevant to Six Sigma in a number of ways. The goals of QFD coincide with that of Six Sigma. These are to continuously enhance customer satisfaction and business performance by improving both the features of the product or service itself, and the planning for a cheaper and faster realization process.

People involved, in whatever level, in Six Sigma activities, need to know about QFD for a number of reasons:

- for familiarization purposes when working in areas where the technique is already deployed;
- for process-improvement purposes, and piloting QFD introduction, when working on projects in areas where the technique is not already deployed in order to make appropriate recommendations;

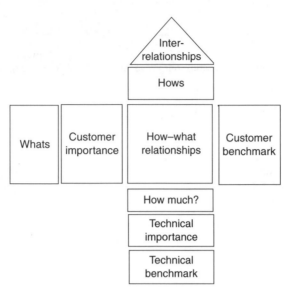

Figure 4.13 General format of the 'house of quality' or QFD diagram

- for direct application by Six Sigma project teams in specific projects as, and when, it is applicable;
- the priority that needs to be given, in Six Sigma activities, due to the impact on business performance of:
  - the high failure rates of products and services when launched in the market-place, currently estimated at some 35–44%;
  - the reduction in costs of the development, planning and realization of products and services, claimed by QFD, of some 30–50%.

What is QFD?[2]

The methodology for ascertaining and deploying the 'voice of the customer' is known by the rather peculiar name of 'quality function deployment'. Colloquially, it is often referred to in more simplistic terms as building the 'house of quality', or rather, the houses of quality by cascading them through the various phases of a product or service.

QFD is a team tool, which systematically captures customer expectations and translates them into relevant technical characteristics of the design of the product, or service, through *each stage* of the realization process.

QFD uses a standard methodology based, at each stage, on the so-called 'house of quality'. The 'house of quality' derives its name from its appearance. The triangular matrix at the top is considered to give it the appearance of a house. Its format and contents are illustrated pictorially, in a general form, in Figure 4.13.

---

[2]QFD is due to Prof. Akao and Prof. Mizuno and was first used in the Kobe shipyards in 1970.

Table 4.7 Initial thoughts for Six Sigma cleaning service improvement project

		How				
		Outsource to single contractor	*Organize tenders*	*Senior contractor on site*	*ISO 9001 accreditation*	*Cleaning specification*
What	Reduced cost	×	×			
	Improved consistency	×			×	×
	Better quality	×			×	
	Minimal in-house involvement	×		×		

The *whats* and the *hows* are two fundamental constituents of the QFD diagram and one can go a long way in structuring Six Sigma projects by just using a simple what/how matrix or table, at least as the starting point. In this way, it can be very useful in other than its more technically complex form. Used in this way it provides an excellent format for Six Sigma problem-solving, process improvement and even for administrative roles such as tabling actions against responsibilities on Six Sigma team projects. For instance, suppose a Six Sigma team is required to develop a skeleton proposal for the improvement of catering services across the divisions of a group of companies. They might well start off by creating a simple initial what/how QFD matrix as shown in Table 4.7.

At the other extreme, a partial QFD diagram for a motor vehicle external rear view mirror is shown in Figure 4.14. This indicates the extent of the work initially involved in QFD deployment. However, once completed it serves as an invaluable database, not only for the development of future models with the transfer of knowledge but also for prioritizing Six Sigma projects for improvement in current models.

How to construct a QFD diagram

Whats

The *whats* are the starting point. They represent a list of the predicted customer needs and expectation for a particular product, process or service. These are expressed in the language of the customer. An example is given in Figure 4.14 in terms of 'good all-round vision' and so on. The whats are crucial to get right as no design can be better than that expressed in the anticipated requirements.

Complementary relationships and trade-offs between hows are entered here

Whats	Hows	Importance scale	Reflectance ratio	Display area	Field of vision	Obscuration	Adjustment range	Adjustment force	Adjuster location	Wind tunnel drag test	Wind tunnel noise test	Time to demist	Deflection force	Complaints/1000 vehs	Customer rating against competitor (1–5)
			O	^	^	v	O	O	O	v	v	v	O		1 2 3 4 5
Good all round vision	Clear vision	5	1	1	1	4						4			O (3)
	No blind spots	5		4	8	4								1	O (4)
	Ok in reverse	3		4	8										O (4)
	Ok on tow	1		4	8										O (2)
No draw backs	Low wind noise	4								4	8				O (5)
	Low drag	3								8	4				O (4)
	Good styling	3													O (3)
User friendly	Easy to adjust	4					4	8	8				3		O (1)
	Stays put	4						4				8	4		O (1)
	Elect. adjust	1													O (2)
	Easy to clean	2													O (5)
How much			40% day:5% night	0.02 m²	85/205 EEC Reqt.	None for 93%	± 8' all directions	12 N	OK for 95%	<0.02 Cd	<2 dB	<100 s	>5 N (max lever pt)		

Technical importance rating entered, and technical performance relative to competitor(s) plotted, here

Figure 4.14 Partial QFD diagram for motor vehicle external rear view mirror

Importance scale

Here, customers rate the importance of each 'what' on a scale that is usually 1 (lowest) to 5 (highest). In Figure 4.14, good all-round vision on tow is rated 1 and no blind spots, 5.

Hows

The *hows* represent the operational requirements chosen to satisfy the 'whats'. They are determined by the organization providing the product or service. There needs to be one or more 'hows' for each 'what'. In Figure 4.14, it will be seen that there is no 'how' for the 'whats' relating to good styling, electrical adjustment or easy to clean. This is because the QFD diagram is incomplete in respect to a set of 'hows' relating to 'system parameters'. Sometimes, the 'hows' are referred to as design requirements, design characteristics or substitute or surrogate quality characteristics.

In Figure 4.14, the 'hows' are categorized under visibility, adjustment and performance headings.

Whats versus Hows

An L-shaped matrix is created by placing the *How* list vertically at right angles to the *What* list. This provides a rectangular area in which the inter-relationship between the 'whats' and 'hows' are then depicted. The strength of these relationships are portrayed either by symbols, or numerical weightings such as 8, 4 or 1, indicating either a strong, medium or weak association. These are entered in the appropriate rectangular cell at the intersection of the row and column containing the items under consideration.

For example, in Figure 4.14, low mirror wind noise has a strong (8) association with wind tunnel noise test, a medium (4) relationship with wind tunnel drag test and none with the others.

How much?

This provides information on how much of each 'how' is required to satisfy the 'whats'. It defines values that are required in the 'how' to achieve the 'whats'. In Figure 4.14, for instance, the drag coefficient, Cd, needs to be < 0.02 and the noise level $<2\,dB$ on wind tunnel tests.

Direction of improvement

This row indicates the direction in which the preferred value would move to reflect improvement in the situation. O indicates nominal is best, arrow up the larger the better and arrow down the smaller the better.

Correlation between the 'hows'

The correlation matrix between the 'hows' form the roof of the house. This shows how each of the design characteristics (the hows) impact upon each other. Here symbols, such as + and −, indicate whether the characteristics complement, or are at cross-purposes with, each other. In the case of the latter trade-offs or compromises may need to be made or the design changed to remove undesirable coupling. An option is to apply TRIZ to remove the contradiction. An example of an adverse relationship would be 'high acceleration' versus 'fuel economy'. A trade-off here could be to increase the 0 to 60 mph time from 6 s, say, to 8 s to retain the fuel economy objective. On the other hand, the relationship between less drag and better fuel economy would be supportive and hence show a positive correlation. Figure 4.14 does not show these relationships.

Complaints/1000 vehicles

This column provides for quantitative feedback from the customer in relation to the 'whats'. In Figure 4.14, it refers to automotive practice that records complaints per 1000 vehicles.

Competitive assessments or benchmarking

In a QFD diagram, two types of competitive assessments are usually present. The first is a customer rating against competition as shown on the right in Figure 4.14. Often the results are plotted against a scale of 1–5. This plot represent customers' perception of ones own product or service against competitions in terms of each 'what'. Sometimes the customer views are quite subjective. One motor vehicle was perceived to accelerate more quickly than another. Actually, the reverse was the case. The feeling was brought about by the fact that the seat in the slower car deflected backwards slightly on touching the accelerator pedal. This gave the false impression of quicker acceleration. This perception was at odds with the actual 0–60 mph times.

This gives rise to a second type of benchmarking that of comparison of the 'how muchs' with competition and of plotting the results similarly to that of the customer competitive rating. These figures are arrived at objectively by tests and calculations.

Technical importance rating

Sometimes, a row at the bottom of the QFD diagram provides a 'what/how' rating similar to that of the customer importance scale for the 'whats'. However, this is calculated for each column of 'hows', by summing, the importance scale value in each row by the appropriate times. Take, Figure 4.14, for example:

Column 1 gives a technical importance rating for 'reflectance ratio' of $5 \times 1 = 5$.
Column 2 gives a technical importance rating for 'display area' of $(5 \times 1) + (5 \times 4) + (3 \times 4) + (1 \times 4) = 41$.

The absolute values of these ratings are of little consequence. It is their relative values that have meaning. They can be used to make trade-off decisions and where to pay emphasis and provide resources.

How to cascade the QFD diagram through the various realization phases of a product or service

The various phases of a product or service will vary. The concept of cascading the QFD diagram through the appropriate phases is illustrated in Figure 4.15 with reference to an automotive product.

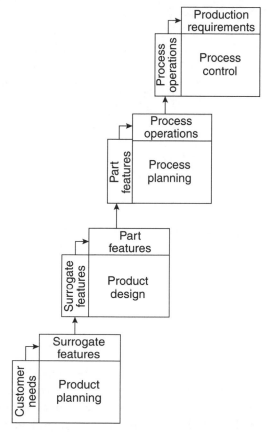

Figure 4.15 Cascade of QFDs through the realization phases of a product

Case study

A case study indicates the direct relevance of QFD to Six Sigma activities even on downstream projects. Figure 4.16 illustrates the cascading of QFD through from the voice of the customer through to component detail manufacture and control. It shows that, for a rear view mirror, the customer identified 'easy to adjust' expectation is first translated into the language of design by the preferred aim of 10 N for the adjustment force. The greatest influence on adjustment force is an 'end slot width' in the adjuster mechanism. This, in turn, is dependent on the continuing sharpness of a tool. The tool sharpness is monitored on an on-going basis by power consumption. As a result of a 'poka yoke' project an 'error proofing' device was installed using a current sensing cut-out device. It is seen that QFD applied in this way can make the whole 'concept to customer' process transparent to all. Here, the primary reason for the shop floor control is traced back to the original customer expectation.

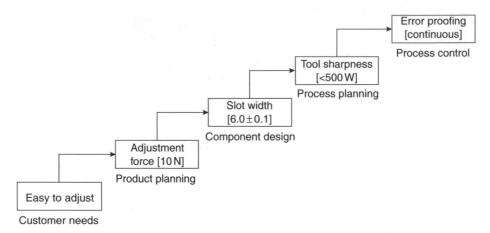

Figure 4.16   The 'voice of the customer' cascaded through to a downstream production operation for a single 'what', that of an 'easy to adjust' external rear view mirror customer expectation

TRIZ

Why TRIZ? The step beyond brainstorming!

TRIZ takes the Six Sigma practitioner well beyond the usual approach to creativity. On being faced with a concern with no known solution the Six Sigma practitioner, quite naturally, first turns to conventional approaches to creative problem-solving such as brainstorming and trial and error methods. With simpler problems these can be highly effective. With complex problems, however, such methods are frequently unsuccessful. They are often hit and miss, time consuming and ultimately, if the brick wall is reached, one can become frustrated and give up trying. This is one situation where TRIZ can become very beneficial in specific Six Sigma project work. The other situation is a wider organizational one where the aims of Six Sigma includes improving the fundamental approach taken at the design stage in order to achieve more effective designs.

With conventional design practice a typical feature that limits the conceiving of an ideal design is the presence of trade-offs. Such compromising of a design occurs, for example, in the case of weight and strength where a low weight and high strength combination is required. The typical design solution to the increasing of strength is to increase weight. In so doing one pays the penalty of an increase (deterioration) in weight to obtain increased (improved) strength. Traditionally, where such adverse interactions occur, the solution is to trade-off one against the other. Such adverse interactions are known in TRIZ as contradictions. Such interactions become evident in both QFD and axiomatic design. In QFD, they manifest themselves in the correlation matrix in the roof of the 'house of quality' and in axiomatic design in the form of coupled designs. When this happens, TRIZ provides a possible solution that does not involve compromising the design with trade-offs. Thus, TRIZ is a complementary tool to both QFD and axiomatic design. In the case in point, the TRIZ solution might be to increase strength without paying a weight penalty by the use of honeycomb structures or composite materials.

Summarizing, TRIZ is a tool that the Six Sigma professional can gainfully use to eliminate system conflicts in a cost-effective manner. The application can take two forms, one, that of problem resolution in specific projects and, two, of prompting upstream personnel to apply the tool in their design activities. Either way, in so doing, it will create product differentiation and competitive advantage.

What is TRIZ?

Creative and innovative ability, like arithmetic, involves use of techniques, which, when mastered, can be used to generate profitable ideas and solutions in Six Sigma activities. Genrich Altshuller (Altshuller, G., 1998) has found that technical problems can be solved by utilizing principles previously used to solve similar problems in other inventive situations. He has developed a universal methodology to do this. His methodology of creative problem solving is known as *TRIZ*. TRIZ has developed from Altshuller's study and categorizing of many thousands of patents. He found that over 90% of the problems met in design work had, in reality, been solved previously by someone, somewhere, using one of *40 fundamental inventive principles*. The percentage breakdown, in terms of levels of innovation, are indicated in parenthesis below.

TRIZ has developed into a set of practical tools for inventing and solving technical problems of varying complexity. TRIZ provides a standardized methodology for technical innovation.

Levels of innovation

Altshuller notes five levels of innovation:

- *Level 1*: a simple improvement of a system. It requires knowledge relevant to the problem (32% of problems found at this level).
- *Level 2*: an invention that includes the resolution of a *technical contradiction*. It requires knowledge from different areas within an industry relevant to the system (45% of problems were found at this level).
- *Level 3*: an invention that includes the resolution of a *physical contradiction*. It requires knowledge from other industries (18% of problems were found at this level).
- *Level 4*: a new technology is developed containing a breakthrough solution. It requires knowledge from different fields of science. It solves the problem

by replacing the old technology with a new technology (4% of problems were found at this level).

- *Level 5*: discovery of new phenomena. A rare scientific discovery (1% of problems were found at this level).

A *technical contradiction* occurs when we improve one characteristic of a system we cause another to deteriorate. For example, to increase the speed of an aircraft a heavier more powerful engine is installed. This additional weight requires a larger wing size with a consequent deleterious increase in drag. A *physical contradiction* occurs when two opposing properties are required from the same entity. An example is the aircraft undercarriage. It needs to be present for take-off and landing and absent during flight. The inventive solution here is 'retraction'. Another example of an inventive 'retraction' solution to a physical contradiction relates to dynamic 'sleeping policemen'. Speed humps in a road that appear only when a vehicle is speeding.

Law of ideality

This law, or axiom, states that any technical system, throughout its lifetime, tends to become more reliable, simple, effective – more ideal. Every time a system is nudged closer to ideality it costs less, wastes less energy, etc. Inventive performance can be judged by its degree of ideality. When a system reaches ideality the mechanism disappears, while the function is still performed.

An example of the exploitation of the Law of Ideality is the farmer in Brazil who ships meat, by air, to the United States of America. Originally, the meat is kept frozen during transport by the refrigeration plant installed in cargo planes. The inventive solution is the cargo aircraft now flies at 15 000–25 000 feet where the air temperature is below 32 °F. The advantage is that no refrigeration plant is now required. This results in less capital cost and more storage space for meat. This utilization of existing resources costing nothing has brought the system close to ideality.

The art (or science) of inventing

Inventing is about removing barriers to ideality. There are a number of ways to make a system more ideal:

- *Increase the number of functions in a system*. Examples are: the sofa that converts into a bed; an entertainment system that contains a radio, tape player and CD player.
- *Transfer as many functions as possible to the working element that produces the final action of the system*. An example is a crimping tool that also cuts wire, strips insulation and crimps the terminal to the wire.

- *Transfer some functions of the system to the external environment.* Examples are: replacing the manual operation of windows in a greenhouse by a temperature-sensitive bimetallic spiral mechanism that operates automatically; the street lamp that switches on and off automatically with the ambient light.
- *Ulltilize internal and external resources that already exist and are available.* Example: utilizing the wiring system in a house to act as an aerial.

TRIZ principles and contradictions

The tools used within TRIZ to overcome technical contradictions are called principles. Principles are generic suggestions for performing an action to, and within, a system. Within TRIZ, 40 principles are used to resolve contradictions in respect of 39 generic characteristics. These are given in matrix format in Altshuller's book on TRIZ referred to above. For instance, *Principle # 19: Periodic Action* has three components:

1 replace a continuous action with a periodic one (impulse);
2 if the action is already periodic, change its frequency;
3 use pauses between impulses to provide additional action.

Examples of the exploitation of this principle are:

1 watering a lawn with a continuous stream of water can cause damage. A pulsating sprinkler eliminates this problem;
2 a warning light flashes so that it is more noticeable than when continuously lit;
3 an impact wrench using impulses rather than continuous force to loosen a corroded nut.

Another illustration of the use of Altschuller's principles is *Principle # 7: Nesting*, which has two components:

1 contain the object within another, which, in turn, is placed within a third object, and so on;
2 pass an object through the cavity of another object.

Examples of the application of this principle are: the telescopic aerial, the lead retracting pencil and the chair that stacks on top of another.

Three steps for solving an inventive problem

Lev Shulyak (who contributed to the TRIZ book referred to) proposes three steps to solve an inventive problem that contains a technical contradiction:

Step 1: analyse the system. This step determines the characteristic that needs to be improved.

Step 2: state the technical contradiction. Identify the characteristic that deteriorates at the expense of the one that is being improved.

Step 3: resolve the technical contradiction. In this step, the 40 principles and contradiction matrix provided in the Altshuller reference given in the bibliography? are used to remove the technical contradiction.

Case studies

A number of successful applications of TRIZ have been reported in the West. Proctor & Gamble historically have registered less than 100 patents per annum. Since introducing TRIZ their patent registrations have rocketed to over 600 patents per annum. The results are manifold. These include the creation of world-beating new-generation products, significant reductions in getting new products to market and a Number 1 world ranking for their contribution to chemical research and technology. In the United Kingdom, Rolls Royce doubled its patents in the first year of deployment of TRIZ. Pilkington, too, found a new way of handling fine sheets of glass based on an application for transporting fragile paper.

TRIZ and Six Sigma

TRIZ obviously has a number of roles to play in the Six Sigma initiative. These are discussed in relation to the three need components of the Kano model, basic, performance and excitement.

First, take basic needs. In pursuit of a 6 Sigma standard the Six Sigma practitioner is highly focused on the reduction of non-conformities. An owner of a motor vehicle would not specify that he/she wants tyres that do not blow out. On the other hand, no design organization would knowingly design a tyre to blow out. The Six Sigma organization, hopefully, would at least, apply conventional failure prevention tools, such as 'potential failure mode and effects analysis' (PFMEA), to attempt circumvent this. The first leading question in PFMEA is 'What can go wrong?' This is explored from the somewhat limited perspective of failure scenarios relating to the PFMEA team's background and experience. However, this, quite naturally, reflects only a part of the possible failure envelope. This is where TRIZ comes in. TRIZ can be used to open up the failure space by asking quite a different leading question, 'How can the tyre blow out'? Or, more generally, 'How can the system be destroyed?' This then becomes an inventive problem to which TRIZ, with its much wider analytical perspective, can gainfully be applied.

Second, consider performance needs. Another role of Six Sigma is to continually improve product/service value by enhancing performance in a cost-effective manner. A stumbling block to progress here is invariably the presence of adverse interactions between characteristics that conventionally result in trade-offs or compromises. Two such instances are the aircraft power versus weight dilemma and the aircraft undercarriage issue discussed earlier. TRIZ is uniquely suited to resolving such conventional technical and physical design limitations by applying its contradiction matrix to such issues.

Third, reflect on excitement needs. Six Sigma personnel, themselves, would be expected to aspire to 'best working practice'. In so doing, they would be obliged to seek to meet latent customer needs and expectations as well as those already brought out into the open. This involves innovation. Innovation can, and should, be achieved by Six Sigma people becoming involved in, or at least ensuring, that consideration is given to potential future product/system/service scenarios and that those with the greatest potential are adopted. TRIZ provides such a mechanism through Altshuller's eight laws of technological evolution.

Taguchi quality engineering

Eight fundamental concepts are set forth by Genichi Taguchi (Taguchi, G., 1985, 1986). These concepts reflect his approach to quality engineering. These concepts are deployed through the process of planned experimentation. Taguchi's fundamental concepts are widely acclaimed. Some statistical criticisms have been levelled at his proposals relating to their application through experimentation. Some of these criticisms concerning experiment design are unfounded in that they arise as a result of a lack of understanding by users. Other valid criticisms relating to analysis of the results are easily circumvented.

The concepts need to be known and absorbed by all Six Sigma personnel before they become involved with upstream development activities. The principal reason for this is that they set out to engender a quite different mindset from that postulated by the founders of Six Sigma (see Concept 1 in particular). Similarly planned experimentation provides a cornerstone of many Six Sigma downstream problem resolution and process improvement activities.

Concept 1: minimize loss by ensuring uniformity around the preferred value

Traditional thinking is often that all products that meet specification are equally good. This enables clearcut decisions to be made. However, Taguchi suggests that this engenders a mind set that inhibits improvement. The Taguchi view is that there tends to be a best point, or target, at which the loss is a minimum with performance deteriorating (and loss increasing) progressively as values depart from the target. He says: 'Quality as perceived by the customer is NOT a go–no go situation. There is an optimum or target value. As the product varies from this point the perception of quality progressively deteriorates until some point, possibly the specification limit, the condition becomes untenable'. This concept is illustrated in Figures 4.17 and 4.18.

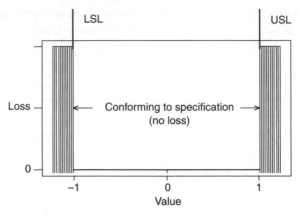

Figure 4.17 The goal post model deprecated by Taguchi. USL, upper specification limit; LSL, lower specification limit. Value refers to a measurement scale not to intrinsic worth

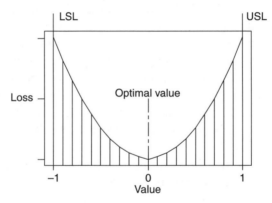

Figure 4.18 Taguch generic loss function model. Value refers to a measurement scale not to intrinsic worth

This idea of targeting on preferred value and minimizing variation may appear rather different from the world-class concept enunciated by the originators of Six Sigma, which is to reduce non-conformities per million opportunities to a level of 6 Sigma. This means, in essence, to ensure that virtually all values are within specification. Aiming for 6 Sigma provides a considerable stretch on that being currently achieved. Even so the mindset of the Six Sigma practitioner should always be that of Taguchi.

Concept 2: design processes/products that produce uniform products economically

The quality and cost of a manufactured product are determined to a large extent by the design of the product and process. This brings out that both manufacturing cost and manufacturing imperfections in a product are determined largely by product/process design. For a given design increased process controls can reduce non-conformities. But process controls cost money. Therefore, it is required to reduce both non-conformities and the need for stringent process controls. This can be accomplished only by improving product/process design.

This concept is directly aligned with the aims of 'design for Six Sigma' (DFSS) and 'design for manufacturability' (DFM).

Concept 3: exploit any non-linear effects of process parameters on performance characteristics

By taking advantage of any non-linear relationship between performance and product or process characteristics, product/process performance variation can be reduced (improved) without tightening manufacturing tolerances or process controls or the given performance can be achieved with more liberal tolerances or controls. Hence, we can achieve either higher quality at the same cost, or similar quality at less cost. This is illustrated by an example in Figure 4.19.

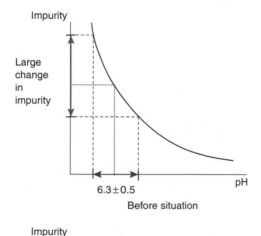

Before situation

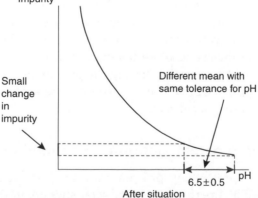

After situation

Figure 4.19 Improvement in performance of product characteristic as a result of changing the setting of a process parameter

A similar result was achieved in a heat treatment operation. By increasing the volume of ammonia, at minimal extra cost, the variation of a key dimension was reduced by a factor of 8.

Concept 4: cure the effect not the cause

Conventionally, Six Sigma practitioners are encouraged, even instructed, to seek out and eliminate root causes of concerns. However, there are many instances where we live with expensive, undesirable situations even when we know the root cause. Why is this? It is because cause removal is too costly. Taguchi proposes in such a situation that we deal with the effect, not the cause. Action should then be taken not to remove the cause but to eliminate or reduce its effect. What kind of countermeasures can be taken to reduce the influence of the cause? Taguchi has an answer to this too. He cites a ceramic tile manufacturing process.

> It was well known that the temperature variation in a tunnel kiln was the root cause of variation in the size of fired tiles. The size variation of tiles in one position in the kiln varied from those in a different position. However, the achievement of a more even temperature distribution was too expensive to contemplate. Instead an experiment was designed to make the product/process more robust to kiln temperature variation. Various tile formulation factors such as, proportion of limestone, agalmatolite and feldspar were investigated with a view to selecting operating levels and recipe proportions which would minimize the difference in shrinkage between tiles loaded in different positions on the cart. By increasing the content of lime in the formulation from 1% to 5% the tile variation was reduced. As lime was one of the less expensive ingredients, this remarkable result was achieved at less cost.

This early Taguchi experimental finding represented a breakthrough in approach that is progressively being more and more exploited in performance-improvement activities. The author was recently involved with a Six Sigma team that successfully exploited this concept when faced with the alternative prospect of proposing a large capital spend on a new higher-performance kiln. Following experimentation with selected process parameters and material constituents some relatively small modifications secured the necessary reduction in variation in dimensions of an insulator during firing in a kiln. It is an extremely useful method for the Six Sigma practitioner, particularly when he/she comes up against a brick wall in terms of excessive expense required to remove a known cause of a concern.

Concept 5: a zero-defect standard is an inadequate goal

A never-ending improvement process requires continuous reduction in the variation of product performance characteristics about their target values.

This will reduce Taguchi-type quality 'opportunity' losses as indicated in Figure 4.18. Almost all products/processes have numerous quality characteristics. It is necessary to concentrate on the identification and measurement of key characteristics. In Six Sigma these are termed critical to quality characteristics (CTQCs). The improvement process depends on knowledge of the ideal values of these characteristics. Performance variation can be evaluated most effectively when the performance characteristic is measured on a continuous scale. All target specifications of continuous performance characteristics should be stated in terms of tolerances about the preferred value. This is frequently not done. Too often one finds specifications written purely in terms of limits. An example is 50–70 N meters. This leaves the fundamental question open, what is the preferred value? Is it 60, or perhaps 50 or even 70? The preferred method is to specify either 60 ± 10, $50 - 0 + 20$, or $70 - 20 + 0$ depending on what is the preferred value. For attribute characteristics a scaling of performance is much preferred to a binary judgement such as good/bad, go/no go, yes/no.

Concept 6: design products/processes robust against operating conditions/use

An example from the food industry illustrates this concept. A caramel product contains some 10 ingredients. The plasticity of the caramel was initially very sensitive to variation in air temperature. An experiment was conducted with a view to developing a recipe whose plasticity was less susceptible to ambient temperature.

Concept 7: Taguchi method is not essentially a problem-solving technique

Initially, most Six Sigma people will start using Taguchi-style experimental designs to solve current problems on existing products/processes/services. However, we should not lose sight of the fact that the Taguchi method is essentially an up-front set of activities that need to be integrated into our way of doing business generally. A key feature of the Taguchi approach is to progressively shift the emphasis from 'online' activities (such as problem-solving) back to the 'upstream' activities of product and process design. Here lies the secret of fluent, economical production of robust products that meet customer expectations for quality and value.

Quality achievement requires 'off-line' methodology that focuses on quality improvement as well as quality evaluation. Taguchi has introduced a three step approach to assign nominal values and tolerances, to product, process and service parameters.

His three-step approach to product/process/service design is:

1 *System design*: the process of applying technical knowledge to produce a basic functional prototype design. This prototype model defines initial settings of product/process/service design features.
2 *Parameter design*: the process of identifying the settings of design parameters to achieve target performance and robustness to sources of variation at minimum cost. His methodology involves the use of two-level experiments.[3]
3 *Tolerance design*: the process of determining tolerances around the nominal values identified by parameter design. His methodology involves the use of three-level experiments.

Case study

An example of the application of parameter design is where 49 designed experiments, many of them involving more than 100 individual experimental runs, were conducted in developing a Japanese photocopying machine. Why? This was done to make the machine robust to a whole range of operating conditions. This was to ensure the machine would make good copies whatever the condition: high humidity:low humidity; high temperature:low temperature; thin paper:thick paper; smooth paper:rough paper; and so on. This is Taguchi's way of embodying quality into products, processes and services.

Concept 8: exploit the three types of product/process parameters

In parameter design one seeks to establish which product/process parameters (called factors) influence the level or variability of output (called response). This leads to three types of design factor:

1 *Control factors*: those that affect the variability of the response.
2 *Signal factors*: those that only affect the level of response.
3 *Null factors*: those that do not materially affect the variability or level of response.

How do we exploit these? First, we establish the control factors and adjust their level to achieve design robustness, in other words to reduce the variability in response. Second, the signal factors, those that affect the level of response but not the variability, are adjusted to bring the response on target. Third, the null

---

[3]Different types of experiments used in Six Sigma project activities are discussed later in the book.

factors are adjusted to the most economic level. Taguchi recommends the use of generic signal-to-noise ratios to analyse the results of such experiments. Such methods have been criticized. It is considered preferable to use simple, straightforward and more readily understandable measures such as mean and standard deviation rather than these generic signal-to-noise ratios. An example is shown later in the book.

Taguchi experimentation

Experimentation is directed to improving the understanding of the manner in which, for example, parameters of a process (mould temperature, riser design, etc.) or properties of a material (Mg, Si, moisture content) affect the performance of a process or a product (e.g. porosity, leakage, shrinkage, yield, etc.). The key to proactive quality improvement at reduced cost is to determine how inputs and process parameters, such as solvent holdout and line speed, affect product-performance characteristics, such as curl and image density.

Essentially, there are two systematic approaches to experimentation:

1 investigate *one factor* at a time approach (expensive, inefficient);
2 investigate *several factors* simultaneously to a factorial design (economic and efficient).

Taguchi did not invent factorial designs (due to R.A. Fisher, UK). However, he has assembled a number of Fisher and Burman and Placket designs in a convenient to use package. These are mostly two- and three-level designs. The most generally used are known, by Taguchi followers, as lattice (L) designs:

- two level: L4, L8, L12 and L16;
- three level: L9, L18 and L27.

Such designs are indispensable for the toolkit of the Six Sigma practitioner. Typical applications of these designs in Six Sigma situations are dealt with later in the book.

Value analysis

What is value analysis?

Value analysis aims at identifying and reducing unnecessary costs. It is function orientated. The aim is to reduce costs without impairing function. Analysis

Table 4.8   Opportunities to apply value analysis in Six Sigma activities

Stage of maturity of a product, etc.	Possible improvement objective
Concept	Improve approach
Feasibility and design	Enhance viability
Realization	Maximize cost-effectiveness
Use	Maximize cost-effectiveness

determines the essential function of the product, process or service under consideration. Then the aim is to ensure it performs its function in the most economical way feasible.

Roles of value analysis in Six Sigma projects

There are many possible opportunities to apply value analysis in Six Sigma activities. The typical scope is shown in Table 4.8.

Functional analysis

Functional analysis is the usual basis for a value-enhancing project. In its simplest form, a function is described in two words: a *verb*, and a *noun*. For example, a starter motor 'converts energy'. A good disciplined approach to value/functional analysis is to list the components of a product together with their individual functions. Two types of functions are often used:

- *Basic functions*. These are functions that the customer wants and is prepared to pay for.
- *Secondary functions*. These are supporting functions, not inherent in the product specification but result from the particular design chosen.

Case study 1

Take a fairly simple example. A pen, with the following product specification: hand-held tool for making indelible marks and a provision for recharging with a marking fluid. The components of one such pen together with costs are shown in Table 4.9.

In Table 4.9, we see that the basic functions make up only 25% of the total cost whereas the secondary functions are responsible for 75% of the cost. Value analysis now concentrates on areas that appear to be of lesser worth, namely, the body and the cap. It would also try to combine some components and eliminate others. A speculative session would provide a list of design alternatives, resulting in a final proposal. This could be on the lines of a ball-point pen with

Table 4.9 Functional analysis with costs of a pen

Part	Basic function	Cost of basic function	Secondary function	Cost of secondary function
Nib	Makes marks	7.5 p		
Nib support			Supports nib, conveys ink	1.5 p
Nib socket			Supports nib, supports reservoir	2.5 p
Reservoir	Stores ink	1 p		
Body			Protects reservoir	12.5 p
Filling lever			Fills reservoir	2.5 p
Cap			Protects nib	5 p
Clip			Assists carrying	1.5 p
Total cost		8.5 p		25.5 p

a considerable overall cost reduction. However, we should pause and reflect upon which market we are aiming for before proposing this. Is it where the customer is concerned only with the functional aspect or, perhaps, interested in a product that also has 'esteem' value? This indicates a role for 'quality function deployment' in conjunction with 'value analysis'.

Case study 2

A further example is shown of value analysis using a matrix layout for a fuse box. Here the multiple functions are related to each individual component. The cost is then obtained for each function of each component (see Tables 4.10 and 4.11).

Potential failure mode and effects analysis

What is a PFMEA?

A PFMEA is a systematic set of activities that identifies and evaluates potential failure modes of a system, product or process, their root causes and effects. It also rank orders potential design and process deficiencies and seeks out and introduces actions that will, as appropriate, eliminate or reduce the chance of the failure occurring. In so doing it increases the probability of detecting (and controlling) the failure at source and also reduces the effect of the failure.

Table 4.10 Fuse box design prior to value analysis

Part	Function											Cost of part	% cost
	Protects circuit	Mounts unit	Holds clip	Provides insulation	Protects fuse	Holds fuse	Makes contact	Provides connection	Secures connection	Protects base	Retains cover		
Base		6	4	2								12.0	13.4
Cover					3.7							3.7	4.1
Fuse	12											12.0	13.4
Fuse clip						12	11					23.0	25.8
Terminal post			3.2					20				23.2	26.0
T. post screw									6.4			6.4	7.2
Terminal washer										3.7		3.7	4.1
Cover screw											3.4	3.4	3.8
C. screw post											1.9	4.9	1.7
Cost of function	12	6	7.2	2	3.7	12	11	20	6.4	3.7	5.3	89.3	
% of total cost	13.4	6.7	8.1	2.3	4.1	13.4	12.3	22.4	7.2	4.1	5.9		100

Table 4.11 Fuse box design after value analysis

Part	Function												Cost of part	% cost
	Protects circuit	Mounts unit	Holds clip	Provides insulation	Protects fuse	Inhibits corrosion	Conveys information	Holds fuse	Makes contact	Retains clip	Conducts current	Provides connection		
Base		4		1.5									8.0	15.6
Cover					1.0	0.6	0.4						2.0	3.9
Fuse (6)	12												12.0	23.4
Fuse clip (8)								6	6				23.0	25.8
Rivet (8)										2	4		6.0	12.7
Lucar (4)												7	7.0	13.7
Lucar (4)			2.5									4	4.0	7.8
Connecting strip												0.25	0.25	0.4
Cost of function	12	4	2.5	1.5	1.0	0.6	0.4	6	6	2	4	11.25	51.25	
% of total cost	23	8	5	3	2	1	1	12	12	4	8	22		100
Mark hi or lo												hi		

It focuses on preventing non-conformities from arising. It is one of the well-known tools for conducting a risk analysis on a system, product and process.

In terms of the Kano model, it should be appreciated by the Six Sigma practitioner that the PFMEA is a tool to reduce customer dissatisfaction not to increase customer satisfaction. The term customer here refers not only to the ultimate customer of the entity but every customer downstream of the event.

Essence of any product or process risk analysis

All too frequently such an analysis is conducted only after a serious failure has occurred. Hence, the emphasis here should be on the term *potential* to indicate that this is a proactive rather than reactive tool. Consequently, the potential failure modes of each system, product, process and service should be determined upstream on the design of the entity at the concept stage and also on the entity realization process. It should be recognized in specification requirements. The preferred result in the event of failure is failure to a safe mode (fail safe). Alternatively, when possible, the product should give warning prior to failure.

From a Six Sigma perspective it provides a means for the Six Sigma practitioner to get off the tread mill of perpetual reactive problem-solving. It provides the 'belt' with the methodology to eradicate the potential for failure in future products, systems, processes and services. It also provides a systematic and comprehensive database that is supportive of diagnosis in reactive problem-solving.

What other similar methodologies are there?

There are a number of failure avoidance methodologies. These include those shown in Table 4.12.

Working model of the PFMEA process

A working model of the PFMEA process is illustrated in Figure 4.20.

Table 4.12 Alternative appoaches to potential failure mode and effects analysis

FTA	Fault tree analysis
HAZOP	Hazard and operability studies
HACCP	Hazard analysis and critical control points
KWA	Key word analysis
RBD	Reliability block diagrams
Poka Yoke	Error proofing

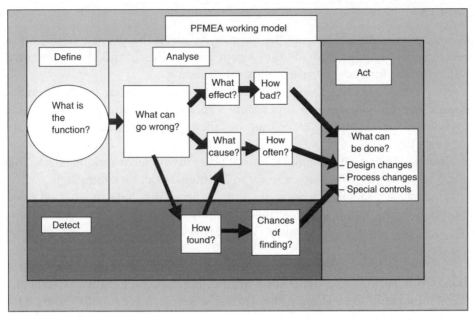

Figure 4.20 Model of the potential failure mode and effects analysis process

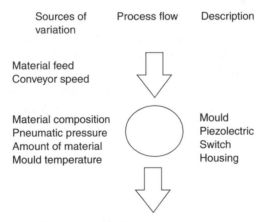

Figure 4.21 Partial flow diagram of process

Steps in the construction of the working model

Define (each operation in the process)

What is the function? First prepare a flow diagram of the process to identify the scope of the PFMEA (Figure 4.21).

Describe each operation being analysed, by function, as verb + noun, for example, mould housing for switch.

Analyse

What can go wrong? Describe the manner in which the process could fail to meet process requirements or the design intent. This is called the potential failure mode, for example, orientation tabs missing.

What effect? Describe the consequences of the failure mode on the operator, equipment and downstream operations. This is called the potential effects of failure, for example, switch not installed properly: headlamp will not generate light.

How bad? For each potential failure mode rate the most serious effect. This is called *severity* [S]. Rate on a 1 (low) to 10 (high) scale, for example, 8.

What cause? State the cause(s) of failure in terms of what can be acted upon to eliminate or control. This is termed potential cause or mechanism of failure, for example, mould temperature below specification, insufficient material injected into mould.

How often? State how frequently each specific failure cause/mechanism is expected to occur. This is termed occurrence [O]. Rate on a standard scale of 1 (very infrequent) to 10 (nearly always), for example, 3 for mould temp., 4 for insufficient material.

Detect

How found? State what current process controls are in place to: prevent the occurrence of the failure mode or detect the failure mode should it occur. This is called current process controls, for example, sampling inspection – 10 per batch – at next operation to check visually for existence of tabs.

What are the chances of finding? Assess the probability that the current process controls will detect each potential cause/mechanism and rate on a scale of 1 (high) to 10 (low). This is called detection [D], for example, 9 for both.

Action

What can be done? Set priorities by calculating a risk priority number (RPN). Act on highest numbers, for example, $RPN = S \times O \times D = 8 \times 3 \times 9 = 216$ for low-mould temp. and $8 \times 4 \times 9 = 288$ for insufficient material.

Act on highest numbers, for example, modify operation, measure material quantity and increase injection pressure and mould temperature (see Figure 4.22).

Chapter highlights

- Six Sigma participants should not be focused purely on minimizing non-conformities to achieve a 6 Sigma level of performance, to the exclusion of the wider concept, that of value enhancement and providing products desired by the targeted customer base.

Process description / Process purpose	Potential failure mode	Potential effects of failure	Severity, S	Potential cause(s) of failure	Occurrence, O	Current controls	Detection, D	RPN = SOD	Action
Op 10: Mould housing (for switch)	Orientation tabs missing	Switch not installed properly	8	Mould temp. below specification	3	Sampling visual inspection, (10/batch), at next operation	9	216	Increase mould temperature
		Headlamp will not generate light		Insufficient material injected into mould	4		9	288	Monitor material quantity, increase mould pressure
Op 20									

Figure 4.22 Specimen partially completed PFMEA form

- Maximum value is achieved when the customer gets the greatest satisfaction from the least amount of resources deployed. Value can thus be enhanced by improving customer satisfaction and/or reducing resource costs.
- Three distinct types of customer needs are recognized in the Kano model that either give rise to dissatisfaction or degrees of satisfaction. These are basic needs (the must haves), performance needs (more is better) and excitement needs (the unexpected).
- Reduction in resource costs can arise not only from reducing the cost of non-conformity but also by cutting the cost of producing good products.
- The power of the 'quality lever' needs appreciation to gain the greatest enhancement of value across the organization. The further upstream an improvement activity takes place the greater the value leverage. This applies to administrative and financial systems as well as products and services for external customers.
- A number of improvement techniques are now available to upstream personnel (e.g. marketing, product and process design, buyers), other stakeholders and Six Sigma personnel.
- To apply the required leverage, relevant people, in the organization, including Six Sigma personnel, need to have a working knowledge of a number of disciplines such as axiomatic design, quality function deployment, TRIZ, Taguchi quality engineering, value analysis and potential failure mode and effects analysis.

Bibliography

Altshuller, G. (1998). *TRIZ keys to technical innovation*, Worcester, MA: Technical Innovation Center.

BSI (2000). *BS EN 12973 Value management*, London: BSI.

CEN/TC 279 (2000). *PD 6663: Guidelines to BS EN 12973: Value management – practical guidance to its use and intent*, London: BSI.

Clausing, D.P. (1994). *Total quality development*, New York: ASME Press.

Senge, P. (1990). *The fifth discipline*, New York: Doubleday.

Suh, N. P. (1990). *The principles of design*, Oxford: Oxford University Press.

Suh, N. P. (2001). *Axiomatic design: advances and applications*, Oxford: Oxford University Press.

Taguchi, G. (1985). *System of experimental design*, New York: Kraus International Publications.

Taguchi, G. (1986). *Introduction to quality engineering*, Tokyo: Asian Productivity Association.

Chapter 5
What competencies are required to drive Six Sigma?

> If a man empties his purse into his head, no man can take it away from him. An investment in knowledge always pays the best interest.
>
> *Benjamin Franklin*

What is meant by competency?

Competency is defined as the key knowledge, skills, abilities, behaviours and other characteristics needed to perform specific tasks.

Six Sigma demands the empowerment of people in an organization. Empowerment is one thing. Making it work to achieve a given objective is another. Prior to the empowering of people in an organization, to perform any new task in a satisfactory manner, three necessary personal requisites need to be satisfied. We have to ensure that they acquire the appropriate knowledge, nurture the correct attitude and develop the necessary skills.

These three features were recognized some 50 years ago and gave rise to the development of a taxonomy of education, training and development objectives (Bloom, B. S., 1956). This taxonomy is the accepted standard for the establishing of training and development objectives. A taxonomy is simply 'a set of classifications which are ordered and arranged on the basis of a single principle or on the basis of a consistent set of principles'. Bloom, and his fellow committee members, decided that the taxonomy be split into three domains, the cognitive, the affective and the psychomotor.

The cognitive domain includes those objectives that deal with the recall or recognition of knowledge and the development of intellectual abilities and skill. Cognitive objectives range from simple recall of material learned to highly original and creative ways of combining and synthesizing new ideas. The American Society for Quality (ASQ) body of knowledge requirements for black

Table 5.1   The major classes of Six Sigma training objectives in the cognitive and affective domains

Cognitive objectives (recall or recognition of knowledge, development of intellectual abilities and skills)		Affective objectives (attitude, feelings, emotion, accepts/rejects)
Knowledge	Remember	Passive response
Comprehension	Understand	Willing response
Application	Apply	Appreciates value: becomes proactive
Analysis	Identify implications	Internalizes value system
Synthesis	Combine and transfer	Integrates values into personal way of life
Evaluation	Judge	

belts is based on the six major classes within the cognitive domain as shown in Table 5.1. The affective domain includes objectives that deal with attitudes and feelings. Affective objectives range from simple passive attention, through willing response, to enjoyment and pleasure in participating and total commitment. The psychomotor domain includes objectives that deal with muscular skill and manipulation of materials and things or some act that requires a neuromuscular coordination.

Whilst the ASQ body of knowledge for black belts is restricted to the cognitive domain it is important to bear in mind that a successful and sustained application of Six Sigma also requires a continuing willingness to participate and the maintaining of a high degree of personal commitment and focus. This involves consideration of objectives in both the cognitive and affective domains. A summary of the structure of these two domains is shown in Table 5.1.

Competency requirements are usually expressed in terms of six levels of cognition as described in Bloom's Taxonomy. These are ranked from the least complex to the most complex.

Six levels of cognition

1 *Knowledge level*: involves the remembering by recognition or recall of facts, terminology, classifications, conventions, principles, criteria, trends, methods, etc.
2 *Comprehension level*: represents the lowest level of understanding of knowledge, namely, a grasp of the meaning and intent of the material. This relates to the ability to understand communications, diagrams, tables, descriptions, etc., without necessarily relating it to other material or seeing its full implications.
3 *Application level*: relates to the ability to apply the knowledge comprehended in a work-related situation. Examples are the application and use of formulae, methods, procedures, principles and theories.

4 *Analysis*: covers breaking down the subject matter into its constituent elements, seeking out the inter-relationships and interactions among the elements and of the way they are organized to form the whole. Here one is expected, for example, to be able to distinguish fact from hypothesis, relevant from extraneous material, to be able to perceive what underlying assumptions are involved and to identify conclusions and supporting statements.

5 *Synthesis*: is concerned with being able to create something, not obvious hitherto, within the limits set by particular problems, opportunities, methods, resources, etc. The outcome might be a communication to inform, describe or persuade; be a plan or proposed set of operations to be carried out; or relate to the discovery or deducing of relationships not previously established.

6 *Evaluation*: is about the ability to make judgements about the value of ideas, proposals, solutions, methods, etc., by using appropriate evidence or criteria. It can involve the ability to detect logical fallacies in arguments and require competence in assessing the reasonableness of statements, documentation, etc.

It is desirable, at a very early stage in Six Sigma planning, to establish competency models for participants. Such competency models would 'describe the most critical knowledge, skills and commitments that underpin and drive superior performance in Six Sigma'.

Competencies for Six Sigma – overview

It is generally accepted that no one should ever be required to work beyond that person's capabilities. Hence, it is essential to ensure that all those participating in Six Sigma activities possess the necessary faculties, aptitude, skills and knowledge. The consequent selection, training and development of potential Six Sigma participants should be based on predetermined competency profiles. Of course, such competency profiles will be tailored to the needs of a particular organization. However, it may be useful to consider those put forward in this chapter as a basis for this tailoring. Typical competencies for people involved in Six Sigma activities are described.

Six Sigma team member – yellow belt

A typical competency model for a yellow belt might include the following:

1 *Job knowledge* – good understanding of his/her work (job/task/process, its inputs, resources used, controls applied , customer expectations and outputs).
2 *Co-operation* – willingness and ability to work with others; readiness to try out new ideas and methods.

3 *Initiative* – resourceful; ready to offer ideas and suggestions about his/her job/task/process.
4 *Personal qualities* – demonstrates understanding, friendliness, adaptability, empathy and politeness in group project activities; has integrity; focuses on and perseveres towards goal attainment; has inquiring mind; has, or is willing and has the ability to develop with respect to:
  (i) *Basic skills* – understanding of basic graphs, tables, flow-charts and the performing of simple calculations in relation to work-related projects;
  (ii) *Six Sigma methods* – understanding of selected basic Six Sigma tools applied to projects in his/her workplace related to both 'soft' skills such as 'brainstorming' and 'team working' and 'hard' skills such as setting priorities using 'Pareto analysis' and 'cause-and-effect diagrams' to facilitate diagnosis.

Six Sigma local project team leader – green belt

A competency model for a green belt could well include features such as that for the yellow belt plus the ability (with appropriate prior Six Sigma development/ training) to:

1 *Initiative* – proactively identify and act on problems and process improvement opportunities within his/her span of operation; initiate projects and take responsibility for their success.
2 *Leadership* – exercise Six Sigma leadership; communicate ideas to persuade and convince others; responsibly challenge existing procedures, practices and policies; lead, develop and motivate his/her Six Sigma team members; build effective project teams with members from diverse backgrounds and personalities.
3 *Resources* – identify appropriate projects; organize, plan, allocate and manage Six Sigma resources; select goal-relevant activities, rank them, allocate time and prepare and follow project schedules; assess skills available and distribute work accordingly, evaluate project performance and provide feedback.
4 *Technical and interpersonal Skills* – select and effectively apply appropriate Six Sigma tools and methodology to a given project; develop appropriate project team members accordingly.

Six Sigma black belt

Overview

The competencies required of a Six Sigma *black belt* are many and varied. The extent of these competencies are such that one has to be very careful not to be guilty of 'saturation bombing' in this regard. Generally, one needs to be selective and progressive by selecting waves of training and development. The ASQ 'body of knowledge' for black belt certification may appear quite forbidding.

However, it does ensure that the certificated black belt does, indeed, possess considerable competency in the field of Six Sigma based continual improvement.

The primary *role* of the Six Sigma black belt is to turn Six Sigma initiatives for improvement, originated by the management, into reality by initiating, managing and delivering high-potential-value Six Sigma projects. To achieve this black belts need a number of competencies. They require the ability to think of new ways to do things and create innovative strategies. Understanding of the business and cultural environment and the tenacity to continuously keep objectives clearly in mind and maintain a focus on results are also a necessity. They must be adept at overcoming obstacles, both technical and organizational, be competent in Six Sigma methods, have planning and time management skills and be proficient in the 'soft skills' of organizing people.

ASQ body of knowledge

The body of knowledge put forward by the ASQ for black belt certification is taken to be an appropriate standard to use as a benchmark. This is particularly relevant to United Kingdom readers as our own Institute of Quality Assurance has a co-operation agreement with the ASQ in the promotion of Six Sigma best practices. An overview of the key topics in the ASQ black belt certification body of knowledge is portrayed as a cause-and-effect type diagram in Figure 5.1. A more detailed version is shown later in this chapter. Some may feel that it is so comprehensive as to be bordering on the extreme, or even over-the-top, as far as their own particular organizational need, or commitment, is concerned. However, one should not be put off by the comprehensiveness of this ASQ body of knowledge. It is as it is for very good reasons, to maximize success and, at the same time, to minimize the risk of failure.

In any event, most people selected to become black belts will already possess a number of these competencies. The development of a certificated black belt

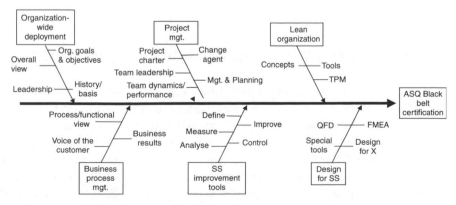

Figure 5.1 Cause-and-effect diagram showing primary elements of the ASQ certificated black belt body of knowledge requirements

can, in any case, be phased in over a period of time, part time or with evening study, in parallel with ongoing Six Sigma activities. Black belt accreditation, however, should become the ultimate aim of all Six Sigma team leaders. Both the ASQ and the IQA run well-established courses leading to such accreditation. The ASQ, for example, have already trained over 1500 people in over 150 organizations. They also make experts available for in-house training, mentoring and coaching.

For those who still find all this too complex to be of much value in their organization then turn to the five simple concepts that define a well-rounded potential Six Sigma black belt. The first is the need for appropriate knowledge and understanding. The second is the ability to apply the necessary Six Sigma technical skill set. Third, there is a need for an awareness of the financial and business implications in any technical decisions that are made. Fourth, there are the interpersonal skills, the 'soft' skills necessary for successful team working and communication. Finally, there is the matter of keeping on building one's competence and commitment in an organization hopefully dedicated to life-long learning and continual improvement.

Elements of the ASQ black belt competency profile

In scanning the elements making up this body of knowledge, or competence profile, some may feel that the Six Sigma initiative is largely made up of pre-existing methods, tools and techniques derived from other fields. This is indeed so. What Six Sigma does is bring a selection of existing world-class tools and best practices together into a cohesive whole. It sets out to provide a complete, self-contained, continual improvement package. The most commonly deployed key elements of the black belt competency profile, and/or those with the greatest leverage on results, are explained throughout this book. Those that are less prevalent, or of lower order in effect, can be found in standard, special to subject, text books.

Organizational-wide deployment competencies

Table 5.2 is a paraphrased overview of the ASQ black belt body of knowledge required for the certification of a black belt in relation to the first limb of the cause-and-effect diagram in Figure 5.1, namely 'organization-wide deployment of Six Sigma'. The universal principles inherent in any Six Sigma organization are discussed in Chapter 6. Six Sigma improvement projects may lead the black belt and the team into any part of the organization. It is, thus, essential that the black belt is familiar with these universal principles applicable to a world-class Six Sigma organization. The black belt needs to be aware of the characteristics of such an organization. He/she can then use such characteristics as a benchmark,

Table 5.2 ASQ black belt body of knowledge: organizational-wide deployment

Organizational-wide deployment	*Cognitive level*
A. Overall understanding of the organization Value of Six Sigma philosophy and goals to the organization Interrelationships between business systems and processes Impact of process inputs, outputs and feedback system on the organization	Comprehension
B. Leadership Leadership roles in the deployment of Six Sigma Black belt, green belt, champion, executive and process owners roles and responsibilities	Comprehension
C. Organizational goals and objectives Key drivers for business; key metrics/scorecards Linking projects to organizational goals When to use Six Sigma improvement methods as opposed to problem-solving tools Purpose and benefit of strategic risk analysis (e.g. SWOT, strengths, weaknesses, opportunities and threats) Risks of suboptimization of a system by optimizing elements Knowledge transfer management	Comprehension
D. History of business improvement: foundations of Six Sigma Origin of tools used in Six Sigma, for example, Deming, Juran, Shewhart, Ishikawa, Taguchi	Comprehension

target, aim, or, maybe, just as a gleam in the eye – to indicate project opportunities to close the gap – something to strive towards.

The origins of the tools used and the role of prominent Gurus in Six Sigma are covered principally in Chapter 3.

Business process management competencies

A paraphrased overview of the ASQ black belt certification 'body of knowledge' requirements for 'business process management' is shown in Table 5.3, which covers the subject matter of the first left-hand side lower limb of the cause-and-effect diagram in Figure 5.1. Most of the topics are covered elsewhere in the book. Other aspects are discussed in this section.

Table 5.3   ASQ black belt body of knowledge: business process management

Business process management	Cognitive level
A. Process vs. functional view Process components and boundaries	Analysis
Process owners, internal and external customers, stakeholders	
Difference between managing processes and maximizing their benefits to the business	
Key performance metrics and appropriate documentation	
B. Voice of the customer Identify different customers; how a project affects internal and external customers; financial impact of customer loyalty	Analysis
Various methods to collect customer feedback; strengths and weaknesses of each approach; key elements re-effectiveness	Application
Graphical, statistical and qualitative tools to analyse customer feedback	Analysis
Translation of critical customer requirements into strategic project areas using QFD or similar tools	Analysis
C. Business results Use of process performance metrics (PPM, DPMO, DPU, RTY, COPQ) to drive business decisions	Analysis
Importance of benchmarking	Knowledge
Financial measures and benefits related to projects; financial models (e.g. NPV, ROI)	Application
Cost and categories of quality; collection, reporting	Application

QFD, quality function deployment; PPM, parts per million; DPMO, defects per million opportunities; DPU, defects per unit; RTY, rolled throughput yield; COPQ, cost of poor quality; NPV, nett present value; ROI, return on investment.

Process versus functional view

What is the meaning of process versus functional view? It is intended to draw attention to the 'fabric' of an organization; to distinguish between the 'warp' and the 'weft'. In a number of organizations, the warp is stronger than the weft. In other words, in a 'warp'-dominant organization power and loyalties are centred within individual departments, each tending to protect its own 'turf'. This is recognized in the typical hierarchical organizational structure comprising marketing, design and development, manufacturing, service, finance, human resources and the like. On the other hand, in a 'weft'-dominant organization the focus, power and loyalties are concentrated in the initiation, development, control and improvement of concept to customer projects and processes. One only has to ask a single question of organization members to determine the relative influence of vertical hierarchies to horizontal project/process activities. The question is. Who do you work for? The answer is invariably 'my boss' with the function/department driven approach or my 'customer' with the process approach.

There is a growing tendency in world-class organizations to progressively concentrate on and strengthen the concept to customer project/process approach to running the business with the consequential flattening of organizational structures. The principal benefit claimed for such a process business model is that it promotes a unified organizational approach to providing customer value rather than suboptimizing in terms of traditional individual departmental interests. In so doing it replaces the obstacle track constituted by departmental boundaries by a fluent flow process as indicated in Figure 5.2.

Bill Scherkenbach (1986), a Deming disciple, reminds us of some of the realities of the boss being the employee's most important customer. The boss gives you an assignment to explain away the increase in this month's warranty figures over last months. This has the adverse effect of putting you off meeting real customers needs for more reliable parts. Your boss tells you that you have enough to do to meet your own department's objectives and do not need to spend our time helping other departments – even though by going upstream and helping other departments who supply yours you will be helping the organization's objectives more effectively. Scherkenbach considers that when the boss is your most important customer, other real customers – those who use your process outcomes – may well be shortchanged and teamwork short-circuited.

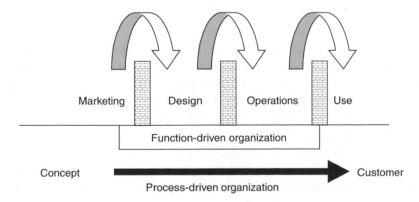

Figure 5.2 Comparison of function- and process-driven organization

Table 5.4 Example of translation of the voice of the customer into critical to quality characteristics

Voice of the customer	Key issues	Critical to quality requirements
Not enough leg room in aircraft	Personal comfort. Existing leg room = 31″	Leg room = 34″
Delivery takes too long	Order cycle time currently up to 1 week	Next day order delivery within 100-mile radius
Bills arrive at different times of the month	Consistency of monthly bill delivery. Currently ±1 week	Bill receipt on same day of month

Voice of the customer

The voice of the customer can be determined in a number of ways. The traditional primary way is through customer complaints. However, this should be looked upon purely as a reactive long stop to things that have already gone wrong. Having said this, much can, and should, be done to ameliorate customer concerns. These include extended warranties, prompt root-cause diagnosis and corrective action, and collection and analysis of customer feedback data. Proactive methods are increasingly being used. These include interviews, focus groups and surveys. With interviews much can be learnt about the point of view of the customer, from the perspective of aspects such as performance measures, product and service attributes. Focus groups involve segments of the customer base. Surveys assess the relative importance and performance of a particular product, service or metric or for benchmarking across a range of competitive products or services. One example, in the automotive field is the J.D. Power survey. In the United States of America, the American Customer Satisfaction Index[1] (ACSI) tracks trends in customer satisfaction over a wide range of companies, government agencies and trade associations. The ACSI customer satisfaction index is based on consideration of customer expectations, perceived quality, perceived value, customer complaints and customer loyalty. It is claimed that ACSI subscribers are able to use the index to calculate the net present value (NPV) of their company's customer base as an asset over time.

The results of customer feedback can also gainfully be used upstream to support the development of customer needs and expectations. Some examples are shown in the matrix of Table 5.4 of the translation of the voice of the customer (VOC) into critical to quality (CTQ) design requirements.

A more recent innovation in this field is a development to enhance customer loyalty that has the name 'customer intimacy'. This is discussed in chapter 6.

[1]The ACSI index is produced through a partnership of the University of Michigan Business School, the American Society for Quality and the consulting firm CFI Group.

Business results

Process performance metrics

Most organizations measure the wrong things from an improvement perspective. Take yield. We all know the yield of our products. But how useful is it as a basis for a Six Sigma project? It is probably not as good as we think. How do you measure your yield? Probably by the formula:

yield % = 100 (good output units)/total input units, or,
        perhaps, % units faulty

These measures of operational efficiency are easy to calculate; the data are readily available and, intuitively, it is very appealing. However, they can provide a major trap for the unwary. They have the ability to mislead and deceive, can mask hidden operations and waste, and furthermore, do not usually provide an effective basis for Six Sigma improvement projects. Why is this? Take the following scenarios:

Scenario 1: two units, A and B, are submitted for functional test. Unit A is fault-free. Unit B has one fault. Conclusion: yield = 50% or 50% units faulty.

Scenario 2: two units, C and D, are submitted for functional test. Unit C has eight faults. Unit D is fault-free. Conclusion: yield = 50% or 50% units faulty.

Using this measure of yield both processing scenarios are of equal performance. However, from a quality, cost of production and improvement potential perspective there is a large difference between the two scenarios. This is because each repairable fault must be detected, diagnosed and appropriate remedial action taken. Even if the faults are not rectifiable (e.g. the units are scrapped), the process is far less efficient in the second scenario than in the first. It can be seen that the simple unit yield measure can be quite misleading.

An improved performance measure, or metric, from a Six Sigma perspective, would be to use the number of non-conformities[2] rather than the number of non-conforming units in the performance expression. Using this measure performance is expressed as 'average non-conformities per unit', namely:

$$\text{average non-conformities per unit (ncpu)} = \frac{\text{total number of non-conformities}}{\text{total number of units}}$$

Thus Scenario 1: ncpu = 2/2 = 1 and Scenario 2: ncpu = 8/2 = 4.

---

[2]Many books and training courses for Six Sigma practitioners use defects instead of non-conformities. However, there is big difference between the meanings of the two terms. The International Standards Organization defines, in ISO 9000, a non-conformity as 'nonfulfilment of a requirement' and defect as 'nonfulfilment of a requirement related to an intended or specified use'. ISO 9000 points out that the term 'defect' should be used with extreme caution as it has legal connotations associated with product liability issues. Hence, conconformity is the preferred term to use in Six Sigma activities.

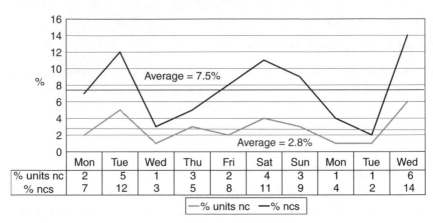

	Mon	Tue	Wed	Thu	Fri	Sat	Sun	Mon	Tue	Wed
% units nc	2	5	1	3	2	4	3	1	1	6
% ncs	7	12	3	5	8	11	9	4	2	14

—% units nc —% ncs

Figure 5.3 Comparison of results from two different performance measures on the same units

Summarizing, whilst simple unit yield may be useful for logistics purposes in manning an inspection, checking or test station it is a misleading performance metric for most Six Sigma projects. Ncpu is more closely correlated with cost, quality and project opportunities.

Case study. Batches of 100 units are checked daily. The results are shown in two ways in Figure 5.3, % units non-conforming (% units nc) and non-conformities per 100 items (% ncs). It would be advantageous from a project selection and diagnostic viewpoint to also list the types of non-conformities together with their numbers and so make a multiple non-conformity chart.

Importance of benchmarking

There are two main reasons for discussing benchmarks and benchmarking in a Six Sigma context. First, benchmarks can be used by management and the Six Sigma practitioner as a basis of comparison of any process with the best in class. Second, benchmarking is a practice that can gainfully be used by the Six Sigma practitioner in eliminating the gap between current practice and best practice. A benchmark is a reference value against which performance may be compared. Examples are the systolic and diastolic blood pressure standard of 120/80, the 20/20 vision standard and the 6 Sigma standard of performance for a particular characteristic. Benchmarking, on the other hand, is a practice that refers to 'the search for, and application of, best practices to secure superior performance'. The overall benchmarking operation is indicated visually in Figure 5.4.

There are many advantages claimed for benchmarking. It reveals the need for improvement, quantifies the magnitude of the change required and indicates

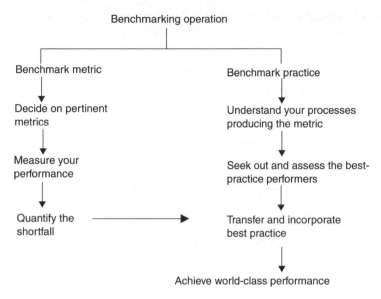

Figure 5.4   Schematic of the overall benchmarking operation

how it can be achieved. It exposes organizations to 'state of the art' practices. In so doing, it induces a culture open to change and continual improvement and helps to instigate a continuous learning process. It stimulates and promotes the involvement and empowerment of members and unleashes, and channels, creative potential. It opens up our perspective from that of seeking virtually error-free performance to that of aiming for world-class performance in terms of important business metrics.

Three parameters form a firm basis for benchmarking. These relate to quality, cost and time. First-time yield (often termed rolled throughput yield, RTY, in Six Sigma speak) provides a measure of process performance, whether it be manufacturing, design or sales (ratio of sales to inquiries). Value-to-cost ratio gives a measure of the ability of any process to provide high value at low cost. Cycle-to-throughput time ratio serves as a measure of efficiency taking into account inventory, downtime and changeover time.

Project management competencies

A paraphrased overview of the ASQ black belt certification 'body of knowledge' requirements for 'project management' is shown in Table 5.5. A number of features quoted in the table are dealt with elsewhere in this book. An example is project charter, dealt with in Chapter 6.

Table 5.5 ASQ black belt body of knowledge: project management

Project management	Cognitive level
A. Project charter and plan	
Elements of project charter and plan	Analysis
Planning tools incl. Gantt chart	Application
Data- and fact-driven documentation incl. spread sheets, presentation	Synthesis
Charter creation and negotiation, incl. objectives, scope, boundaries, resources, project transition and closure	Analysis
B. Team leadership	Application
Team initiation; launch elements; purpose, goals, commitment, ground rules, roles and responsibilities, schedules, mgt. support, team empowerment	
Team member selection; appropriate knowledge, skills	
Team stages; stages of team evolution; storming, norming, performing, adjourning, recognition	
C. Team dynamics and performance	
Team-building techniques; basic steps in team-building goals, roles and responsibilities	Synthesis
Team-facilitation techniques; coaching, mentoring and facilitation techniques to guide a team and overcome problems	Application
Team-performance evaluation; measure progress to goals.	Analysis
Team tools, for example, nominal group technique, force field analysis	Application
D. Change agent	Application
Managing change using appropriate techniques	
Organizational roadblocks; overcome structures and cultures that inhibit change	
Negotiation and conflict resolution techniques including brainstorming, consensus finding	
Motivation techniques that support and sustain member participation and commitment	
Effective and appropriate communication techniques to overcome resistance	
E. Management and planning	Application
Tools such as affinity, tree and activity network diagrams, interrelationship digraphs, prioritization matrices, and process decision programme charts (PDPC)	

Project and team leadership

Overview

People talk about the need for a participative leadership style to secure involvement in Six Sigma projects. This is an over-generalization. Any of four leadership styles may be required depending on the situation.

A leadership style is how one behaves when one is trying to positively influence the performance of others. There are four styles of interest:

Directing: for people who lack knowledge in Six Sigma methods but who are enthusiastic and committed. They need direction and supervision to get them started.

Coaching: for people who have the knowledge but lack commitment. They need direction, supervision, support and praise to build their esteem and involvement in decision-making to restore their commitment.

Supporting: for people who have the knowledge but lack confidence or motivation. They do not need much direction because of their intellectual skills but support is necessary to bolster their confidence and motivation.

Delegating: for people who have both knowledge and commitment, who are able and willing to work with little supervision and support.

The need for leadership arises when a number of people join together in a Six Sigma project with common aims and objectives. The belt needs not only to co-ordinate and motivate team members but also ensure that all those people affected by the project are kept on board. Leadership achieves its results through authority that is recognized and accepted by those who are involved. Authority can be divided into five areas, which, in practice, tend to blend into each another. These are:

1 *Authority by fear*. Authority has the power to inspire by fear. However, when it reaches the point where fear is the dominant reaction then authority defeats itself. Fear breeds anxiety that undermines quality of performance.
2 *Organizational authority*. This will only ensure that the essential effort as defined in the mind of each participant will be applied. The extra effort that will achieve outstanding success will only be achieved through other forms of authority.
3 *Intellectual authority*. This is possessed by a black belt who has knowledge that makes a contribution to the aims of the team. It earns for its possessor respect and recognition from others.
4 *Personal authority*. This is based on trust, respect and loyalty because of the personal standing of the black belt in the eyes of the team and those affected by the project.
5 *Inspirational authority*. No black belt can be an outstanding leader unless he has a sense of purpose, a dedication to the Six Sigma cause.

It is essential that the black belt strives to develop in himself, or herself, the ability to lead by intellectual, personal and inspirational authority. A black belt who has strength in all three will not only be an effective Six Sigma team leader but will also exert a significant influence on all people affected by Six Sigma projects. Personality is the effect we have on others. It is the reaction we generate in other people by the impact of our personal characteristics and behaviour on their senses. Whereas our character is what we really are our personality is what we choose to project as ourselves. Success as a Six Sigma black belt is highly dependent on one's ability to project an acceptable personality. If you want to strengthen your personality you will need to identify and analyse what your own judgements of yourself are. If it is vague, ill defined, or not consciously recognizable at all, the starting point is to bring it into focus. Habitual thinking of a lifetime cannot be changed overnight. If one is somewhat indecisive, shy, unsure of oneself, or lacking in confidence the change will not take place immediately. Why not? You may well resolve to. But as soon as you meet people you know, and who know you, there is a strong possibility you will revert to type. There are basically two steps in changing one's self-image:

– identify and analyse the picture you hold of yourself;
– consciously simulate and act out the role and personality you wish to develop.

A Six Sigma belt needs to be capable of self-expression. To organize and motivate people the belt has to communicate effectively. Many people know their subject well but have difficulty in putting their knowledge into a logical and interesting sequence of words. The black belt will deal with people of different interests, for example, those at different levels of the organization. At some levels they think in terms of 'money' and at other levels in terms of 'things'. A key to effective communication is to 'know and understand your recipient'. This is indicated in Figure 5.5.

OK

Not OK

Figure 5.5   Be understood

A simple but useful method of making a start is to put down questions and answers under the three headings:

- *descriptive*: the *facts* relating to the subject;
- *emotive*: how you and others may *feel* about the subject;
- *motivational*: what you want people to *do* as a result of what you are saying.

Summarizing, a black belt takes on the role as champion of Six Sigma. A champion has the multiple tasks of leader, manager and facilitator to varying degrees depending on the nature and complexity of the project being undertaken. The black belt leads people, manages projects and facilitates decision-making.

Team-member selection

To achieve success in any Six Sigma project through effective team working we need: expertise in the appropriate area (e.g. design, operations, procurement); the correct mix of skills and a variety of personalities, working styles or behavioural styles in the project team. Whilst the need to have the appropriate technical and operational knowledge and skills in the team is obvious, the requirement to have a balance of behavioural styles in the team is not so apparent. Also, when these various working styles are present in the team, the project leader needs to acknowledge that the members behave and react differently from one another and need to be treated as such if the best is to be drawn out of individual members and team interactions. If these styles are identified and understood by the black belt, then trust, rapport and credibility can be established with each member of the team, team roles can be delineated and team interactions can be managed to the benefit of all. Four specific predominant styles, or behavioural patterns, are identified. These are the driver, the persuader, the analyst and the amiable. These styles are a simple but effective way of describing the way that a person with a particular style may interact with others in a work situation. Remember there is no one best style. A well-handled mix of styles in a team is beneficial. Team members need also to be aware that if his/her behavioural style causes problems within the team then this will be counterproductive from that person's viewpoint. The important message is to learn to manage and use your style positively to achieve the best results by adjusting your own conduct to make others feel more comfortable with you and for you to better understand and tolerate the behavioural patterns of others. This can involve adjusting your own style frequently to deal with different situations. This ability to adapt to different interpersonal situations is called behavioural flexibility. The key to successful team working is to recognize these individual styles, play to the strengths of individual team members and minimize the effect of their weaknesses.

The driver

The driver likes to be in charge/in control. He/she is result orientated, competitive, forceful, direct, active, assertive and decisive. He/she prefers freedom to operate. In a team situation he/she can be demanding, impatient, unsympathetic and have low tolerance to feelings and attitudes of others. When challenged and under stress the driver can show a tendency to being a bully, by becoming overbearing and dictatorial.

There is a need to be precise and well organized in dealings with the driver. It is preferable to ask such questions that allow the driver to discover the solution rather than telling him/her what to do. Base your discussions on facts, not opinions.

The persuader

The persuader is typified by being a people person, spontaneous, gregarious, stimulating, enthusiastic and personable. He/she can tend to be a risk taker, undisciplined concerning time, opinionated and dramatic. Under stress the persuader tends to verbally attack the person causing the stress.

He/she expects things to be entertaining and fast moving. Encourage the persuader to develop ideas. Pin down specifics on any agreed course of action. Do not expect a high degree of dependability.

The analyst

This is the well-organized precise fact finder, disciplined with time, one who enjoys problem-solving. He/she tends to be orderly, methodical, industrious and focused on specifics. In a team situation he/she can often be looked upon as over-cautious, critical and uncommunicative. Under stress the analyst moves into an unproductive style and tends either to resent and withdraw or to protract the issue by demanding more information.

Be systematic and organized in dealing with the analyst. Give the analyst time to validate what he/she is being told.

The amiable

This person is relationship orientated, warm and friendly, adaptive, likes stability and avoids risks. He/she tends to be helpful, co-operative, supportive and dependable. He/she may appear to be uncommitted and to hide true feelings in an effort to conform. Under stress the amiable person tends to go into an unproductive style mode that is to give in or submit and silently resent.

Make an effort to get the amiable person to separate out what he/she actually wants from what he/she thinks you want to hear. Give personal assurances concerning actions that involve a degree of risk.

Team stages of evolution

The ASQ body of knowledge refers to the '-orming' team development model developed by Bruce Tuckman of the USA Naval Medical Research Institute who recognizes four stages of team development. These are forming, storming, norming and performing.

Forming stage

The forming stage relates to the initiation of a new project team when members come together for the first time. This is a critical stage particularly with respect to feelings on issues of trust and degrees of collaboration, a degree of scepticism about the possibility of being manipulated and some apprehension at what they may be letting themselves in for. The management style to use at this stage is a structured empathetic one. Ensure all members are encouraged to participate without fear or ridicule. Draw out members who are withdrawn and isolate themselves from other team members. Encourage communication. Create a charter covering the purpose of the project and formulate team roles and methods of team operation and project realization.

Storming stage

This relates to the project stage where some members of the team may begin to feel uncomfortable as they realize the complexity of the work ahead and may show signs of confusion or frustration that can manifest itself in dissention and argument with other team members. The leadership style to use in this phase is that of moderator or mentor. Manage dissent. Avoid setting up win–lose situations between team members. Advise and develop methods both of team working (soft skills) and how to tackle the particular project in hand (hard or technical skills). Ensure proper resources are available to undertake the project.

Norming stage

Team members begin to feel comfortable in their role and with one another at the norming stage. The black belt can begin the process of delegating and set challenging project assignments.

Performing stage

At this stage members are all 'singing to the same hymn sheet' and it is all systems go regarding the project in hand. Here the leader focuses on goals, measures of task accomplishment and maintains momentum. He shows that members are valued. He bears in mind the 'five most important questions in the world' as quoted by Michael Le Boeuf (1986), namely:

The five most important words in our language are 'You did a good job'.

The four most important words are 'What is your opinion?'

The three most important words are 'Let's work together'.
The two most important words are 'Thank you'.
The single most important word is 'We'.

Team dynamics and performance

There are two major team-related functions of every black belt: project functions, to keep the team focused on the project in hand, and team relations functions, to maintain constructive team relations among members and to keep diverse individuals working together as a team. The task functions are discussed in Chapter 6. Good team relationships involve respect for the knowledge each team member possesses and a degree of tolerance in putting up with and accommodating different ways of working, habits and foibles of other members.

Team relations functions

Six specific team relations functions are discussed:

1 *Encouraging*: being friendly, warm and responsive to others; accepting others and their contributions; giving others an opportunity for recognition.
2 *Expressing team feelings*: sensing feeling, mood, relationships within the team; sharing one's own feelings with other members.
3 *Harmonizing*: attempting to reconcile disagreements; reducing tension; getting people to explore their differences.
4 *Modifying*: modifying one's own position, when one's own idea is involved in a conflict, to maintain team cohesion.
5 *Gate-keeping*: attempting to keep communication channels open; facilitating the participation of others.
6 *Evaluating*: assessing team functioning and performance; expressing standards to achieve; measuring results; evaluating degree of team commitment.

Brainstorming

A brainstorming team normally comprises up to eight members. The method of operation is structured and the members are required to observe certain rules of conduct. The primary aims are to create a safe environment in which ideas can be voiced without fear of ridicule and to create an atmosphere that stimulates positive thinking and encourages the flow of ideas. In a Six Sigma brainstorming session members can take on one of three roles:

1 *Client*: who has the problem to be solved or process to be improved.
2 *Facilitator*: who steers the session in a prescribed way.
3 *Participants*: all other members whose sole function is to help the client solve his/her problem.

There is a standardized method of operation, the:

- client describes the problem, indicates measures already taken and suggests area in which help is required;
- facilitator writes the problem on the flip-chart or board in 'How to ...' headline form;
- facilitator encourages a flow of ideas from all participants that are written in headline form, starting with an active verb, on the chart or board; at this stage there is no evaluation and therefore no criticism;
- facilitator may, if considered necessary for understanding, invite participants to enlarge on their ideas;
- client ultimately reviews each idea in turn by firstly stating the useful features of each idea; he/she thus protects the originator of the idea and encourages sensitive participants whom criticism might discourage;
- client then selects what he considers to be the best idea; if further assistance is required from the team in developing this idea it is then expressed in the 'How to ...' form as a further problem to be solved.

Change agent

Cultural patterns

Each and every organization has evolved its own cultural pattern. Any new members are expected to adapt to that pattern. Any perceived threat to the established cultural values is resisted. Any proposed change in culture will be assessed from the point of view of the threat it poses to the existing culture? Such threats to the existing culture can be identified at each level of an organization. For the management it involves a completely different style of managing with the associated risks and uncertainties. White collar people may view it as an invasion of their monopoly of power. Technologists, designers and the like may object to having to use a more disciplined approach, become more transparent in their decision-making and lay their activities wide open for scrutiny by multi-disciplined teams. All will have to learn a completely new ball game.

Expectations and approach

With the general resistance to change in the existing cultural pattern we should expect only a modicum of real support at the start in overcoming roadblocks. This will not be resolved by edict or debate but by demonstration on pilot projects. This movement in single file, and not across a broad front, has many advantages. It means that the training and development involved can take place in waves. It also provides an opportunity to manoeuvre and change tack if this is found necessary in the light of experience. This, too, accommodates differences in business priorities and enthusiasms of the people involved.

Handling resistance to cultural change

Juran has listed a number of points to bear in mind in introducing change. These include: provide participation, spring no surprises, start small; keep it fluid; create a favourable climate; weave the change into the present culture; work with the informal leadership of the existing culture; treat people with dignity; and finally, be constructive (positive not negative).

Six Sigma improvement tools: competencies

A paraphrased overview of the ASQ black belt certification 'body of knowledge' requirements for 'Six Sigma improvement tools' is shown in Tables 5.6–5.8 in terms of the five project stages used in standard Six Sigma. These five stages, define, measure, analyse, improve and control are discussed in Chapter 6 and

Table 5.6   ASQ black belt body of knowledge – improvement tools: 1

Six Sigma improvement tools (1 of 3)	*Cognitive level*
Define stage	
A. Project scope	
Project definition, incl. Pareto charts, process (macro) maps	Synthesis
B. Metrics	
Primary and consequential metrics, incl. quality, quality costs	Analysis
C. Problem statement	
Problem statement, incl. baseline and improvement goals	Synthesis
Measure stage	
A. Process analysis and documentation	
Process maps, written procedures, work instructions, flow charts, etc.	Analysis
Process input and output variables and their relationships using cause-and-effect diagrams, relational matrices, etc.	Evaluation
B. Probability and statistics	
Validity of statistical conclusions; descriptive vs. inferential studies; population parameter vs. sample statistic	Evaluation
Central limit theorem and relationship to inferential statistics, confidence intervals, control charts, etc.	Application
Basic probability concepts including independent and mutually exclusive events; multiplication rules, etc.	Application

Table 5.6 *(Continued)*

Six Sigma improvement tools (1 of 3)	Cognitive level
C. Collecting and summarizing data	
Types of data: variables vs. attributes; conversion of one to the other	Evaluation
Measurement scales: nominal, ordinal, interval and ratio	Application
Data-collection methods such as check sheets, data coding, automatic gauging	Evaluation
Techniques for assuring data accuracy and integrity such as random sampling, stratified sampling, sample homogeneity	Evaluation
Descriptive statistics re. dispersion, central tendency frequency and cumulative frequency distributions	Evaluation
Graphical methods: depicting relationships with stem and leaf, box and whisker and scatter plots and run charts, etc.	Evaluation
Depicting distributions with histograms, normal probability and Weibull plots, etc.	
D. Properties and applications of probability distributions	
Poisson, binomial, normal, chi^2, t and F distributions	Evaluation
Hypergeometric, bivariate, exponential lognormal and Weibull distributions	Application
E. Measurement systems	
Attribute screens, gauge blocks, calipers, micrometers, optical comparators, and tensile strength, titration eqt. etc.	Comprehension
Measurement system analysis. Bias, repeatability and reproducibility, measurement correlation, linearity, % agreement, precision/tolerance, precision/total variation, using ANOVA and control chart methods for non-destructive, destructive and attribute systems	Evaluation
F. Process capability	
Process capability studies: identification of characteristics and specified tolerances: developing sampling plans for verifying stability and normality	Evaluation
Natural process limits vs. specification limits; process performance metrics such as percent non-conforming	Evaluation Evaluation
Process capability indices: *Cp* and *Cpk*	Evaluation
Process performance indices: *Pp, Ppk* and *Cpm*	Evaluation
Short-term vs. long-term capability	Evaluation
Process capability with non-normal data	Application
Process capability for attribute data: sigma value	Application

Table 5.7   ASQ black belt body of knowledge – improvement tools: 2

Six Sigma improvement tools (2 of 3)	*Cognitive level*
Analyse stage	
A. Exploratory data analysis	
Multi-vari studies: charts; sampling plans	Application
Measuring and modelling relationships between variables; regression including hypothesis testing; simple linear correlation: confidence intervals, correlation vs. causation;	Evaluation
diagnostics, analysis of residuals	Analysis
B. Hypothesis testing	
Statistical vs. practical significance; significance levels, power, type 1 and type 2 errors	Evaluation
Sample size for given hypothesis test	Application
Point and interval estimation; efficiency and bias of estimates	Analysis
Tests for means, variances and proportions	Evaluation
Paired comparison parametric hypothesis tests	
Goodness-of-fit tests: chi^2 tests	
Analysis of variance (ANOVA)	
Contingency tables: statistical significance	
Non-parametric tests, incl. Mood's median, Levene, Kruskal–Wallis, Mann–Whitney	Analysis
Improve stage	
A. Design of experiments (DoE)	
Independent and dependent variables; factors levels; response, treatment, error and replication	Comprehension
Planning and organizing experiments; objectives, factor selection, response measurement methods	Evaluation
Design principles; power and sample balance, replication, order, efficiency, randomization, blocking, interaction and confounding	Application
One-factor vs. multi-factor experiments	Evaluation
Full-factorial experiments; construction; computational and graphical methods of analysis	
Two-level fractional factorial experiments, incl. Taguchi designs	
Taguchi robustness concepts; controllable and noise factors; signal-to-noise ratios	Analysis
Mixture experiments; construction and graphical analysis	Analysis
B. Response surface methods	
Steepest ascent/descent experiments	
Higher-order experiments, e.g. Central Composite, Box Behnken	Comprehension
C. Evolutionary operation (EVOP)	
Application and strategy	

Table 5.8 ASQ black belt body of knowledge – improvement tools: 3

Six Sigma improvement tools (3 of 3)	*Cognitive level*
Control stage	
A. Statistical process control	
Objectives and benefits, e.g. performance control,	Comprehension
special vs. common causes; selection of critical	Application
characteristics; rational subgroups	
X-bar and R, X-bar and s, individual and moving range,	
median, p, np, c and u charts	
Control chart analysis	Analysis
Pre-control	
B. Advanced statistical process control	
Short-run SPC, EWMA and moving average	Comprehension
C. Lean tools for control	
5S, visual factory, kanban, poka-yoke, total productive	Application
maintenance	
D. Measurement system re-analysis	
Improvement of measurement system with process	Evaluation
capability improvement	

shown in extended form pictorially in Figure 6.8. It is seen that there is a considerable body of statistical knowledge required for certification of an ASQ accredited black belt. The practical application of the more generally used techniques in Six Sigma projects are covered in British Standard 600 (SS/3:BSI, 2000) at the black belt level of understanding. The pocket size Memory Jogger (Brassar, B. and Ritter, D., 2000) [available in the United Kingdom from the Institute of Quality Assurance] also covers the more fundamental statistical methods in a very practical manner. This, or a similar guide, for example, the *Process improvement pocket advisor* (Qualpro, 2000) should be in the hands of everyone involved in the Six Sigma initiative.

Discussion of the extensive statistical methods covered in the ASQ body of knowledge for black belts is confined to essential basics.

Overview

To think statistically will one day become as necessary ... as the ability to read and write ...

H.G. Wells

That day has arrived! Daily we are bombarded with statistics. In the purely personal (and passive) sense we need to think statistically if only to combat the plausible deceptions that are frequently practised on the innocent. In the more positive business sense it is essential for everyone not only to develop a 'feel' for data, but, particularly with the current data explosion and our commitment to never-ending improvement to:

- Nurture an attitude change to statistics, to encourage others to look on it as a lively, fascinating and penetrating tool; a tool for unmasking prejudice and for providing valuable insights into our problems/opportunities. Too often statistics is looked upon as uninspiring and excrutiatingly dull and sometimes forbidding or yet even frightening. Some even say insulting things about statisticians themselves. It has been said, 'a statistician is someone who does not have the personality to become an accountant'. However, in Six Sigma, we need to keep both accountants and statisticians on-side. We must get away from these negative thoughts and outlook and convey the vitality of the statistical approach to our colleagues so that they will not only use it but enjoy so doing.
- Develop skills in the methodology of collecting, organizing and presenting data, as well as common-sense interpretation using largely pictorial methods–with the minimum of mathematics/statistical theory.

It is vital not only to learn the statistical techniques described but also to appreciate how and when to apply them.

What is statistics?

The term statistics has a double meaning:

- Data itself (e.g. payroll statistics) or measured derived from statistical data (e.g. net sales billed).
- Methods for the study and evaluation of data. This can be divided into five categories:
  - *collection*: by counting or measuring;
  - *organization*: presentation in a form suitable for drawing logical conclusions;
  - *analysis*: the extraction of relevant information from which numerical descriptions can be made (e.g. average, standard deviation);
  - *interpretation*: drawing conclusions from analysis of data often involves prediction (inference) concerning a large amount of data from information on a small sample (e.g. quoting of faults in parts per million with a sample of 50);
  - *decision-making*: taking action in the light of the interpretation.

Alternatively, statistics can be divided into two categories:

- *Descriptive statistics*: essentially involving the collection, organization and presentation of data so that the information content is most readily communicated.

- *Inferential statistics*: essentially involving the drawing of conclusions from a sample about a body of data (a so-called population), which has not been completely collected.

Samples

From cost/benefit considerations it is often necessary to take decisions on the basis of a small portion of the total information that could conceivably be collected. This portion is known as a sample. In order to structure the sampling approach we need to be clear about a few specific terms. These are:

- *task objective*: the purpose of sampling;
- *population*: the whole group or set of objects we want information about;
- *unit*: any individual member of the population;
- *sampling frame*: a list of sampling units; the frame can be a list of all individual units or groups of units;
- *characteristic*: the feature that is being assessed in the units in the sample;
- *sample*: a part or subset of the population.

Sampling

There are many methods of taking samples. The main ones are:

- *Random*: gives each unit in the population the same chance of being chosen. If the units are numbered consecutively a table of random numbers may be used to obtain the sample.
- *Systematic*: here a sample is drawn to some predetermined plan such as: a designed experiment [e.g. orthogonal (balanced) array]; an SPC (statistical process control) procedure (e.g. 5 per hour); folo (first off–last off) in a set-up-dominant production system.
- *Stratified*: when a population is known to be heterogeneous, in relation to the characteristic under study, it is divided into strata and samples of units are drawn from each strata.
- *Cluster*: here the population (e.g. Ford of Britain) is divided into a convenient number of clusters (e.g. Bridgend, Dagenham, Liverpool).
- *Quota*: is chosen by deciding how many of each type or class of unit is to be in the sample (e.g. any 10 nurses, 5 administrative personnel, 15 doctors).

Data collection methods

Data can be collected in many different ways. The more common are:

- *direct observation*: potentially good accuracy, but could affect the measurement;
- *experiment*: good when active intervention is possible; highly efficient designs are available;

- *routine reports*: much data are routinely collected, for example, in the name of 'due diligence'; frequently feedback is open-loop;
- *interviewing*: (face to face and telephone) good in skilled hands, could induce bias;
- *questionnaires*: (postal) cheap, low response rate, introduces bias;
- *questionnaires*: (self-administered), for example, application forms: cheap, good response rate.

Collection formats

Data can be collected in many forms. Four principal scales are in use:

- *nominal*: data are placed in categories only; for example, acceptable/not acceptable, by colour (e.g. black, red or blue); type of fault (e.g. mis-shapes, broken, etc.); or sex (male, female).
- *ordinal*: data are ranked to some criterion; for example, excellent, good, average, fair; private, corporal, sergeant; grade A, grade B.
- *interval*: data are measured on a numerical scale; for example, temperature. We can add or subtract but not form ratios; for example, take two temperatures:
  $A = 50\,°F = 10\,°C : B = 68\,°F = 20\,°C$.
  Ratio $A/B = 50/68 = 0.74$ in F. But $A/B = 10/20 = 0.5$ in °C.
- *ratio*: as interval with the added feature that the ratio of any two values is independent of the unit of measurement; for example, weight is a ratio variable.

Basic statistical measures

The most commonly used statistical measures are those that measure central tendency (setting of a process or level of a characteristic) and variability.

Central tendency

Three measures are relevant:

- *arithmetic mean (or just mean or average)*: the total of the values divided by the number of values;
- *median (mid-value)*: the central value when the data are ranked in order of size;
- *mode*: the most frequently occurring value.

Variability

The two most relevant measures are:

- *range (R)*: is the difference between the smallest and largest values in the data;

- *standard deviation* (*s*): is best determined using a scientific calculator using the σ_{n-1} key.

Case study

Comment on the relative performance of two suppliers who have each provided five samples of wire for testing for breaking strength. Results were: A, 390, 405, 386, 412, 397; B, 450, 375, 468, 350, 536.

	Measure	*Supplier A*	*Supplier B*
Level	Mean	398	436
	Median	397	450
Variability	Range	26	186
	Standard deviation	11	75

The table shows that supplier A produces the more consistent product. However, the average value of supplier A is less than that of supplier B.

Pareto diagram for prioritizing

A Pareto diagram is a simple graphical technique for displaying the relative importance of features, problems or causes of problems as a basis for establishing priorities. It distinguishes between the 'vital few' and the 'trivial many' and hence focuses attention on issues where maximum quality improvement is secured with the minimum effort. The Pareto diagram displays, in decreasing order, the relative contribution of each element (or cause) to the total situation (problem). Relative contribution may be based on relative frequency, relative cost or some other measure of impact. Relative contributions are shown in bar chart form. A cumulative line may be added to show the cumulative contribution.

The procedure is:

- select the concern to be rank ordered and the measure (e.g. frequency, cost) and gather data;
- list the elements from left to right on the horizontal axis in order of size;
- set up an appropriate vertical scale on the left-hand side and above each classification draw a rectangle whose height represents its size;
- set up a 0–100% scale on the right-hand side and draw a line from the top of the tallest bar, moving upward, on a cumulative basis from left to right.

An example is shown in Figure 6.11.

Process flow charting

The flow chart is used in an approach called imagineering. (What life would be like if we did the right things in the right sequence right first time.) Here, the people with the greatest knowledge about the process frequently:

- draw a flow chart of the steps the process actually follows;
- draw a flow chart of the steps the process should follow if everything worked right first time;
- question whether the process is really necessary and, if so, how it could be done differently. (Are we doing the right things?)

A process flow chart is a pictorial representation showing the steps of a process in sequence. It frequently describes the key process activities, their sequence and who is responsible for them. The flow chart has many applications. The principal one is in investigating opportunities for improvement by gaining a better understanding of how the various stages in a process relate to one another.

A typical flow chart is shown in Figure 6.9. A variation of the flow chart is shown in Figure 6.10. This flow chart shows the key process activities, their sequence, and who is responsible for them.

Cause-and-effect diagram for diagnostic work

The cause-and-effect diagram is used where it is required to brainstorm and show pictorially cause-and-effect relationships and the root causes of a problem. It is frequently called a fishbone diagram (because of its shape) or an Iskikawa diagram (after its creator). There are several types of cause-and-effect diagram, based on the formation of the main branches (categories), including general 4 M (manpower, machines, materials, methods) or 4 P (people, procedures, plant, process) and those constructed in terms of process steps and sequence. A typical cause-and-effect diagram is shown in Figure 5.1.

Graphs to show pictorial relationships

A graph is a picture of the relationship between two variables. There are various forms of graphs; however, certain general principles apply.

Since graphs depend on visual interpretation they are open to every trick in the field of optical illusion. Scale manipulation, for example, can considerably affect the dramatic impact of a graph. Four points should be borne in mind when constructing graphs to ensure the communication of information with clarity and precision. These are:

1 all graphs should have a clear, self-explanatory title;
2 all axes should be clearly labelled; units of measurement should be stated;

3 the scale on each axis should be such as to avoid distorting or suppressing information;
4 the independent variable should be on the horizontal axis.

There are many types of graph. The principal ones are:

- *Arithmetic (linear)*: this is the most familiar type of graph and is easily identified by the fact that both horizontal and vertical scales are arithmetical (linear).
- *Scatter diagram*: when one variable is plotted against another to see how they are related it is known as a scatter diagram.
- *Log-linear*: semi-logarithmic graphs are used to display rates of change; a constant rate of change will appear as a straight line.
- *Log–log*: these are used to express learning curves (relationships) in straight line form.
- *Probability plot*: this transforms a regular pattern of variation (e.g. normal or skew) into a straight line. This is very useful when presenting capabilities of processes.
- *Nomograph*: a nomograph provides a graphical solution to formulae.

A typical graph is shown in Figure 5.3.

Statistical process control for Six Sigma

Principal role in Six Sigma

Process monitoring with statistical process control, through the medium of control charts, is an invaluable tool in Six Sigma activities for a number of reasons:

- For establishing current process behaviour at the project formulation stage.
- For diagnostic work during the project, by indicating unusual 'out-of-control' behaviour in the form of:
  - adverse effects, which can be used to determine and eliminate their causes;
  - beneficial effects, which can be exploited to secure an improved performance.
- For monitoring processes, on completion of a project, to:
  - secure the gains achieved;
  - provide the basis for calculating process capability and universal benchmark indices of performance such as Cps and $Cpks$.
- For providing a common language, at all times, for communication of process behaviour, throughout the organization and its supply and customer base.
- It provides answers to three vitally important business questions:
  1 Is the process stable (in control)?
  2 What is the performance (capability) of the process?
  3 Is there evidence of significant improvement?

The control chart

The principal tool of SPC is the control chart. The control chart is an extension to the simple run chart. It distinguishes between two types of variation:

- *special cause variation*: a source of variation that is not present all the time but which arises from specific circumstances;
- *common cause variation*: a source of variation that affects all the individual values of the characteristic being studied.

It is important to distinguish between the two as the action required to remove a special cause (fixing a specific concern) is fundamentally different from that required to reduce common cause variation (improving the process perform-ance, or capability, as a whole). If a special cause is present the process is said to be 'out-of-control'. In such a case, it is necessary to stabilize the process by bringing it back into control. Special causes are usually identified with a con-trol chart by four standard criteria:

- any point outside the control line;
- a run of seven points all above/below the centre line;
- a run of seven intervals up/down;
- any obvious non-random pattern.

Examples of the application of these criteria are shown in Figure 5.6.

Control charts for attribute and measured data

Standard control charts are available to handle both attribute data and variables data. Essentially, there are two classes of control chart, those for attributes

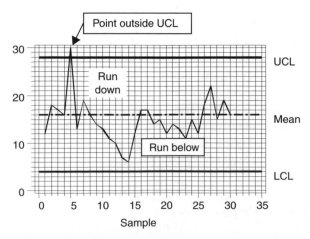

Figure 5.6 Out-of-control conditions

(qualitative data) and those for measurements (quantitative data). *Attributes* are process outcomes that are classified into two categories: item passed or failed, fastener present or missing, open-circuit or short-circuit. Such occurrences can be counted or classified and used in attributes control charts. *Variables* are those product characteristics or process parameters that are measured. Examples are length in millimetres, resistance in ohms, closing effort of a door in Newtons and the torque of a fastener in Newton-meters.

Attribute control charts

Four classes of attribute control charts are used depending on whether the sample size is constant or variable and the measure used is, say, non-conformities or non-conforming units. This is illustrated in Table 5.9.

It may appear peculiar to see the symbols such as c, u, np and p used to describe the different types of attribute charts. The symbols were initially chosen somewhat arbitrarily. However, their main advantage now is that they are now in standard use throughout the world. The average value of the symbol is indicated by placing a bar across the top of the symbol. Thus, the average of c is denoted by $\bar{c}$ or c_{bar}.

It is necessary to clearly distinguish between a non-conformity and a non-conforming unit:

- *Non-conformity*: a fault such as a ding, a dent, porosity or a scratch. It is possible to have more than one non-conformity on an item or unit. The c and u charts apply.
- *Non-conforming units*: a unit that is non-conforming due to one or more non-conformities. The np and p charts apply.

Control limits for attribute charts

Formulae are available for calculating control limits for attribute charts. Alternatively, to avoid the use of such formulae upper and lower control limits can be read off the graphs in Figure 5.7.

Guidance in the use of Figure 5.7 is now given:

For constant sample size: use directly.

Example: If average = 9: enter at average = 9, exit at UCL = 18.

Table 5.9 The four classes of attribute chart

Attribute control chart	Non-conformities	Non-conforming units
Constant sample size	np chart	c chart
Variable sample size	p chart	u chart

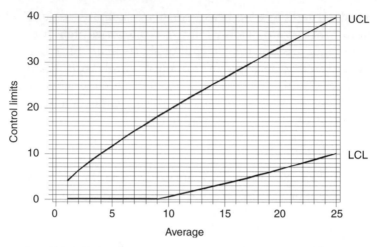

Figure 5.7   Graph for determining control limits for attribute control charts

For variable sample size (proportion chart): enter at (average proportion × average sample size). After exit; divide by average sample size to get control limits.

Example: if proportion = 0.03 and sample size = 500: enter average at 0.03 × 500 = 15

For UCL exit at 26: UCL = 26/500 = 0.05; LCL = 3.5/500 = 0.00.

Measured data control charts

The most common form of measured data control chart is the average ($\overline{X}$) and range (R) chart. Two graphs are plotted on the same base line, one for $\overline{X}$ (average) and the other for range (R). The $\overline{X}$ (average) chart monitors the setting, or level, of a process in relation to the preferred value, or aim. The range chart monitors the precision of the process (see Figure 5.8). Control limits are derived thus:

$$\text{UCL}_R = D_4\overline{R} \qquad \text{LCL}_R = D_3\overline{R}$$
$$\text{UCL}_{\overline{X}} = \overline{\overline{X}} + A_2\overline{R} \qquad \text{LCL}_{\overline{X}} = \overline{\overline{X}} - A_2\overline{R}$$

where the constants D_4, D_3 and A_2 are related to sample size, n, as shown in Table 5.10.

Case study

A case study illustrates the application of measured data control charts. The subgroup size = 4 for the $\overline{X}R$ chart plotted. Th mean is equal to 99.91 and the average range is equal to 6.125. The chart is seen to be 'in control'.

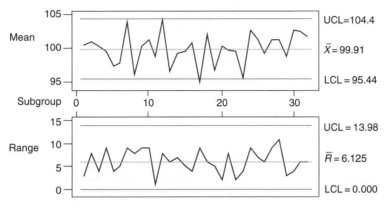

Figure 5.8 Example of mean and range control chart

Table 5.10 Constants for determining control limits for measured data control charts

n	2	3	4	5	6	7	8	9	10
D_4	3.27	2.57	2.28	2.11	2.00	1.92	1.86	1.82	1.78
D_3	–	–	–	–	–	0.08	0.14	0.18	0.22
A_2	1.88	1.02	0.73	0.58	0.48	0.42	0.37	0.34	0.31

For sample sizes below 7, there is no lower control limit.

Process capability and process performance

The four possible states of any process

In the SPC section, control charts were considered purely in terms of process control. A process 'in control' may, or may not, be acceptable in terms of an imposed specification. Here, we go a stage further and consider the process also in terms of capability and performance of performing to specification. The four possible states of any process are shown in Figure 5.9.

Capability and performance indices

Capability and performance indices are in widespread use to provide a standard universal benchmark of process capability or performance in relation to specified requirements. The three main capability indices for a stable process with a Normal distribution, are:

$$Cp = \frac{\text{specified tolerance}}{6 \text{ standard deviations}} = \frac{U - L}{6 \text{ standard deviations}}$$

$$Cpk_U = \frac{U - \text{mean}}{3 \text{ standard deviations}}$$

The four states of any process		Control (stability)	
		Not OK	OK
Capability (performance)	Not OK	Eliminate special causes reduce common causes	Reduce common causes
	OK	Eliminate special causes	Ideal situation monitor at low level

Figure 5.9   The four possible states of any process

Table 5.11   Table for determining the relationship between range and standard deviation

n	2	3	4	5	6	7	8	9
d_2	1.13	1.69	2.06	2.33	2.53	2.70	2.85	2.97

$$Cpk_{\mathrm{L}} = \frac{\mathrm{Mean} - L}{3 \text{ standard deviations}}$$

where U is the upper specification limit and L the lower specification limit.

The standard deviation can be found from the $\overline{X}R$ control chart using the formula: standard deviation $= \overline{R}/d_2$, where d_2 is given in terms of control chart subgroup size (n) in Table 5.11.

These capability indices are applicable for a stable process where individual values follow a bell-shaped 'normal' distribution. If insufficient data has been gathered to establish stability the indices are then called performance indices, Pp, Ppk_{U} and Ppk_{L}. The same formulae are used as with the Cps. This manner of distinguishing between the definition of capability and performance is somewhat arbitrary. However, this notation has been standardized by the International Standards Organization and is now used throughout the world.

The Cp process capability index relates a standardized process spread to the specified tolerance interval. It does not take the location (e.g. mean) of the distribution into account. The Cpk indices relate both the process variability and the location (setting) of the process in relation to the specification nominal and the upper and lower specification limits. Table 5.12 provides an estimate of the parts per million (ppm), or percentages (%), outside the upper and/or lower specification limits provided Cpk_{U} and/or Cpk_{L} is known for a stable process with a Normal distribution.

Table 5.12 Relationship between *Cpk*s and ppm out-of-specification

3Cpk_U and 3Cpk_L	Parts per million and percentages outside upper/lower specification limits									
	0.0	0.1	0.2	0.3	0.4	0.5	0.6	0.7	0.8	0.9
6	0.001 ppm									
5	0.29 ppm									
4	32 ppm→	21	13	8.5	5.4	3.4	2.1	1.3	0.8	0.5
3	1350 ppm→	988	687	483	337	233	159	108	72	48
2	2.3% →	1.8	1.4	1.1	0.8	0.6	0.5	0.4	0.3	0.2
1	16% →	14	12	10	8.1	6.7	5.5	4.5	3.6	2.9
0	50% →	46	42	38	34	31	27	24	21	18

Case study

The control chart of Figure 5.8 is used in this case study. The characteristic is in-control with mean = 99.91 and average range = 6.125. A sub-group size = 4 was known to be used. Suppose the specification is 105.0 ± 10.0. The distribution of individual readings is estimated to be Normal.

What is the capability of the characteristic in relation to the specification?

Hence the standard deviation = $\overline{R}/d_2$ = 6.125/2.06 = 2.97

$$Cp = \frac{\text{specified tolerance}}{6 \text{ standard deviations}} = \frac{U - L}{6 \text{ standard deviations}} = 20/(6 \times 2.97) = 1.12$$

$$Cpk_U = \frac{U - \text{mean}}{3 \text{ standard deviations}} = (115 - 99.91)/(3 \times 2.97) = 1.69$$

3 Cpk_U = just over 5. Using Table 5.12, approximately 0.29 ppm are expected above the upper specification limit. This equates to an upper limit Sigma value of 6.5:

$$Cpk_L = \frac{\text{Mean} - L}{3 \text{ standard deviations}} = (99.91 - 95)/(3 \times 2.97) = 0.55$$

3 Cpk_L = 1.65. Using Table 5.12, some 5% are expected below the lower specification limit. This equates to a lower limit Sigma value = 3.1.

Experimentation and Six Sigma

Overview

Planned experimentation is often referred to as DoE, for Design of Experiments. It is a very important tool in the deployment of Six Sigma projects. This is so for a number of reasons. By using readily available experimental designs it is possible to significantly improve our understanding of the way in which:

- features and build characteristics of a product affect product performance;
- parameters of a process (e.g. line speed, depth of cut, metal temp) affect process yield;
- constituents of a material (e.g. moisture content, Si, Mg) affect its performance properties.

These relationships are then to be used to make significant improvements in product, process and service performance. We can go a long way in achieving this using very economical standard experimental designs that often involve only simple pictorial methods of analysis. In general, there are two kinds of approach that can be taken in Six Sigma projects in establishing relationships between product features and process variables, on the one hand, and performance, on the other. These are:

- *Observational approach*: where variations that occur naturally during day-to-day operations are monitored and analysed. Statistical process control is used to listen to the process in this way.
- *Experimental approach*: where planned experiments are conducted and the results analysed statistically. Here we are proactively opening up a conversation with the process rather than passively listening.

With the experimental approach there are also two main courses open: *change one experimental feature or factor at a time*, keeping everything else constant or conduct a *multi-factor experiment* in which multiple factors are changed simultaneously to a predetermined pattern.

Single-factor experimentation versus multi-factor experimentation

Any designed experiment involves changing from one set of conditions to another, to a predetermined pattern, and the effect determined. The things that are changed are called *factors*. The conditions to which the factors are changed/set are known as *levels*. The value of the outcome is termed the *response*. The change in the response as a result of a change in factor level is termed an *effect*.

A case study is shown to bring out the differences between the traditional method of adjusting one factor at a time and the much more revealing multi-factor experiment.

Case study

The question posed to a Six Sigma team in the midst of a project was thus. *Is a modified machine performing significantly better than the original?* Two possible decisions are considered.

Table 5.13 Results of a single-factor, two-level experiment

Batch	Machine	Operator	% out-of-spec	Average % out-of-spec	Conclusion
1	Original	Betty	4.6	Original m/c =	Retain
2	Original	Betty	5.4	5% average	original m/c
3	Modified	Betty	8.7	Modified m/c =	(with 5%
4	Modified	Betty	9.3	9% average	out-of-spec!)

The machine is called a 'factor' and as two types of machine are compared the factor is said to be at two levels. Hence, this is called a one-factor two-level experimental design. The % out-of-spec is termed the response.

Table 5.14 Results of a two-factor, two-level experiment

Run	Machine	Operator	Out-of-spec %	Average %	Conclusion
1	Original	Betty	5	Original m/c = 5	What
2	Original	Joe	5		conclusion do
3	Modified	Joe	1	Modified m/c = 5	we now draw?
4	Modified	Betty	9		

As machines and machinists (factors) are now involved and there are two of each (levels) this is known as a two-factor, two-level multi-factor experiment.

Decision 1: Perform a single-factor experiment to compare machine performance. Use the day shift machinist, Betty, for convenience. Joe is on nights. Run the experiment with Betty, over two batches for each machine, and measure the percentage of output not meeting the specification. Results are given in Table 5.13.

The natural conclusion from this experiment is to retain the original machine.

Alternative decision: Perform a multi-factor experiment using both operators. Again run the experiment over four batch runs. This involves the identical amount of resources being expended. Results are given in Table 5.14.

In this experiment it is seen that two factors, each at two levels, are changed simultaneously to a predetermined design. This is a more efficient design than the previous one. The plot in Figure 5.10 shows the difference in the operators' performance on the two machines. This is known as an interaction plot. It shows quite a different story than in the previous experiment. It is seen that both machinists have a similar performance on the original machine, at 5% out-of-spec (Sigma level = 3.15). With the modified machine the average performance of the two machinists indicates no improvement. There is still 5% out-of-spec. The Sigma level has not changed. There is one big difference between the two designs. This multi-factor experiment clearly reveals a difference between machinist

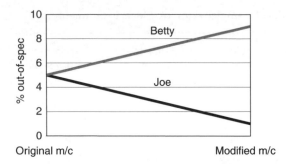

Figure 5.10 Interaction plot for two-factor, two-level experiment

Table 5.15 Design layout in matrix form

Factors		Level	
		1	*2*
A	Machine	Original	Modified
B	Operator	Joe	Betty

performance. Whilst Betty is performing less effectively with the modified machine, the reverse is true for Joe. He is performing at a much improved level of 1% out-of-spec (Sigma = 3.8).

If Joe's knack of using the modified machine can be transferred to Betty then the modified machine appears to offer considerable improvement. This is a different result from that reached with the previous experiment. The layout of this design is shown in Table 5.15, which shows a balanced design for both factors and levels. This type of design is known as orthogonal.

The standard L4 two-level orthogonal array

We will now go from the particular to the general. What we have just done is to use one of the simplest standard experimental designs. It is called a Lattice 4 run (L4), two-level, orthogonal array.

The L4 array can be used in two ways:

- *Design 1*: two-factor, two-level with interaction, known as a full factorial.
- *Design 2*: three-factor, two-level without interaction, known as a fractional factorial.

The usual design layout of an L4 is shown in Table 5.16. Columns 2 and 3 are used for factors A and B. Column 4 can be used in either of two ways. First, purely as an analysis column to determine the extent of the interaction between A and B. Second, it can be used to explore the effects of a third factor, C, if it is considered that interactions are going to be negligible. The response is entered into column 5.

Table 5.16   Layout for standard L4 design

Runs	Factors			Response
	A	B	AB (or C)	
1	1	1	1	
2	1	2	2	
3	2	1	2	
4	2	2	1	

Table 5.17   L4 case study layout

Runs	Factors			Response
	A	B	AB	
1	1 (orig)	1 (Joe)	1	5
2	1 (orig)	2 (Bet)	2	5
3	2 (mod)	1 (Joe)	2	1
4	2 (mod)	2 (Bet)	1	9

An example of the use of the layout, in Table 5.16, for the case study just completed is now shown in Table 5.17.

In Table 5.17, it is seen that in Run 1, for instance, factors are set at levels A1 and B1, namely the original machine with Joe as machinist. The result achieved is 5% out-of-spec. The column AB is used only for later analysis of the interaction. We have already come to a conclusion on the results shown in Table 5.17. However, we will conduct a standard analysis to indicate the approach taken with more complex designs.

A effect = average of responses to A1s − averages of responses to A2s
   $= 0.5(5 + 5) − 0.5(9 + 1) = 0$

B effect = averages of responses to B1s − averages of responses to B2s
   $= 0.5 (5 + 1) − 0.5(5 + 9) = −4$

The AB effect is best determined by a matrix type layout:

	B1	B2
A1	5	5
A2	1	9

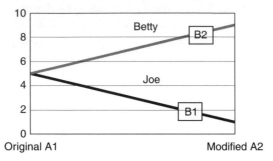

Figure 5.11 Interaction plot for case study

Table 5.18 Layout for standard L8 design array

Run	Column						
	1	2	3	4	5	6	7
1	1	1	1	1	1	1	1
2	1	1	1	2	2	2	2
3	1	2	2	1	1	2	2
4	1	2	2	2	2	1	1
5	2	1	2	1	2	1	2
6	2	1	2	2	1	2	1
7	2	2	1	1	2	2	1
8	2	2	1	2	1	1	2

These effects would usually be portrayed graphically, to assist in communication to non-experts in experimentation, as shown in Figure 5.11.

Standard L8, two-level orthogonal array

The L8 standard two-level orthogonal array has eight runs and has the layout shown in Table 5.18.

When you learn the secret of the L8 array you will be well on the way to successful Six Sigma experimentation. The secret lies in the interaction table shown in Table 5.19.

For example, Table 5.19 shows that the interaction between column 1 and 2 is in column 3; the interaction between column 1 and 4 is in column 5 and the interaction between column 2 and 5 is in column 7.

Four different useful designs are possible with the L8 array. The choice will depend on the number of factors chosen for experimentation and the

Table 5.19 Interaction table for L8 to facilitate different designs

1	2	3	4	5	6	7
(1)	3	2	5	4	7	6
	(2)	1	6	7	4	5
		(3)	7	6	5	4
			(4)	1	2	3
				(5)	3	2
					(6)	1
						(7)

assumptions made regarding possible interactions:

- *Design 1*: seven factors, A, B, C, D, E, F and G, with no interactions. This design is often useful for initial screening where many factors are involved.
- *Design 2*: three factors with all interactions clear of one another, A in column 1, B in column 2 and C in column 4. The two-factor interactions between these are found thus: AB in column 3, AC in column 5 and BC in column 7. The ABC interaction is in column 7. This is a full factorial design that isolates factors together with all their interactions.
- *Design 3*: four factors with all main effects clear of two-factor interactions.
- *Design 4*: five factors clear of selected two-factor interactions.

Range of standard two-level designs

The potential value of the most commonly used experimental designs in Six Sigma activities, the two-level, L4 and L8 designs have been illustrated. Other standard two-level designs are available to deal with larger numbers of factors, for example:

- L12 for up to 11 factors with no interactions;
- L16 for up to 15 factors with no interactions, four factors with all interactions, five factors with all two-factor interactions and eight factors clear of all two-factor interactions.

Black and green belts with little or no previous experience in formal experimentation are advised to practice using the L4 and L8 designs before progressing to larger or more complex designs.

Multiple-run experimentation

Why multiple runs? In practice, it is usually advisable to obtain more than one result for each combination of factor levels. Multiple-run experimentation opens

Table 5.20 Layout of, and results achieved on, a multiple run L8 experiment

Run	Column							Results			Average	Standard deviation
	A	B		C								
1	1	1	1	1	1	1	1	5	6	7	6	1
2	1	1	1	2	2	2	2	4	10	7	7	3
3	1	2	2	1	1	2	2	13	12	11	12	1
4	1	2	2	2	2	1	1	13	16	10	13	3
5	2	1	2	1	2	1	2	14	12	13	13	1
6	2	1	2	2	1	2	1	15	12	9	12	3
7	2	2	1	1	2	2	1	6	7	8	7	1
8	2	2	1	2	1	1	2	3	6	9	6	3

up a new dimension in Six Sigma process improvement. It is then possible not only to establish the effect of a change in level of a factor on the mean but also on the variation (range or standard deviation). We can then do two things:

- optimize the setting/level of response (maximizing, nominalizing or minimizing the mean);
- increase precision by minimizing variation (reducing the standard deviation).

A case study illustrates this.

Case study

A critical dimensional characteristic has an out-of-spec performance. The objective is to meet, or better, a specification of 13.0 ± 5.0, with an average ± 4 standard deviations. The process characteristic is currently performing at 6.0 ± 12.0.

Step 1. Define key factors and levels, A, B and C at levels 1 and 2. If, for example, A relates to temperature, level 1 could be 120 °C and level 2140 °C.

Step 2. Design and run experiment. An L8 was chosen with factors A, B and C in columns 1, 2 and 4. The other columns will then each contain one two-factor interaction. Replicated results are to be obtained with three specimens per run. This will enable both the mean and standard deviation to be calculated. The results[3] are shown in Table 5.20.

Step 3. Analyse the results. Here the analysis is done twice: once in terms of the mean, which we want as close to 13 as possible, and then again in terms of the standard deviation, which we need as small as possible. The summary analysis of the results is shown in Figure 5.12.

---

[3] The actual results have been simplified, to ease calculations, in showing the principles involved.

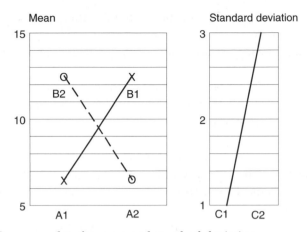

Figure 5.12 Response plots for mean and standard deviation

Figure 5.12 summarizes the salient results of the analysis of Table 5.20. It shows that factor C affects only the standard deviation and an interaction between factor A and factor B affects the mean. Conclusions may now be drawn. Either A1B2 or A2B1 provides the highest mean at an expected 12.5. C1 provides the lowest standard deviation with an expected value of 1. Proposals for future operation would be either A1B2C1 or A2B1C1, depending on which is the more economic arrangement.

The expected performance would then be 12.5 ± 4.0. This is better than the performance initially aimed for. The net effect of this project is to improve the mean from 6.0 to 12.5 and the standard deviation from 3.0 to 1.0. In terms of performance indices, expected Sigma values and ppm outside of specification limits:

- Pp has improved from 0.56 to 1.67.
- Ppk_U has improved from 1.33 to 1.83. (from 32 ppm above the USL to less than 0.29 ppm).
- Ppk_L has improved from −0.22 to 1.5 (from nearly 75% below the LSL to 3.4 ppm).
- The corresponding upper-limit Sigma values improved from 5.5 to 7.
- The corresponding lower-limit Sigma values improved from 0.84 to 6.

Summary

The value of multiple-factor, multiple-run and multiple-level experimentation is illustrated in a number of ways:

- Creating awareness that when the cause is unknown, or when the cause is known but its removal is costly, we can make the process 'talk to us'.
- Achieving this by experimentation where we intentionally produce various possible causes (by changing the levels of factors with the potential of affecting the response) and see how the process reacts (by studying the effects at the various combinations of factors and their levels).

- Illustrating the concept of 'robustness' by: introducing noise factors into the experimental design.
- Exploiting non-linearity relationships between factors and response.

All the designs covered so far can be analysed using simple arithmetic with a user-friendly pictorial presentation of results in the form of response plots. From a black and green belt perspective, however, it is essential that:

- A multi-discipline team is formed at the outset, with relevant process know-how, in order that the best available technical and operational knowledge and experience is used to deduce which factors, and at what levels, experiments are to be run.
- Good housekeeping and discipline is maintained during the running of the different factor combinations to ensure there is no confusion in what level to apply in each run.
- Traceability is maintained throughout the experiment particularly if the product is transferred between departments, or even companies at different locations, during the process (e.g. a foundry operation where the results cannot be assessed until after machining in a different company).
- statistical advice is at hand to deal with concerns and the finer points of experimentation.

Other standard designs and analysis methods

Other standard designs are available for Six Sigma projects. These include:

- Three-level designs for investigating the effects of tolerancing and non-linearity. Typical of these are L9, L18 and L27 arrays.
- Placket–Burman optimal designs.
- Response surface designs such as central composite and Box–Behnken.
- Mixture/blending designs.
- Evolutionary operation (EVOP) designs.

More sophisticated methods of analysis are also available such as analysis of variance (ANOVA), tests for significance and Daniels' probability plots. Generic signal-to-noise ratios should be avoided.

Lean organization competencies

A paraphrased overview of the ASQ black belt certification 'body of knowledge' requirements for 'lean organization' is shown in Table 5.21. The main content of this table was discussed in Chapter 3.

Table 5.21   ASQ black belt body of knowledge: lean organization

Lean organization	Cognitive level
A. Lean concepts	
Theory of constraints	Comprehension
Lean thinking: value, value chain, flow perfection, etc.	
Continuous flow manufacturing (CFM)	
Non-value added activities: inventory, space, inspection,	Application
rework, transportation, storage, etc.	Comprehension
Cycle-time reduction using kaizen methods	
B. Lean tools	
Visual factory, poka-yoke, standard work, SMED, etc., in	Application
areas outside of DMAIC control	
C. Total productive maintenance (TPM)	
Concepts	Comprehension

Table 5.22   ASQ black belt body of knowledge: design for Six Sigma

Design for Six Sigma (DFSS)	Cognitive level
A. Quality function deployment (QFD)	
QFD matrix	Analysis
B. Robust design and process	
Functional requirements	Comprehension
Noise strategies	Application
Tolerance design	Analysis
Tolerances and process capability	
C. Failure mode and effects analysis (FMEA)	
System, design and process FMEA	Analysis
D. Design for X (DFX)	
Design for cost, manufacturability, producibility,	
test and maintainability, etc.	Comprehension
E. Special design tools	Knowledge
TRIZ, axiomatic design, etc.	

Design for Six Sigma competencies

A paraphrased overview of the ASQ black belt certification 'body of knowl-edge' requirements for 'design for Six Sigma' is shown in Table 5.22. The main content of this table was discussed in Chapter 4.

Chapter highlights

- Six Sigma demands the engagement of people in the organization. An essential prerequisite of engagement is the nurturing of attitudes, the acquisition of knowledge and the development of skills.
- Six Sigma competency is defined as the key knowledge, skills, abilities and behaviours needed to satisfactorily perform appropriate Six Sigma tasks.
- Training and development objectives to meet competency requirements are classified into three domains, cognitive (relating to intellectual abilities and skills), affective (reflecting attitude and feelings) and psychomotor (dealing with muscular skill, co-ordination and manipulation).
- The cognitive domain is graduated into six levels of attainment in ascending order, knowledge of, comprehension, application, analysis, synthesis and evaluation.
- Competency levels for yellow, green and black belts need to be pre-established.
- The American Society for Quality required body of knowledge for certification of black belts is used as a 'gleam in the eye' benchmark.
- Black belt competency requirements cover a number of areas. These are overall understanding of the organizational, business process management, project management, Six Sigma improvement tools, lean organization and design for Six Sigma.
- Important basic Six Sigma 'common language' tools include:
  - statistical process control (SPC), for monitoring and ensuring process stability;
  - process capability analysis (PCA) with capability (Cp family) and performance (Pp family) indices for first-time quality profiling,
  - experimentation (DoE), using standard economic designs, for creative problem-solving and securing process and product improvements.
  - SPC, PCA and DoE form a trilogy that enables the Six Sigma practitioner to attain, and sustain, the ultimate goal of aiming for preferred value and minimizing variation.

Bibliography

Bloom, B. S. (1956). *Taxonomy of educational objectives*, London: Longman.
Brassard, M. and Ritter, D. (2000) *Pocket guide of tools for continuous improvement*, Goal/QPC, Methuen.
BSI/SS3 (2000). *BS 600; guide to the application of statistical methods*, London: BSI.
Le Boeuf, M. (1986). *The greatest management principle in the world*, New York: Berklet Books.
Qualpro (2000). *Process improvement pocket advisor*, Knoxville: Qualpro.
Scherkenbach, W. (1986). *The Deming route to quality and productivity*, Rockville, MD: Mercury Press.

Chapter 6

What are the options for tailoring and implementing Six Sigma?

I cannot say whether things will get better if we change, what I can say is that
they must change if they are to get better

Lichtenberg

What does a truly Six Sigma organization look like?

What does a truly Six Sigma organization look like? We need to know so that
we can then use such characteristics as a benchmark, target, aim or, maybe, just
as a gleam in the eye – to indicate project opportunities to close the gap – something to strive to. Imagine what life would be like if one's own organization
was truly Six Sigma?

The principles that characterize a Six Sigma organization

A Six Sigma organization is made up of people who: know what needs to be done,
have *purpose*; want to do it, have motivation and *commitment*; have the Six Sigma
capability to do it, *capability; learn* from what they are doing and continually
improve to do it, take *action*. These five principles that are universally applicable
to any Six Sigma world-class organization are shown pictorially in Figure 6.1. The
elements within each principle provide the black belt and management generally
with a common lens through which to address a variety of project objectives in the
various functions of, and processes within, any organization.

Purpose

Questions to be posed in respect of purpose include:

1 *Mission and shared vision*. Does the mission reflect a top-level commitment to
   the Six Sigma process? Is the mission aimed at creating synergy and shared

The elements within each principle provide a common lens through which to address a variety of project objectives within the various functions of the organization.

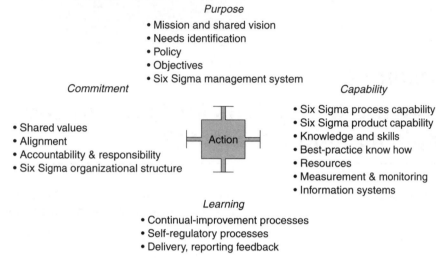

Purpose
- Mission and shared vision
- Needs identification
- Policy
- Objectives
- Six Sigma management system

Commitment
- Shared values
- Alignment
- Accountability & responsibility
- Six Sigma organizational structure

Action

Capability
- Six Sigma process capability
- Six Sigma product capability
- Knowledge and skills
- Best-practice know how
- Resources
- Measurement & monitoring
- Information systems

Learning
- Continual-improvement processes
- Self-regulatory processes
- Delivery, reporting feedback

Figure 6.1   Principles and elements of a Six Sigma organization

values to influence the mind-set and behaviour of all? Do members know and have a sense of involvement with the mission of the organization?

2 *Needs identification.* Is the Six Sigma process aligned with the needs of the organization and its stakeholders? Is there a process to continually align the mission of the organization with stakeholders' needs?

3 *Policy.* Has the Six Sigma breakthrough strategy been adopted as a business initiative? Do members understand the policy with respect to their actions and decisions? Are members actively encouraged to take part in the Six Sigma process?

4 *Objectives.* Has the organization developed a set of objectives that reflect its mission and policies? Do objectives specify Six Sigma goals and the time frame of performance expectations? Are objectives established with the people responsible for achieving them? Are objectives revisited and revised in the light of learning, experience and continual improvement?

5 *Six Sigma management system.* Does the management system deploy the Six Sigma strategy in a unified and focused manner? Has Six Sigma implementation and deployment guidelines been established? Has an appropriate infrastructure been created to ensure continuity of the Six Sigma process? Is every member accountable for understanding and implementing Six Sigma methods?

Commitment

1 *Shared values.* Do members of the organization share commonly held values about how they should meet their Six Sigma commitments? Do these

common values reflect the involvement and commitment of members? Are the values explicitly stated? Do the actions of members reflect these stated values?

2 *Alignment.* Is there a high level of open communication and trust between people in the organization? Is this level of communication and trust reflected in open dialogue concerning conflicting objectives and priorities? Are reward systems compatible with the objectives and values of the organization? Do mistakes and conflicts get openly addressed, or are there underlying frustrations and cynicism?

3 *Accountability and responsibility.* Is there clarity on who is responsible for the development of the Six Sigma implementation road-map? Is there clarity on who is responsible for the execution of Six Sigma deployment plans? Is there clarity on who is responsible for the identification, selection, execution and follow-through of Six Sigma projects? Is there clarity on who is responsible for the realizing of targeted benefits.

Capability

1 *Six Sigma process capability.* Are there effective procedures in place to seek out, and secure, opportunities for improvements in process capability to Six Sigma standards?

2 *Six Sigma product capability.* Are the principles of 'Design for Six Sigma' deployed effectively to secure product Six Sigma capability?

3 *Competency.* Are members trained in what they need to know to achieve Six Sigma objectives? Is there continued upgrading of Six Sigma knowledge and skills? Are specialist skills available to Six Sigma project teams? Are Six Sigma project teams formed on the basis of aptitude, knowledge and skills?

4 *Best-practice know-how.* Is the practice of others reviewed and assessed to establish whether 'best practices' can be adapted/applied throughout the organization? Are benchmarking practices used?

5 *Resources.* Are financial and physical resources available to support the organization in achieving its Six Sigma objectives. Is there clear communication when lack of resources may prejudice achievement of a Six Sigma objective?

6 *Measurement and monitoring.* Are Six Sigma performance measures established for each important characteristic? Is there ongoing monitoring of performance against measures? Are measurement results analysed for patterns and trends? Are gap analyses done in relation to Six Sigma requirements and action taken where and when appropriate? Are processes subject to continual improvement analysis?

7 *Information systems.* Are communications effective vertically and horizontally throughout the organization? Are there information systems to track key performance metrics, and to analyse data by trend and pattern?

Learning

1 *Continual-improvement processes.* Are continual-improvement processes established, such as process evaluation, preventive and corrective actions? Are ideas for improvement of processes actively sought after and followed through? Are measurements and results communicated to relevant people? Is there a focus on detecting trends and patterns in events and values that may have a significant impact on the organization? Are appropriate Six Sigma tools, techniques and methods understood and correctly deployed?

2 *Self-regulatory processes.* Do people in the unit learn from their mistakes and their successes, and take action from that learning? Does the unit conduct self-assessments to assess Six Sigma performance and opportunities for improvement? Are communications, and supporting values of trust, adequate to support real learning and constructive dialogue? Do people in the organization reflect on the adequacy of their learning processes, and take action to improve their abilities?

3 *Customer feedback.* Is feedback obtained from customers, both internal and external, on the product or service delivered? Is this information fed back to, and acted upon by, relevant people?

What are the first steps to take?

There are a number of options for tailoring and implementing Six Sigma. It is advisable to take a number of features into consideration before deciding on the best approach to take in the deployment of Six Sigma in an organization. A convenient starting point is frequently an assessment of the strengths, weaknesses, opportunities and threats posed. This is known as SWOT analysis. Strategic review is an alternative. An example was shown for Invensys in Chapter 1.

Decide on the project focus(es) for Six Sigma

The four options

In setting up business performance improvement projects we need to be aware of, and exploit, the various approaches that can be taken. This is particularly pertinent to the Six Sigma initiative as the set goal is often 6 Sigma, namely fault reduction to no more than 3.4 faults per million opportunities. Whilst this singular objective is entirely laudable and can lead to considerable 'bottom line' savings there is a danger that an undue focus on this one aspect can create a mind-set that inhibits other than purely reacting to failures to meet requirements. In so doing many important opportunities for improvement may be neglected. Best-practice Six Sigma practitioners will recognize the four facets, or dimensions, of continual improvement in business shown in Figure 6.2,

Figure 6.2 The Six Sigma options to improve business performance

which indicates that the four possible but quite different facets of the Six Sigma continual-improvement initiative relate to:

1 The type of *response* we take, whether it is reactive, proactive or both.
2 The *nature* of the initiative. Are we are seeking breakthrough and/or incremental improvements?
3 The *business focus*. Is the prime focus on enhancing customer relationships, product leadership or operational excellence?
4 The *organizational approach*. Is it to be at the strategic level, cross-functional and/or local to each workplace.

A business that wishes to be recognized as one of organizational excellence will readily appreciate that these different facets are *and* ones not *or*. All aspects, with varying degrees of focus, will be addressed in a world-class organization. Each focus is now discussed at the appreciation level.

Option 1 – type of response: reactive, proactive or both?

The numerical definition of a 6 Sigma critical quality characteristic is one that is performing at a level of 3.4 faults per million opportunities. This represented a stretch goal for Motorola, the originators of Six Sigma, in the late 1980s. This suited their *reactive* approach to defect levels current at that time. There is no doubt that, in most organizations, reactive problem-solving projects still have a major role to play. For example, in the automotive industry the J.D. Power annual survey lists customer problems in the first 90 days of ownership of a new motor vehicle. The most recent survey indicates that, for the seven major manufacturers in the survey, complaints are running at some 134 per 100 vehicles. The complaints range from 152 to 107 between the worst and the best manufacturer.

Warranty costs too are estimated to run at some $400–700 per vehicle. Of course, these are very simplistic measures of quality, and many other characteristics are taken into account in the assessment of vehicle worth to the owner. Massive efforts have made in the automotive sector, over a number of years, in terms of quality system standards and associated drives for excellence in quality, under such slogans as 'quality is job one'. In spite of this, quite obviously, there is still considerable scope for quality-improvement initiatives purely in terms of the elimination of faults. As Bill Ford, the Chief Executive Officer of Ford, has said 'quality is not something you can declare victory on'.

Since the early Motorola days with Six Sigma, whilst the name Six Sigma and the 6 Sigma numerical goal has been retained, the methods and approach have rapidly evolved. There is now an increased focus on 'front end' activities where there is substantially greater leverage for improvement. The consequence is that the Six Sigma initiative now has a much wider vision in that proactive approaches to business improvement form an ever-increasing element. This, in turn, demands a significant increase in, and broadening of, the skill profiles of Six Sigma practitioners. Methods such as 'quality function deployment' (QFD), value analysis (VA), potential failure and effects analysis (PFMEA), Taguchi style quality engineering, design of experiments (DoE), evolutionary operation (EVOP), design for X (X = cost, producibility, etc.), inventiveness methods such as TRIZ, axiomatic design and benchmarking now come prominently into play. These are reflected in the body of knowledge specified by the American Society for Quality (ASQ) for the certification of Six Sigma black belts.

Option 2 – Business focus: customer, product or operational?

Successful Six Sigma practitioners will also need to have a good understanding of the three business focuses indicated pictorially in Figure 6.3.

The key features of these three different business strategies are:

1 Focus on improving customer awareness and understanding (colloquially this relationship is known as customer intimacy) by:
   - creating a deep and understanding knowledge of, and relationship with, its customers;
   - being geared to tailoring offerings to niche customers;
   - assimilating, and responding promptly and effectively to, customer needs, expectations and aspirations.
2 Focus on product leadership by:
   - creating trail-blazing products;
   - encouraging ingenuity and innovation in unexplored territory with loosely knit and flexible organizational structures;

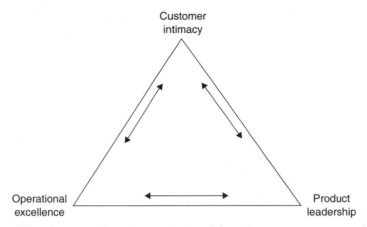

Figure 6.3 What is your primary organizational focus?

- accepting the possibility of initial lack of user friendliness, some failures and waste as the price to pay for not inhibiting inventiveness, risk-taking and entrepreneurship.
3 Focus on operational excellence, to aim to be the lowest cost supplier, through:
    - designing product for economic manufacture, realization and delivery;
    - standardizing and limiting the range of products offered;
    - securing economies of scale;
    - optimizing and standardizing processes;
    - attacking all forms of waste.

It is considered by some that of the three strategies 'customer intimacy' has the greatest potential for establishing a sustained advantage in a competitive marketplace. This is particularly so for the small business. It is often impossible to compete with the larger-scale mass producers in terms of operational efficiency and cost. In relation to product leadership a competitive advantage is unlikely to be sustained for much time as replicas tend to appear quite quickly. It is also felt that any organizational unit, at any given point of time, should focus on just one of these three core competencies whilst including aspects of the other two needed for success.

Option 3 – Nature of projects: incremental or breakthrough?

Continual-improvement projects are frequently expected to deliver only small incremental changes in performance to existing processes. On the other hand, *breakthrough* projects are often looked upon as one-off type acts of innovation and creativity that produce major pay-backs. This is considered to be a false scenario. It is one that gives rise to limited horizons for Six Sigma activities.

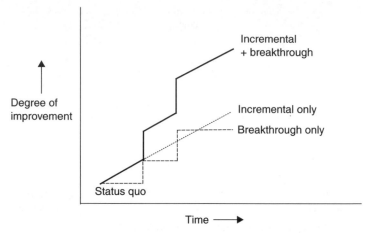

Figure 6.4   Six Sigma continual improvement can be made up of incremental and breakthrough elements

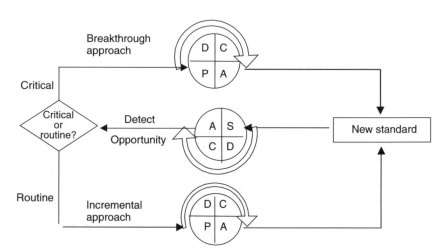

Figure 6.5   Pictorial indication of how the dual approach to continual improvement can be achieved. PDCA = plan, do, check, act; SDCA = standard, do check, act (*Source*: Kozo, Koura, Total quality control, vol. 42, no. 3, 1993, p. 273)

We should be looking at continual improvement as repeated improvements of any size from whatever origin. Both types of continual improvement are essential in any organization committed to achieving world-class standards of performance. The importance of this on the extent of improvements achieved is indicated in Figure 6.4. Breakthroughs are shown simplistically as occurring instantaneously and increments by sloping lines.

Figure 6.5 gives a pictorial indication of how the dual approach to continual improvement is achieved. The emphasis on, and importance of, incremental as opposed to breakthrough projects may well change according to circumstance such as the maturity of the sector, industry, organization, technology, product or service with which one is concerned.

Option 4 – Organizational approach: strategic, cross-functional, day-to-day?

Three major management-led approaches to performance improvement in an organization are important from a Six Sigma initiative perspective. These are strategic management, cross-function management and day-to-day management.

Strategic (Hoshin) management

Strategic management focuses on the key issues required for success of the overall business. It may be recognized under different names, such as Hoshin management, Hoshin planning, Hoshin Kanri or simply policy management or strategic planning. Hoshin Kanri is derived from two Japanese words, Hoshin refers to compass or pointing the way. Kanri refers to management or policy. Hence, Hoshin Kanri sets out to point everyone in the organization in the right direction. One might ask of what relevance is all this to Six Sigma? There are a number of reasons. Hoshin management provides a principal focus for vital Six Sigma activities that are aligned to the overall success of the organization. It not only provides the focus by setting goals it also sets out and manages both the means and the manner in which results are to be measured. In essence, Hoshin management takes the form of the Deming PDCA (plan, do, check, act cycle).

- *Plan.* A top management team first assesses the organization's strengths, weaknesses, opportunities and threats (SWOT analysis). Second comes the creation, or updating, of the vision and mission of the organization. It is expected that the vision statement will describe where the organization sees itself a few years down the road. Hopefully, in a Six Sigma sense, it will not only provide all members of the organization with a clear understanding of their important role and expected contribution but also seek to inspire and provide a fresh impetus to those who may have become somewhat jaded and are finding their present job rather irksome. Third comes prioritization, the selection of a few items that represent opportunities for breakthrough projects. Fourth detailed plans are generated to achieve breakthrough performance. It is crucial that the plans include targets, the ways and means to achieve the targets, the time frame, control points for the targets to which they relate and check points for the various ways and means. Finally, the ways and means are negotiated and agreed with the various functions in the organization affected.
- *Do.* Deploy the plan by cascading it vertically throughout the organization. In the United States of America, this is commonly known as 'catch-ball'.

Note that managers affected by the hoshin plan may now have the responsibility for three types of management: that for normal routine day-to-day affairs involving local Six Sigma projects together with cross-functional Six Sigma projects and hoshin responsibilities. Hence, they and their people are directly aligned with the strategy of the organization in seeking and achieving performance improvements today, tomorrow and into the forseeable future.

- *Check.* Monitor both control points and check points.
- *Act.* Implement solutions, standardize changes and disseminate learning throughout the organization.

Effective hoshin management considerably enhances the influence of hoshin-based Six Sigma activities on overall business performance.

Cross-function management

Cross-function management is concerned with enhancing the fabric of an organization by strengthening and sustaining the horizontal weft to complement the vertical warp provided by hoshin management. It is concerned with performance-improvement issues that demand cross-functional initiation, co-operation and co-ordination. To be successful it requires that the managers involved ensure that the interests of the organization transcend departmental interests. It contrasts with day-to-day management in that it is concerned, in the Six Sigma sense, with particular aspects of management that demand horizontal multiple function acquiescence and activity such as 'quality cost reduction', 'reduction in time to market of new product', 'improved manufacturability/ deliverability of new designs of products/services'. The instigation of this form of management requires the formation of a team of managers from each function within the organization. Team members should be familiar with the Six Sigma philosophy and methods at least at the appreciation level. Next follows selection of the cross-function to be managed. Quality cost reduction could well form a useful initial project in the absence of any other strong runners. The management team would then be well advised to delegate the project field-work to a black belt run Six Sigma team, reflecting the various interests involved, who are familiar with the deployment of improvement projects.

Effective cross-function management considerably enhances the prospects of successful deployment of Six Sigma projects that affect more than one department.

Day-to-day management

Day-to-day management focuses on the routine operation and control of processes within their remit. In a best-practice organization, it is expected that day-to-day management also addresses local improvements that can be made within their sphere of managerial control. In a Six Sigma organization, day-to-day management would be responsible for green belt run projects run in their departments. A word of warning is necessary in respect to these local projects. One has to ensure that performance improvements in the processes of a particular department do not have an adverse impact on organizational performance by degrading results in another department. An example of this could be the purchasing department buying from a non-approved lowest-cost supplier to the detriment of the quality and reliability of incoming components destined for assembly operations. A feature of day-to-day management that differentiates itself from the other forms of management is the expectation that an ongoing management operating and measurement system, based on a control plan, will be in place and routinely deployed. Such a control plan should include monitoring of process parameters as well as output performance. The reason for this is that process control is enhanced and process output performance improvement only becomes possible when the effect of process parameter variation on output is understood and exploited.

How to set up a Six Sigma infrastructure

Having decided what is expected of Six Sigma in an organization and which options are to be focused on, at least initially, the next step is to consider the type of infrastructure required to drive the initiative. Of course, the actual infrastructure will depend on the size and complexity of the participating organization, the stage of maturity of deployment of Six Sigma and the decisions already taken regarding expectations and approach options. A typical Six Sigma infrastructure consisting of mentors/master black belts/champions, black belts, green belts and yellow belts was discussed in Chapter 1.

Mentor/master black belt/champion(s)

Choice of a mentor/champion

The choice made here for this appointment(s) will be the most critical to the success of the whole operation. The principal reason for this is that the implementation of Six Sigma involves change in an organization. Most organizations can be expected to resist change. Furthermore, if change is achieved, there is a susceptibility for it to be a transient state, because of a strong tendency to return to the status quo. This is an inherent characteristic of any established organization particularly one that is based on the culture of conformance in terms of organizational structure, systems and personal behaviour. Such systems can be expected to have developed immune systems, which, acting naturally and very subtly, attempt to kill change. Change too needs to be achieved with due deference to the sensibilities of the workforce particularly in a situation where scarce resources are concerned. Hence, Six Sigma change management is frequently a very delicate task and always a challenging one.

What is expected of a mentor/champion?

Different organizations will have different perceptions of the mentor role; however, there will be many common factors. The dictionary definition of a *mentor* is 'an experienced and trusted advisor or guide'. In Six Sigma, the role of the mentor extends beyond this. In keeping with the desirability of keeping the organizational structure as flat and lean as possible the mentor will often be expected to act as a Six Sigma *co-ordinator* and *facilitator* and frequently also as the Six Sigma *champion* in a particular area of the company. In some cases the role may even extend to that of *guru*. This where:

- a *co-ordinator* causes things and people to function together as parts of an inter-related whole;
- a *facilitator* makes thing easy, or easier;
- a *champion* supports the cause;
- a *guru* is looked upon as a source of wisdom, or knowledge, an influental leader.

The usual role of such a mentor is to nurture the Six Sigma process and ensure that it is rolled out across a business unit, site or organization. He/she paves the way for change and champions the operation. Normally, this person selects, initiates and co-ordinates projects, ensure Six Sigma participants are appropriately trained in both people and technical skills, acts as mentors for black belts and provides project support by breaking down any barriers and ensuring resources are available.

This role is obviously critical to the success of the Six Sigma initiative in a particular organization.

Mentors and Six Sigma projects

Six Sigma activities are project based but not in the traditional one-off way of constructing a bridge or installing a computer system. Six Sigma projects are participatory, team based (often cross-functional/departmental) activities aimed at the continuous improvement of the effectiveness and efficiency of processes, products and services. Consequently, the mentor may be involved in:

- shaping project goals; setting clear objectives;
- identifying, negotiating for, and obtaining the necessary resources;
- building teams, roles and structures; gaining support and sponsors;
- ensuring the development of team member Six Sigma skills and sense of commitment;
- establishing and maintaining good lines of communication with all interested parties;
- seeing the bigger picture; keeping things moving within that perspective.

Mentor's check-list for setting up Six Sigma projects

– What is the agreed purpose of the project?
– Have similar projects been done before? With what result?
– Who actually owns the process(es) involved?
– Is/are the owner(s) supportive even acting as sponsor(s)?
– Who is to select the project team and team leader?
– What is the scope, and limits, of the team's remit?
– What resource constraints are there?
– Who mainly gains from the project?
– What is the potential from a business viewpoint?
– Where is opposition (overt or covert) likely to come from? Why?
– Who will pick up the reins when the project is successfully completed?

Mentor's check-list for managing Six Sigma projects

– Establish and agree the nature of the project and yardsticks of measurement of performance.
– Get the correct mix (skills/knowledge/personalities) in the project team.
– Negotiate time for team project work. (How will the team balance time between project and other responsibilities?)
– Ensure resources/facilities/meeting/working space for the team. Clarify to whom they are responsible.
– Break down complex projects into manageable elements. Create project milestones.
– Keep lines of communication open between mentor and team and mentor and other interested parties. Keep the project visible.
– Arrange access to expert advice/training as and when necessary.
– Generate enthusiasm, maintain it in face of set-backs, and publicize success.

Mentors check-list at end of each Six Sigma project

– Remember the team have emotionally invested in the project to a great degree. Ensure that the process of emotional divestment leaves positive vibes – feelings of accomplishment.
– Thank the team and all others who have contributed.
– Let interested parties know what good results have been achieved. Consider facilitating a project presentation by the team.
– Check whether the results on this project can be applied beneficially elsewhere.
– Ensure that the gains achieved will not be eroded. Install a monitoring system on ongoing performance.
– See that a project report is prepared by the team so that others may gain from their experiences and accomplishments.
– Start a new project.

Black Belts

Black belts are effectively leaders of multi-disciplined project teams. They normally apply the Six Sigma approach and methods to cross-function and the more complex projects. As indicated in Chapter 5, they need to be fully trained in both people and technical skills. In large, totally committed organizations, there tends to be of the order of one full-time black belt per hundred employees. Having said this the reality in Europe is that this situation is the exception rather than the rule.

Green and yellow belts

Green and yellow belts normally work on Six Sigma projects, as part of their usual job, in areas of their personal expertise. They form part of a Six Sigma project team. Green belts may lead Six Sigma projects within their own work area. Both green and yellow belts need specific competencies, as described in Chapter 5, and so usually need formal training in Six Sigma tools and techniques prior to involvement in Six Sigma projects. Green belts make up some 1 in 20 of employees in large committed Companies.

A particular Six Sigma infrastructure

As an illustration, one particular initial infrastructure chosen by a multi-site European organization takes the form shown in Figure 6.6.

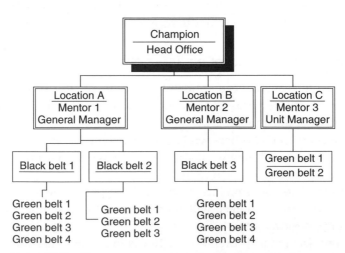

Figure 6.6 An initial Six Sigma structure for a European multi-plant organization

Development of required competencies in Six Sigma participants

Overview

Having established an embryonic concept of the type and number of people to become involved, at least initially, it is essential to ensure that everyone involved has the required competencies. This normally involves some, up-front, training and development. A number of organizations offer public and tailored in-house development programmes in Six Sigma. If only a very small number are involved initially it is more economic to send them as delegates on a public course. However, if a sufficient number are involved consideration should be given to the adoption of an in-house development programme as, from a technical and administrative viewpoint, this offers many advantages. These advantages include the tailoring of the Six Sigma programme to the particular needs of one's own organization, and access to the external trainer/developer for guidance/mentoring/championing during the initiation period.

Typical in-house development programme

Overview

A typical in-house training programme consists of three phases: phase one, Six Sigma awareness and programme introduction; phase two, technical training; and phase three, project work, assessment and belt certification. A key feature of the Six Sigma development programme portrayed in Figure 6.7 is the combining of workshops, and training modules with the setting up, carrying out and presenting of live in-company Six Sigma projects. The modules and workshop are participatory and centre on team and individual learning, delivering 'best-practice' Six Sigma methodology using a practical and structured approach. This enables participants to immediately apply the principles and practices of Six Sigma to their project work. Modules and workshop are *specially designed* to meet the corporate objectives of the client, the individual needs of the participants and the required elements of the programme. This provides tailoring flexibility and improved effectiveness, coupled with significant economic benefits to the client. It also ensures training is linked to achieving specific goals and that it is consistent with the management style of the client and the culture of the organization.

The delivery methodology is varied with formal tutorials interspersed with innovative practical break-out sessions, case studies and team projects. This ensures a comprehensive understanding and implementation capability. Delegate interaction is encouraged throughout. Each module and workshop is led by experienced professional engineers and is supported by a comprehensive A4 interactive workbook for each participant together with a pocket-size memory jogger of key points for subsequent ready reference.

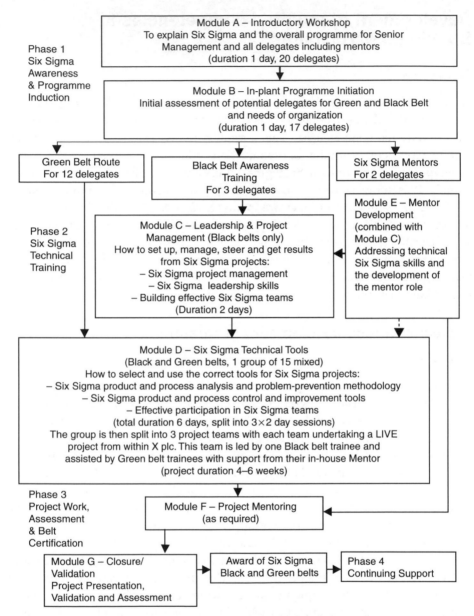

Figure 6.7 Outline of typical in-house Six Sigma development programme

The hallmark of the integrated development programme is the efficient and effective dissemination of that knowledge and development of those skills, in a user friendly manner, that can be put to immediate use by project teams in projects that have a significant impact on the 'bottom line'. The programme illustrated is typical. In practice, such programmes are always tailored to the needs and expectations of individual clients.

Phase 1: Six Sigma awareness and programme introduction

Phase 1 of the programme consists of a one day in-plant programme initiation together with a 1-day introductory workshop delivered at appreciation level.

Module B: in-plant programme initiation

The in-plant programme initiation involves:

- meeting the client's management and nominated mentors to explain the overall programme and to determine the aspirations of the client with regard to Six Sigma;
- an introduction to the potential black and green belts to ensure their suitability and capability, to assess their current aptitude, skills, experience and potential and provide the opportunity for discussion of any reservations or concerns;
- familiarization with the client's organization;
- presentation and any necessary refining of the overall programme to address the specific requirements of the client's organization and personnel involved;
- preliminary discussion of probable potential initial projects to be undertaken and their implications both for the development programme and the provision of the necessary resources by the client.

Module A: introductory workshop

The 1-day introductory workshop comprises a briefing at appreciation level including:

- What is Six Sigma? Six Sigma the benchmark. Six Sigma the improvement process. Six Sigma the statistical measure.
- What is the Six Sigma philosophy, infrastructure and methodology?
- What kind of Company culture is required to make Six Sigma thrive?
- Where did the Six Sigma process originate?
- What is the importance of Six Sigma benchmarks?
- What makes the Six Sigma approach different to previous approaches?
- Why are an increasing number of world-class organizations becoming committed to the Six Sigma process, the philosophy, the infrastructure and the methodology?
- What type of benefits can be expected with a successful application?
- What pitfalls are to be avoided?
- What are the key elements of a successful application?
- What knowledge and skills are needed by participants?
- How do we achieve desired results on projects through team-working?
- Why is it important to standardize our disciplined approach?
- What techniques and methods are available to teams?
- Why is it desirable to choose tools that are user friendly and robust?

- What is the role of a mentor, a black belt and a green belt?
- Why do we need the development programme and how we an make use of the ongoing support?

Phase 2: Six Sigma technical training

Phase 2 workshop modules follow different routes for the training of Six Sigma black belts and Six Sigma green belts. (A *black belt* is the leader of a project team responsible for applying the Six Sigma process. A *green belt* is a person, with knowledge of Six Sigma methodology and skills in Six Sigma tools and team working who participates in a project team applying the Six Sigma process.) The development programme for mentors is tailored to the assessed needs on an individual basis. Core elements include:

- Why world-class organizations use statistics: to determine and aim for preferred value; to identify and continually reduce process variation; to improve operational efficiency and increase value to customers.
- Developing a statistical thinking mind set: integrating it with business thinking.
- The three components of statistical thinking: process focus, understanding variation, using data to guide actions.
- Statistical method as an integral part of management: the four issues to be addressed.
- What managers should know about statistics: the five principles.
- Responsibility matrix for process improvement.
- Continual improvement: why is it important? essential ingredients; are we doing it? how to make it happen; improvement management.

Module C: leadership and project management (normally black belts only)

The black belt route begins with a 2-day Module C entitled Leadership and Project Management consisting essentially of three elements on how to set up, manage, steer and get results from Six Sigma projects together with the core elements of the mentor programme:

1 *Six Sigma project management*: how to select the correct projects; fix project performance and time goals; develop project performance measures and set project milestones; acquire data.
2 *Six Sigma leadership skills*: how to lead the team; choose the appropriate situational leadership style; facilitate, co-ordinate, champion; effective communication and self-expression. The four working styles. What is your working style? Project.
3 *Building Six Sigma project teams*: how to get the correct team mix; motivate and get the best out of members; set ground-rules for operation; develop

measures of team progress; manage team dynamics; nurture the team and maintain momentum; structure team problem-solving sessions; recognize the eight hallmarks of a good team.

4 *Selected core elements of the mentor programme.*

During this module black belt trainees will be encouraged, through selected course mini-projects, to focus on and start developing a structured approach to their chosen Six Sigma projects, on the basis of their previous experience and the skills and knowledge gained. This will be shared with other trainee black belts through mini-project presentations and interactive discussions.

Module D: Six Sigma technical tools (black and green belts)

Module D, which is part of both the black and green belt route, is split into 3×2 day sessions and deals with how to select and use the correct methodology and tools for projects. Principal constituents of this module are:

- *Basic Six Sigma team tools and techniques*: Warm up. Case study; *Data collection and sampling methods*; flow charting, team tasks. *Identify and quantify an opportunity or problem*; check sheets, tables, pictograms, bar charts, pie charts, cluster diagrams, team tasks. *Prioritize, analyse and diagnose*; Pareto, process mapping, cause-and-effect diagrams, affinity and tree diagrams, matrix diagrams, histograms and dot plots, scatter diagrams, team tasks. *Develop countermeasures, monitor results, hold gains*; CEDAC diagrams, 5 S's, graphs, trend lines, team tasks. Warm down.
- *Structured Six Sigma process-improvement methodology and related tools*: Methodology for problem-solving versus methodology for continual process improvement. Seven-stage process-improvement approach: identify and quantify the opportunity; define the process and the scope of the project; analyse the current process; envisage future process, probe; generate and assess alternatives and recommend changes; try out and verify effectiveness of changes; implement changes, standardize; hold the gains.
- *Structured Six Sigma problem-solving methodology and related tools*: Approach to error prevention. Counter-measures for various error types. Eight-stage problem-solving approach: identify and quantify the problem; assign project team; gather and analyse data and establish measures; diagnose cause(s) and ascertain whether cause is sporadic (special) or endemic (common); address causes; develop action plan; implement plan and prevent recurrence; start another project.

Module D also includes specialist support elements typically linked to the Six Sigma process. The extent and depth of treatment of these elements will vary according to client need. This is to avoid mental overload on the part of the trainees. It is also in the best interests of a key training objective which is to address the appropriate knowledge and skill requirement for each role, at the time it is required, to ensure the most effective application. A comprehensive in-depth treatment of some elements will be phased in later, if required, at the appropriate stage of a project. Typical specialist support elements that will be addressed are:

- *Statistical process control* (SPC); basics of control charts, variables and attributes; how to interpret various patterns of variation; identifying special and common cause variation.
- *Process capability analysis* (PCA); measures, *Cp* and *Cpk*, ppm; benchmarks of performance.
- *Measurement system analysis* (MSA); establishing resolution, bias and precision including repeatability and reproducibility.
- *Experimentation* (DoE); one factor at a time; multi-factorial designs, full factorial, fractional factorial, response surface; evolutionary operation.
- *Failure mode and effects analysis* (FMEA); *fault tree analysis* (FTA); *key word analysis* (KWA); *hazard analysis and critical control points* (HACCP); *error proofing* (Poka Yoke).
- *Design for Six Sigma.*

Throughout Module D the Six Sigma teams will be encouraged to focus on, and continue the development of a structured approach to, their chosen projects. This will be shared with other teams through mini-project presentations and subsequent interactive discussions. All teams ultimately prepare a proposed detailed plan of action for their first in-house project. This Six Sigma project plan is presented, by each team, to appropriate client mentors and other interested parties on the completion of this module for assessment with a view to approval.

Phase 3: project work, assessment and belt certification

Six Sigma in-house project

Following approval each team undertakes a *live* project within its own organization. Each team is made up of trainee green belts and is led by a trainee black belt. The external trainer provides assistance in the initiation, set-up and planning of, and the projection of milestones for, each project together with advice on the technical approach to be taken.

On-going project mentoring and reviews

The external trainer provides support, in conjunction with the client's mentor, during the course of the project. Interim project reviews will be undertaken as appropriate.

Project presentation, validation and assessment

A project report will be prepared by the client's Six Sigma teams. These will be presented to the external trainer for preliminary assessment 14 days prior to the presentation date. An in-plant presentation will then be made followed by a project validation process and black and green belt accreditation process.

Award of Six Sigma black and green belts

The award of black belts and green belts is based on the final validated project reports; objective evidence of satisfactory participation in and completion of the scheduled training modules and project work and oral examination (viva voce) of each candidate for black or green belt. Successful candidates will be awarded a certificate attesting to their status of Six Sigma *black belt* or *green belt*, as appropriate, signed by the Chartered Engineer Examiner.

Phase 4: continuing support

A key element of this training programme is the continuing support offered to the client. This may take, for example:

- providing supplementary practitioner-level training for *black belts* and *green belts* in related subjects such as quality function deployment, value analysis/ engineering, and lean manufacturing;
- providing more in-depth training for black belts and green belts in core specialist subjects as the need presents itself on a project-by-project basis;
- supporting the internal training conducted on further waves of Six Sigma participants;
- training of *yellow belts* (yellow belts are people who will be directly involved with Six Sigma team projects);
- ongoing mentoring on Six Sigma projects;
- participation, guidance and assistance in the further development of the Six Sigma process across the client's organization;
- supporting the client in ensuring a critical mass of people in the organization are receptive to the change in culture often required to produce acceptance of the change to be brought about by introducing and developing the Six Sigma process.

Start off with a few pilot projects?

Launching Six Sigma in a real-life situation

The reality in Europe is that the situation of one black belt per hundred or so employees, or any structured hierarchical approach to Six Sigma, is the exception rather than the rule. It is not unusual, even in medium to large organizations that profess to be actually deploying Six Sigma, to find that they are doing this with just one black belt, and this frequently not even on a full-time basis. A major sticking point appears to be where to fit Six Sigma into an established organization already well endowed with very useful fully fledged functions, with their associated structures. Such functions may include people already engaged in statistical process control, other continual-improvement initiatives, quality-excellence programmes, quality and reliability departments, ISO 9001, quality function deployment, failure mode and effects analysis, lean activities and the like. Finding the most appropriate solution for a particular organization faced with such a situation can be a real dilemma. One could well argue, on a technical basis, that Six Sigma embraces all such best practices and thus should be the focal point for such activities. However, responsible management faced with the situation, quite naturally, is reluctant to risk giving up the substance for the promise however convincing and impressive the potential gains that Six Sigma might appear to bring. Initiating and completing a few successful pilot projects is probably the best way to secure progress in such a situation. However, before deciding on this pilot-project approach, one could well heed the course taken by organizations at the leading edge of Six Sigma in Europe. Four organizations are taken to illustrate this. They are Land Rover, Perkins Engines, Invensys and Northern Ireland Electricity.

Land Rover and Perkins Engines

Two organizations in the United Kingdom, Land Rover and Perkins Engines, who are both firmly committed to Six Sigma, vied for the top spot in the MX 2002 manufacturing excellence awards. Land Rover, the winner, has successfully integrated Six Sigma with a number of other continual-improvement initiatives. These include virtual prototyping, integrated system review, the Ford (a la Toyota) manufacturing system, lean production, leadership development and in-station process controls. They are currently training some 14 black belts and 60 green belts. Significant savings are being realized. For instance, things gone wrong (TGW) per thousand vehicles in-line have dropped by 27%. Land Rover has also recently won the award for the most improved brand within Ford.

The Perkins Engines story is very similar to Land Rover. At Perkins they are well on the way to getting some 1% of the staff trained as black belts. This is being achieved alongside other business-improvement initiatives such as total quality, Kaizen, strategic planning and extensive personal development programmes. They have recognized the need for this broad-based approach to meet the growing demands of the marketplace. This has manifested itself, for example, by key customers who are demanding some 9% year-on-year product cost reductions. Demonstrable savings include over 30% improvements in the production process together with significant improvements in delivery and inventory performance.

Invensys

The Chief Executive's November 2002 review stated that over 1000 leaders have been trained to manage improvement projects. The first 11 projects alone encompass expenditure of some £83 million. There is a target of 10% savings.

Northern Ireland Electricity

In quite a different sector, Northern Ireland Electricity (NEI) became the first utility outside of the United States of America to adopt Six Sigma. NEI was a UK Business Excellence Award finalist in both 2001 and 2002. Its Director of Business Improvement states that the excellence model and Six Sigma are the two main drivers for ongoing change with senior managers taking a leading role in both. For example, some 37 managers are Six Sigma champions.

Overall situation in the UK

Focusing now on the other almost half of British organizations, namely those in the £5 to £20 million turnover size, who do not even have any type of quality-management system. Of those who do the system is largely deployed in departments directly associated with the final product, such as manufacturing. One could well ask what hope is there of such organizations becoming committed to any system let alone a Six Sigma one. On a more optimistic note, a recent UK Institute of Quality Assurance survey shows that the Six Sigma initiative, a relatively new concept, is just as popular already as well-established systems such as 'business excellence'.

The most generally deployed quality system in the United Kingdom is the ISO 9000 series of quality system standards. Even so this system is largely contained to departments directly associated with the final product, such as manufacturing. Other functions such as finance, human resources and marketing generally appear to be devoid of any form of quality management system. The recently issued ISO 9001:2000 is both *process based* and focuses on the need for *continual improvement*. The progressive take-up of this new standard is thus likely to stimulate the more aware and successful organizations to embody the Six Sigma initiative within the structure of their modified quality-management systems.

The generic Six Sigma project road-map

We are now ready to start off with one or more pilot projects. A standardized approach to the conducting of Six Sigma projects is recommended. This establishes a common language base not only across one's own organization but also with the supply and customer base. As indicated in Chapter 1, the Six Sigma generic project road-map recommended, consists of eight stages. These stages are discussed below. Alternatively, Juran's universal steps for breakthrough described in Table 3.8 are equally applicable.

Project charter, plan and roadmap

A generic eight-step road-map for Six Sigma project activity was discussed briefly in Chapter 1. This is represented in visual form in Figure 6.8. This is looked upon as an improved extension on the five-step road-map used in

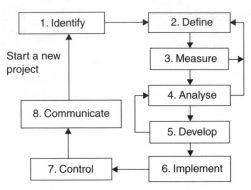

Figure 6.8 Eight-step road-map for generic Six Sigma projects

standard applications of Six Sigma and which is the subject of the ASQ body of knowledge discussed in Chapter 5. There will be some difference in method and approach depending on the nature of the project. This will arise for two principal reasons, namely, whether the project is concerned with problem-solving or process improvement. An illustration of this is given in Table 1.6.

Step 1: identify the project

Six Sigma projects should always be directed at the achievement of business objectives. However, the choice of a particular Six Sigma breakthrough project will depend on a number of factors. These include

- the make-up and experience of the project team;
- whether the focus is on industrial processes or administrative ones;
- the level at which the project is aimed: corporate, operations or task level;
- project selection is on a 'top-down' or 'bottom-up' basis;
- aiming at so-called 'low-hanging fruit'; namely processes that can be fairly easily improved and which have an immediate performance pay-back;
- criteria such as: low-yield processes; high inspection costs, capacity problems, customer dissatisfaction, poor supplier quality or delivery, design concerns.

Whatever factors are involved, the first step in Six Sigma process-improvement projects is to view any task or job in the organization as a process, with its associated inputs, resources, controls and outputs. Identify the proposed Six Sigma project in outline form. Examples are shown. 'Reduce time of delivery of motor vehicles from customer point of order from 17 to 23 weeks to, at most, that of our principal competitor, namely 12 weeks'. Reasons: loss of potential customers; cancellation of orders. 'Reduce stock from 20 to 12% by value'. Set up a preliminary team to define the project.

Step 2: define the project

A project definition would be expected to contain as a minimum:

1 A concise statement that defines and quantifies the problem or process performance improvement task, identification of the performance measures and measurement sources, together with a description of the current performance of the undesirable characteristic(s) and an affirmation of the project goals.
2 A definition of the critical to quality characteristics (CTQC) and who is impacted by them. These ideally will be classified in three ways in terms of 'basic essential CTQCs', which are a critical priority for improvement to prevent non-conformance; 'performance CTQCs', which improve product or service competitiveness; and 'customer delighter CTQCs'. These types of CTQCs are shown pictorially in the Kano model described in Chapter 4.
3 A definition of the process giving rise to the CTQCs under consideration. This is usually presented visually as a flow diagram. There are a number of features expected in such a process map. These include components such as the supplier(s), the task or process itself, the process controls, resources deployed, the outputs, the customer(s) and the primary and secondary owners of the process. An example of such a flow diagram is shown in Figure 6.9. Additionally, it is often extremely useful to show pictorially three variations of such a process: one, what the process is thought to be; two, what it actually is; and, three, what it should be like.
4 A presentation of a business case for the project. Key elements of such a case include: why the project should be authorized; the potential business payoff together with a risk assessment; the resources to be sanctioned; project scope, roles and responsibilities together with a project plan and activity and event milestones.
5 Seek approval to set up a project team, with appropriate resources, to proceed.

The consequent project as set out and agreed is known in Six Sigma parlance as the project charter.

Example

Define flow of work activities with key interfaces for the process under consideration as a possible first Six Sigma project for an administrative team led by a green belt. See Figure 6.9.

Step 3: measure current process performance

Again several steps are often required for this stage. These include:

1 Identify quantitative process parameters and product or service characteristics to be measured and those qualitative attributes that need to be observed

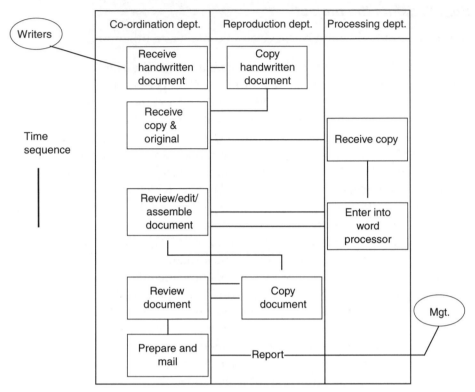

Figure 6.9 Example of flow of work with key interfaces and ownerships

and decisions taken on whether they are present or absent. Confine this to key product and service characteristics and process parameters related to the Six Sigma project. Extend it to both performance measures and the quantifying of sources of variation.

2 Develop a data-collection plan and collect data. A well thought out collection plan forms a sound basis for subsequent diagnosis and analysis. Ask yourself questions using what, why, where, who and how. Prior to the development of the data-collection plan make sure that you are familiar with the various methods of sampling and data collection and the variety of collection formats readily available to the Six Sigma practitioner.

3 Ensure the capability of the methods used for collecting the data. This may involve assessing bias, repeatability and reproducibility of measuring systems and ensuring that operational definitions are stipulated and sound decision criteria established for attribute characteristics.

4 Collect just sufficient data to establish a sound basis for identification and quantification of principal sources of variation and project-related performance characteristics of the process, product and/or service.

Determine baseline capabilities for CTQCs. Some points of caution are appropriate at this stage. It is often recommended that one universal metric 'Sigma', be used here. However, this can be quite misleading other than as a very coarse relative indicator of end performance. This is discussed in detail in Chapters 5, 7 and 8. It is advisable, on the grounds of using a universally accepted standard language, to use the internationally prescribed capability and performance indices Cps, $Cpks$, Pps and $Ppks$ for measured data. *NPHOs* or *NPMOs* (nonconformities per hundred or million opportunities) [see ISO 3534-2 (TC69:SC1, 2003)] should be similarly used for attribute data. These indices are applied only after appropriate criteria have been established relating to targeting, patterns of variation and stability issues.

Example (Figure 6.9 project)

Customer expectations. The Six Sigma team interviewed a cross-section of managers, who receive reports, to establish expectations. Accuracy and timeliness were the primary concerns. Units of measure are number of errors and throughput time in days.

Supplier expectations. The Six Sigma team also interviewed the production and distribution personnel. Timeliness (document submitted before 10.00 hours) and completeness of the document request form (100% fields completed) was preferred.

Current performance. In terms of actual turnaround time and number of errors it was found that:
- 8% of text procesing jobs were reworked; this delays document delivery time by half a day;
- 20% of reproduction jobs were reworked; this delays delivery time by 1 day.

Step 4: analyse/probe the process

Approaches include:

- focus on sources and types of error; simplification activities; interactions at interfaces; bottlenecks; lack of internal control; error rates per activity; throughput and processing time per activity; rework and scrap per activity;
- construct control charts to determine if causes are sporadic or endemic;
- identify causes of variation with a view to eliminating sporadic causes of variation and reducing principal endemic causes;
- seek out the relationships between process parameters and process performance to exploit improvement opportunities.

In probing a process/task/activity one is encouraged to question it from every conceivable angle in a structured way. The 5W2H method is proposed. This stands for the 5Ws, what, why, where, when and who; and the 2Hs, how and how much. These are brought out in Table 6.1.

Table 6.1   The 5W2H method of probing processes

5W2H	Description	Question
What?	Subject matter	What is being done? Can task be eliminated?
Why?	Purpose	Why is the task necessary? Clarify the purpose
Where?	Location	Where is it being done? Does it have to be done there?
When?	Sequence	When is the best time to do it? Does it have to be done then?
Who?	People	Who is doing it? Should someone else do it?
How?	Method	How is it being done? Is there a better way to do it?
How much?	Cost	How much does it cost now? How much will it cost after improvement?

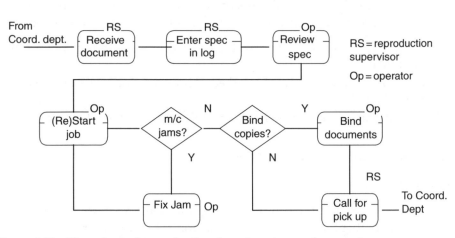

Figure 6.10   Flow chart of reproduction department copy document process

Example (Figure 6.9 project)

A flow diagram was constructed focusing on internal process opportunities. For instance, the team concentrated initially on the 'copy document' process with the results shown in Figure 6.10.

Step 5: develop the improved process – pilot and verify

We are now in a creative phase in which inventiveness and creativity is brought into play by the use of the question 'what else?' Key 'what else' pointers for creating an improved process are shown in Table 6.2.

Table 6.2 List of 'what else' questions to improve a process

Eliminate	The ultimate solution after removing the need
Reverse	For example, lower instead of lift
Sequence	Change
Link/separate	Join/take apart
Enlarge	Reduce
Concentrate	Disperse
Add/remove	For example, adding of extra slot on Philips head screw
Replace/substitute	For example, avoid waiting delays and empty movement
Parallel/sequential	Do more than one thing at the same time

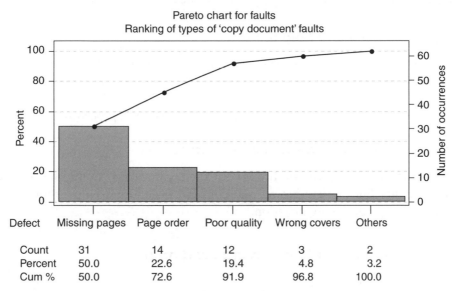

Defect	Missing pages	Page order	Poor quality	Wrong covers	Others
Count	31	14	12	3	2
Percent	50.0	22.6	19.4	4.8	3.2
Cum %	50.0	72.6	91.9	96.8	100.0

Figure 6.11 Pareto diagram of 'copy document' faults

Review results of process assessment and investigation and generate improvement alternatives. Rank improvement opportunities based on customer needs, internal business objectives, benefit/cost ratio, potential for improvement and resources required to implement the change. Choose. Pilot and validate. Perform cost/benefit analysis. Recommend solution. For each high-priority opportunity discuss and agree actions and timeframes with stakeholders.

Example (Figure 6.9 project)

The Six Sigma administration team gathered data on the causes of rework over a period. A Pareto diagram (Figure 6.11) showed that 73% of the rework was due to missing pages and pages out of order. This was attributed to 'machine jams'. This was made *priority one*. The root cause was 'cut and paste' pages being fed into the machine. The simplest solution was considered to be to secure all sides of such pages with transparent tape. This was piloted and found successful with a 30% reduction in cycle time.

Step 6: implement the changes – achieve breakthrough in performance

For each high-priority opportunity, discuss and agree actions and timeframes with stakeholders. Juran has drawn attention to the need for careful planning prior to implementation. This is because implementation of process improvements involves change, and change has two facets: the technical impact and the impact on people. The latter one is frequently not taken into full account. This can have serious consequences. Accordingly, there is a prior need to explain the reasons for change to all those affected so that prior agreement and support is secured.

Step 7: measure and hold the gains

Measure the new performance level and hold the gains. Institute controls to hold the new level of performance. Monitor the process to make sure unforeseen problems are resolved and the solution continues to be effective. Institutionalize the change and modify appropriate operating instructions and procedures.

Step 8: exploit the achievement in other areas

Standardize similar processes throughout the organization. Communicate the achievements. Start a new project and consider expanding the concept of Six Sigma throughout the organization.

The Six Sigma problem-solving road-map

The eight stages here, become:

Stage 1: identify the problem

State what the problem is about. State what is wrong now. State what is to be achieved. Specify measures of success. Describe constraints.

Example

What the problem is about	Double overhead cam manifolds
What is wrong now	Leakage
What is to be achieved	Reduced leakage
Measure of success	lower levels of impregnation and scrap
Constraints	Product is in production. Production levels are not to be compromised

Stage 2: clarify the problem and the approach

In conjunction with the process owner(s) determine the terms of reference for the project. Select the project team. Find out what has been tried previously to solve the problem. Determine the method of approach to be taken.

Example

Terms of reference	Conduct an in-house study that is self-contained. For instance, no waiting time for external machining required
Project team	Multi-disciplined; including foundry personnel, metallurgist, process engineer and inspector
Previous attempts	Several previous attempts unsuccessful by changing one process variable at a time to see the effects
Method of approach	Multi-factor experimentation

Stage 3: measure the extent of the problem

From analysis of available data and by probing further, as necessary, determine the severity of the problem in business terms and how the performance is measured operationally. Is this method of measurement satisfactory. What is the extent of the problem in technical terms?

Example

Severity of problem re. business	£62 000 per year on an on-going product
Performance measures	% leakers; % impregated; % scrap
Measurement method OK?	Yes for project purposes
Problem extent, technically	Average 4.5% scrap; 10.7% rework (impregnated)

Stage 4: analyse concern and determine causes

Analyse the process giving rise to the concern. Use methods appropriate to the particular problem (e.g. brainstorming, cause-and-effect diagrams, control charts, process variation analysis, Pareto and CEDAC diagrams, trend analysis, experimentation). Determine cause(s) of the problem.

Example

Analyse the process	Process control charts monitoring the process indicate that the problem is endemic rather than sporadic
Methods used (1)	Cause-and-effect diagrams through brainstorming by the project team as indicated in Figure 6.12. Following consideration of the cause-and-effect diagram, by the

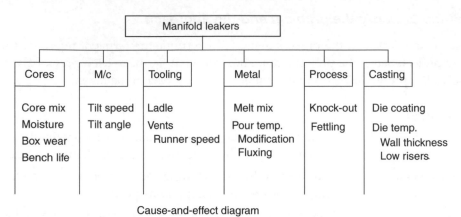

Cause-and-effect diagram

Figure 6.12 Brainstormed cause-and-effect diagram for manifold leakers

	project team, a number of factors were chosen as the more likely causes of manifold leakage. These were the factors: Melt mix, modification, pour temperature, die temperature, tilt speed, die coating and fluxing
Methods used (2)	The team decided to run an L8 multi-factor experiment with a seven-factor, two-level, eight-run factorial array. Each factor was run at two levels during the experiment: level 1 current setting; level 2 new possibly better setting. Each run was over two shifts with two dies. Production was 75/die/machine/shift. Response was % yield in respect to leakers
Determine causes	Results of the experiment indicated that there was no significant die-to-die variation. Five of the seven factors appeared to have a significant impact on yield. In order of importance these were: die temperature, pour temperature, tilt speed, melt mix and die coating. Four of these five factors gave better results at the new trial settings.

Stage 5: develop action plan

Determine from the analysis which solution is optimal, and why. Conduct trial run with the preferred solution. Review results and decide proposed future course of action.

Example

Optimal solution	The experiment shows that the optimal solution in terms of yield is obtained with four factors at new levels
Why?	Predicted results for yield at the new levels are: reduction in scrap rate for leakers from 4.5 to 0.8%;

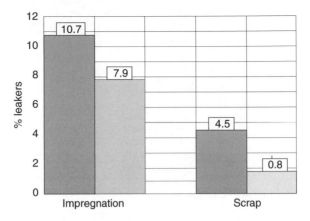

Figure 6.13 Manifold project fault rate reduction

	reduction in rework rate (impregnation) from 10.7 to 7.9%; see Figure 6.13.
Trial run validation	These results were validated in a pilot confirmation run
Results review	A decision was taken to discuss the findings with the process owners with a view to implementation.

Stage 6: implement plan to prevent recurrence

Discuss the preferred solution with the process owners and implementers. Introduce changes smoothly by planning and explanation. Monitor progress. Install controls to maintain the improved performance.

Example

Agree preferred solution	Permanent changes in the four factors were agreed with the foundry operations manager and the metallurgists involved
Plan changes	Changes were introduced smoothly
Monitor	A control chart was introduced to monitor yield in terms of scrap and rework

Stage 7: measure, control and hold the gains

Ensure that the new level of performance is maintained as standard practice. Measure and communicate gains in business terms.

Example

| Maintenance of new level of performance | The yield is continually monitored using a statistical process control chart with the new yield as the performance centreline |

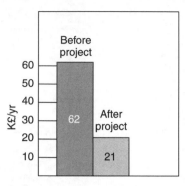

Figure 6.14   Manifold project cost savings

Business gains   The savings, on this one line alone is £41 000 per year at the current rate of production. See Figure 6.14.

Stage 8: exploit the achievement in other similar areas

Seek out similar situations where this solution may be gainfully transferred.

Example

Possible to extend solution ?   This project was conducted on a single manifold line for one customer who instigated the approach and the Six Sigma initiative. Comparable products are made for other customers. It is to be determined whether a similar solution can be extended to these lines.

Expand the Six Sigma initiative

The time has now arrived to review the results of your initial projects. Hopefully, the results will be such that the decision taken will be to expand the concept of Six Sigma across the organization.

The creation of a thousand forests is in one acorn

Ralph Waldo Emerson

Chapter highlights

● First imagine what a truly Six Sigma organization looks like. It has purpose, shows commitment to shared values, has the capability and engages in continual learning and improvement.

- To achieve such an organization, the first step is to consider the options for tailoring and implementing Six Sigma in the light of a prior selection of key business areas that present the best opportunities for improvement.
- Early business decisions need to be taken as four Six Sigma project focuses are possible:
  - Are we going to concentrate exclusively on reducing nonconformities or include also the possibility of improving process effectiveness and efficiency, particularly upstream where they offer the greatest leverage?
  - What is the principal business focus? Is it on enhancing customer relationships, product dominance or on becoming the lowest-cost supplier?
  - Is the expectation that Six Sigma projects will yield savings of an incremental or breakthrough nature?
  - Are the Six Sigma projects intended to deal primarily, or exclusively, with business strategic issues, cross-functional matters or be contained to the addressing of local concerns?
- What kind of Six Sigma infrastructure is to be set up? This will depend on whether a local or broad-based organizational approach is to be taken. A normal infrastructure consists of champions/master black belts/mentors together with black and green belts.
- The choice of Six Sigma champion(s) who usually acts as mentor, facilitator, co-ordinator and guru is critical to the success of the initiative.
- Prior to deploying the Six Sigma initiative, it is essential to ensure that all participants have the required competencies. The ASQ body of knowledge for black belts has been taken to be a benchmark. A number of organizations offer in-house training and development programmes leading to belt certification. They are also available to assist in getting stakeholders and interested parties on-side by helping to create the culture necessary for Six Sigma to operate successfully. If a pilot run is envisaged initially, and it is considered that only a very few people need development, recourse to external public seminars may appear more feasible.
- When deploying Six Sigma it is advised that a standardized generic project road-map be followed. Establishing this common approach and language will greatly assist communication within and between organizations. The eight-step road-map proposed is preferred to the conventional five-step DMAIC road-map followed by many Six Sigma practitioners. Some fine-tuning of the generic road-map will be necessary depending on whether the project is concerned with problem-solving as opposed to process improvement.

Bibliography

TC69:SC1 (2003). *ISO 3534-2, Applied statistics vocabulary*, Geneva: ISO.

Chapter 7

Is the Six Sigma statistical model technically sound?

> 'When I use a word', Humpty Dumpty said, in a rather scornful tone
> 'it means just what I choose it to mean – neither more nor less'.
> 'The question is', said Alice, 'whether you can make words mean
> so many different things'. 'The question is', said
> Humpty Dumpty, 'which is to
> be master – that's all'
>
> *Through the looking glass, Lewis Carroll*

Overview

Purists challenge the statistical component of the Six Sigma model on the grounds that it is, at worst, fundamentally flawed and, at best, based on very tenuous grounds. There are a number of reasons for this. The critique and response to the critique given in this chapter are prompted by four constructive and positive considerations:

- to place potential users in a better position to deal with technical queries on the standard Six Sigma statistical model as they arise;
- to point out frailties in the conventional or original Six Sigma statistical model and to propose more appropriate metrics where required by a particular situation;
- to indicate the probable marketing reasons for the model that has given the initiative its name; and
- to put this matter of model frailty into proper perspective in relation to the merits of the overall Six Sigma business initiative.

There are five very controversial aspects of the Six Sigma statistical model that are criticized, cause confusion, and hence prompt discussion and resolution:

1 the different use of the universally accepted term denoting standard deviation, the Greek term *'sigma'*;
2 the method of the linking of 6 Sigma to a claimed world-class performance standard of 3.4 defects per million opportunities;
3 the claim that 3.4 defects per million opportunities represent world-class performance;
4 the use of the term defects when non-conformities or undesirable events is intended;
5 the multiple meaning of the term 'opportunity'.

Let us deal 'head-on' with the most significant criticisms of the Six Sigma model. The critique and response in the body of this chapter are dealt with in as non-statistical a manner as possible. A more statistical approach, to justify the conclusions drawn is given in the Chapter 8. These criticisms are dealt with either by explaining and justifying the rationale, advising in interpretation and application, and/or proposing alternative approaches in particular circumstances.

Sigma versus *sigma*

Criticism

The originators of the Six Sigma initiative use a unit of measurement, a 'Sigma', to measure performance, the higher the value of Sigma the better the performance. For example, a 6 Sigma process is rated better than a 5 Sigma one. This meaning contrasts with the standard statistical meaning and usage of the term, *sigma*. The symbol, *sigma*, a Greek letter symbolizing a statistical measure of variation, termed the standard deviation is in universal use. The lower the value of the standard deviation, *'sigma'*, the less the variation present and the better the performance of a characteristic. The opposing meanings inevitably cause confusion. This confusion can be compounded as the internationally accepted standard *'sigma'* provides the derivation of the Sigma metric used in Six Sigma projects and also the relationship between non-conformities per million opportunities and the Six Sigma, Sigma.

Throughout this book, to distinguish between the two uses of the term the Six Sigma 'Sigma' is represented by an upper case initial letter thus, 'Sigma'. The standardized conventional use of the term is represented wholly in lower case italic, thus *'sigma'*.

Response to criticism

An advantage of the Sigma measure is its simplicity and practicality. This appeals to all those who do not wish to get too embroiled in statistical niceties but just want a simple readily understandable scale of performance measurement.

The fact that 6 Sigma denotes something better than 5 Sigma and that 5 Sigma is better than 4 Sigma, and so on makes good practical sense to them and they are quite prepared to run with it.

Others, who are already actively engaged in the application of statistical process control, will readily understand the use of Sigmas in a different way to *sigmas* but may feel uncomfortable and uneasy with both the frailty of the underlying concept and the outcome. This is because an alternative soundly based approach is available with the use of the internationally defined measured data process capability indices such as *Cp*. A *Cp* of 3 indicates less variation than a *Cp* of 2, and so on. Such measures require the pre-establishment of both process stability and a knowledge of the underlying pattern of variation.

Linkage of Sigma value to defect rate

Criticism

The value of Sigma is linked to a 'defects per million opportunities' value in a pseudo-statistical manner in two ways. Two gross assumptions are made.

1 The pattern of variation of the characteristic is symmetrical and bell shaped. This pattern is termed 'normal' or Gaussian distribution by statisticians.
2 A drift in one, unspecified, direction of the value of a characteristic amounting to 1.5 standard deviations.

Response to criticism 1

It should be noted that the use of the term 'normal' here is not that of 'usual' but rather just a statistical name given to a particular distribution. In the technical sense it is quite appropriate to state, quite categorically, that: 'in diagnostic activities leading to process improvement and in the estimation of process performance *normality of data* should never be assumed'. An erroneous assumption of normality can, and undoubtably will, lead to false trails and take one 'up the garden path' in Six Sigma project-improvement activities.

Having said this, we need to recognize that a lot of people throughout the world do and have being doing so, very successfully in the control of processes, for a great many years. Walter Shewhart (Shewhart, W. A., 1931) introduced statistical quality control charts for both measured and attribute data. Standard action control limits on such charts are set, quite simply, at ±3 *sigma* (standard deviations) of the measure plotted. This is so for both measured and attribute characteristics. The assumption is that the data are 'normal' when it is patently not for range and standard deviation charts and frequently not for measured individuals and attribute ones. Such procedures are, in general, used throughout the world, and are specified by the International Standards Organization (ISO) and the British Standards Institution in various standards. Examples are

ISO 8258 (TC69/SC4, 1991) and BS 5702-1 (BSI:SS/4, 2001). This approach is justified, purely for control purposes, not on statistical grounds but rather on pragmatic and economic ones. However, it cannot be tolerated for knowledge-gaining purposes, with performance improvement in mind, where the aim is to better understand what makes a process really 'tick'.

From purely practical considerations two circumstances arise, one with measured data and the other with attribute data. In Six Sigma project activities each measured data situation should be taken on its merits. In many instances the assumption of 'normality' is invalid. For instance, geometric form variation (e.g. eccentricity, parallelism and taper), particle size, fatigue results, lateness, time to pay bills, waiting time for a service, and most situations with a natural zero or with single-sided limits can give rise to non-normality. Significant distortion of an intrinsically normal distribution can also occur if a process is affected by special causes, step changes or drift in the mean.

In the case of attribute data, we have a different picture altogether. Assumptions based on 'normality' often have little statistical relevance in estimating performance or in improvement projects relating to go/no go, yes/no, good/bad attribute situations. Non-symmetrical patterns of variation are the norm rather than the exception. Examples of such instances are:

- a paint area where non-conformities may take the form, say, of gun spits, scratches, blisters, sags and runs;
- balloting and other systems using punched cards having hanging, swinging, dimpled and pregnant chads;
- form completion where errors may arise due to, incomplete information, wrong information, incorrect spelling, illegible writing;
- absenteeism: sick, holiday, wilful;
- casting faults: pinholes, porosity, flaws, cracks, shrinkage.

Response to criticism 2

The relationship between Sigma value and faults per million opportunities is based on a drift in one direction only of the characteristic under consideration. The value of this assumed drift is set at 1.5 standard deviations (*sigma*). On the face of it, this is contrary, in all respects to good standard practice. This is to target on preferred value, minimize variation (namely *reduce* the value of the standard deviation, *sigma*) and only estimate performance on the basis of process stability and a knowledge of the underlying pattern of variation. However, it is eminently reasonable to expect some variation about the preferred value even with the best of systems. The general assumption of a drift of 1.5 standard deviations is said to be based on actual experience. One should bear in mind that the actual value will depend on individual circumstance related both to the nature of the characteristic in question and the efficacy of the control system. The concept is also difficult or impossible to relate to attribute situations where terms such as 'preferred state' (e.g. free from blemish) and 'minimum acceptable state' (minor blemish tolerable) may be used.

Overall response to criticism

Taking this discussion into account, two recommendations are made:

1 The Six Sigma 'Sigma' is a simple measure that has gained wide acceptance. It has strong marketing and motivational merits if taken at face value. On these bases it seems reasonable to go along with this, provided its use is restricted to providing convenient, but arbitrary, overall indicators of performance or stepping stones to improvement.
2 One should, most certainly, not go along with the tenuous link between Six Sigma 'Sigma' and real *sigma* via the general assumption of 'normality' of data and a pre-ordained offset in a single unspecified direction. It is imperative that organizations committed to, or intending to commit themselves to, the Six Sigma initiative do not assume 'normality' of data, or a drift of 1.5 standard deviations from nominal, either in performance assessment or in their improvement activities. The acceptance of this will, most certainly, impair diagnostic ability and lead to misleading assessments of reality in any given situation.

What are the potential inadequacies in the use of Six Sigma 'Sigma' when used for technical purposes that justifies such statements? There are a number of inadequacies. The 1.5 *sigma* permissible drift in a single direction can well, in itself distort the pattern of variation. This presumption of normality and permissible drift also conflicts with standard practice in the quality field in respect of three tenets, which is to: target on preferred value, minimize variation and only estimate performance on the basis of a knowledge of:

– process stability and the underlying mean and pattern of variation in each individual characteristic under consideration in the case of measured data; and
– process stability and the average VPM (values per million opportunities) both in totality and in terms of types and nature of nonconformities, or other, often undesirable, events, in the case of attribute data.

One should also probe whether any drift is in one direction only and, if so, which? This can have quite serious financial consequences. For example, for a machined outside diameter, undersize could give rise to expensive scrap, and oversize to inexpensive rework. It many cases, it might also be more logical to allow the permissible movement in the process mean to be half above and half below nominal, namely ±0.75 *sigma* here. This, of course, would give rise to a different total VPM in terms of Sigma. For instance, 6 Sigma would equate to less than 0.29 VPM below and above the specification limits, giving under 0.58 VPM in total, rather than the 3.4 VPM given by the standard Six Sigma statistical model.

There is also the question when the preferred value is not centrally situated in relation to the specification limits, for example, minimum or maximum rather than nominal is best. A further issue arises when the specification limit is single sided. And a much larger issue emerges when we are dealing with attribute data rather than measured data as the whole concept of the relationship between Sigma and non-conformities through *sigma* is challenged.

From a process improvement viewpoint, the core messages for measured data are, never assume a pattern of variation and never assume a particular offset from the mean. Always determine what the actual mean and pattern of variation actually are. Use measures appropriate to the actual circumstances and exploit the potential for improvement that this key knowledge provides. With respect to attribute data, the key messages are, separate out the types of events, attributes or non-conformities, determine their relative frequency and degree of adverse impact on business performance. Use measures appropriate to the actual circumstances. Search out root causes and exploit the potential for improvement on a cost-effective basis.

Table 7.1 shows the relationship between the commonly used Sigma value and defects per million opportunities in numerical terms.

Figure 7.1 shows the relationship between Sigma in terms of nonconformities, or values, per million (VPM). It shows that the steps to improvement progressively get larger as perfection is approached.

Table 7.1 Relationship between values per million (VPM) outside of a limit in terms of Sigma values as exposed by the originators of Six Sigma

Six Sigma 'Sigma value'	VPM above upper limit	VPM below lower limit	Total VPM non-conforming
1	691 462	6297	697 759
2	308 538	233	308 771
3	66 807	3.4	66 810
4	6 210	Near 0	6 210
5	233	Near 0	233
6	3.4	Near 0	3.4

Columns 2 and 3 are transposed if the shift in mean is in the opposite direction. This table is based on normally distributed measured data with bilateral specification limits symmetrical about the nominal. A process offset of 1.5 standard deviations from nominal is assumed. Many Six Sigma texts assume (incorrectly) non-conformities only against the limit to which the process has shifted. VPM = values per million. This term, or non-conformities per million, is used in preference to defects per million as used by the originators of Six Sigma. Reasons for this are given in page 217.

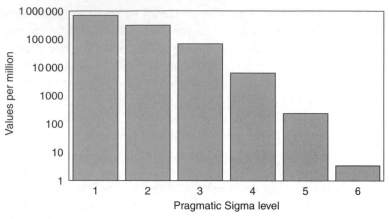

Figure 7.1   Non-conformities (values) per million in terms of Sigma value: stepping stones to improvement

What constitutes world-class performance?

Criticism

What is the justification for the Six Sigma claim that 3.4 defects per million opportunities represent world-class performance? Why set 3.4 as the 'gleam in the eye'?

Response to criticism

World-class performance

In short, it is patently obvious that there is no one universal world-class performance standard, per se, for a particular characteristic, process or project. Benchmark standards will inevitably vary from situation to situation. For instance, the benchmark time standards for a 'donkey derby' will differ greatly from that of a 'Formula One' motor race. However, the concept is appealing for characteristics where there is some commonality from the viewpoint of operational requirements.

Some may remember the more ambitious slogans supporting past quality-improvement initiatives such as 'right first time every time', 'zero D' and the like. Philip Crosby has proclaimed zero defects as the only performance standard. Joseph Juran, in contrast, has consistently taken the view that we should always strike a balance between effort and return by making value judgements. Edwards Deming has cautioned us that setting numerical goals without a road-map to reach the objective has an opposite effect to that intended. More recently, the Ford Motor Company, amongst others, have pioneered the development and application of process capability indices, such as Cp, Cpk_U and

Cpk_L for assessing the performance of measured data characteristics and minimum parts per million non-conforming for attribute characteristics. These have gained wide acceptance and are standardized by the International Standards Organization, in the standard ISO 3534-2:2003; Statistical vocabulary and symbols: Part 2: Applied Statistics. Requirements exist, too, to display a commitment to improve capability consistent with the operational philosophy of continual improvement in quality and productivity.

Marketing

Step one in marketing is to create a brand name, a distinctive mark of ownership, that will create a simple but strong image impelling people to buy in. In this respect, it is useful to bear in mind that surpassing something already well known and successful in its own right, in the same field, would give a considerable marketing edge to the concept. Let us put ourselves into this position. Suppose one wants to market some well-known statistical-based process-improvement and problem-resolution techniques together under one umbrella. What might be a suitable brand name with the connotation of extending the limits of existing best practice coupled with a well-known performance metric that could readily provide markers of progress towards the goal? Ford, amongst others in the application of the Deming philosophy, were already leading the way with demanding that their supply base and their assembly and manufacturing plants world-wide demonstrate a minimum capability from their measured data processes. This was set at least ±4 *sigma* capability during production, and a ±5 *sigma* potential performance during development.

A ready solution might be seen to be apparent. Six Sigma could provide a convenient marketing label that would be seen, on the face of it, to put clear water between it and existing best practice. One dilemma arises. True 6 Sigma, in standard statistical usage terms, equates to 0.002 parts per million non-conforming. That could be looked upon as too large a stretch even for world-class organizations. A simple answer to this is to permit the process to drift in the direction of one of bilateral specification limits, say, by 1.5 standard deviations. This would provide a more realistic world-class standard of 3.4 parts per million nonconforming. Hence:

Six Sigma the benchmark = 3.4 non-conformities per million opportunities

It has been established at this level, presumably, primarily for sound marketing purposes and its motivational merits, rather more so than for intrinsic merit. After all 6 Sigma has more of a ring about it than the more statistically valid 4.5 Sigma it actually represents. Packaging it, in statistical clothing, to create a little smoke and mirrors and so fog the issue, then naturally follows. In all probability it will then be accepted with little question, by a large proportion of people either potentially or actually committed to the Six Sigma initiative.

These remarks are not made in a derogatory sense but in a sense of realism of the world we live in and the recognizing of the need for good marketing if one is to achieve 'lift-off' of any new concept. It is accepted that all this may be considered most objectionable, particularly from a purely statistical and technical viewpoint, to some. However, it is suggested that we do not dismiss Six Sigma purely on these grounds for three very cogent reasons:

- one, the needs of successfully marketing a novel concept;
- two, the enormous successes and cost savings claimed with Six Sigma;
- three, because there is far more to Six Sigma than the statistical component discussed in this chapter.

Need for sustaining Six Sigma

If we, for a moment, consider the situation from a different angle, that of successful introduction, operation and sustaining of a continuous-improvement process or quality initiative, it has to be admitted that most such ventures have failed to become a recognized way of life. Take 'quality circles' for instance. In spite of a very promising 'lift-off' it failed to reach escape velocity and fizzled back to earth after a very short life span. The quality Gurus such as Deming, Juran, Crosby and Taguchi, for instance, have all left their footprint to varying degrees. Methodologies, such as statistical process control, quality function deployment and formal experimentation, have been or are often implemented in a fragmented manner without achieving their full potential. What is the secret of sustained success that has eluded these eminent quality practitioners?

Taking account of this historical experience and observing the ways of modern marketing will help us understand and appreciate the successful business approach adopted by the originators of Six Sigma in promoting the Six Sigma concept.

Step 1: The need to create a brand name, a distinctive mark of ownership, that will create a strong image impelling people to buy in has already been discussed above.

Step 2: Register the name 'Six Sigma' in an attempt to keep competitors at bay.

Step 3: Define the core organizational and technical competencies required to drive continual improvement.

Step 4: Create an awareness through articles, books, promotions, pilot programmes and the like. Get large well-known organizations, such as General Electric, to commit themselves to Six Sigma, achieve success and extol its virtues.

Step 5: Recognize the short life span of previous attempts in this field of endeavour. Take the necessary steps to create some form of infrastructure to perpetuate the process. Preferably this infrastructure should be a novel one that would also be appealing, stimulate interest and encourage involvement. Why not Judo-like belts? What a brilliant idea!

Why misuse the term 'defects'?

Criticism

Why misuse the term 'defects' with all its product liability connotations in the expression linking Sigma value to performance, for example, stating that 6 Sigma performance represents 3.4 defects per million opportunities.

Response to criticism

The continuing misuse of the term 'defects' is indicative of a certain naivety and too ready acceptance of, and perpetuation by, many Six Sigma authors and trainers of somewhat casual and amateurish utterances by the originators of Six Sigma. This does not bode well for the future of a process that demands high levels of ingenuity and perceptivity for significant improvements in value to be realized.

There is no rational justification for the use of the term 'defects' in this expression. Do not use the term 'defects' for general usage. Replace it, where applicable, by the more cumbersome, but preferred term, 'non-conformities'. However, in Six Sigma improvement projects one is not always confined to dealing with non-conformities as such. Sometimes the term 'non-conforming items', 'events' or 'values' is more appropriate. Organizations are advised to take heed of ISO 9000:2000 *Quality management systems – Fundamentals and vocabulary*. ISO 9000 states that the term 'defect' should be used with extreme caution. It warns us that the distinction between defect and non-conformity is important because of its legal connotations, particularly those associated with product liability issues. To minimize risk it is strongly recommended that in the phrase 'defects per million opportunities' defects be replaced by 'non-conformities (or more generally, events) per million opportunities' in Six Sigma applications.[1]

What is a critical quality characteristic?

Criticism

Just what is intended when one expresses Sigma value in terms of 'defects' or non-conformities per million 'opportunities'? How can the term 'opportunity' be consistently applied given that it relates to a single, so-called, 'critical-to-quality characteristic' (CTQC) in a product? Just what is a critical-to-quality characteristic?

Response

The definition of *opportunity* is critical to the establishment of a metric or benchmark. However, just what is meant by non-conformities, values or events, per

---

[1]Non-conformity is defined in ISO 9000 as 'non-fulfilment of a requirement'.

million *opportunities*? For instance, take a quality or inspection audit of office cleaning services in a number of similar blocks. What is to be the performance measure? Are we to measure in terms of non-conformities per block, non-conformities per room, or perhaps, non-conforming blocks or non-conforming rooms. Each would give a different result. Here, too, there is the opportunity for different types of non-conformities to occur in each room, such as, carpet not vacuumed, cabinet not dusted, waste bin not emptied, desk not tidied, and so on. There could also be more than one instance of a given type of non-conformity in each room, for example, three waste bins not emptied or carpet only partially vacuumed. Hence, the dilemma is further compounded. The originators of Six Sigma state that an:

> opportunity for a nonconformity relates to a single *Critical To Quality Characteristic* (CTQC) of a product or process not to the total product or overall process.

As such, if it is said that a product such as a motor vehicle or aircraft is Six Sigma it does not mean that only 3.4 non-conformities are present per million vehicles or aircraft. It does mean that if there are, say:

- 1000 critical-to-quality characteristics within the vehicle each at 6 Sigma, the vehicle itself can be expected to contain, on average, just over three non-conformities per 1000 vehicles; and
- if there are 5000 such characteristics each at 6 Sigma then this yields some 17 non-conformities per 1000 vehicles.

How many critical-to-quality characteristics would you estimate there are on Concorde? What margin of error would you place on that estimate? Would your colleagues agree? What do you conclude from this?

Non-conformities per million opportunities, NPMOs, are expressed in equation form as

$$\text{NPMO} = \frac{\text{Total number of non-conformities per unit}}{\text{Total number of opportunities per unit}} \times 1 \text{ million}$$

An alternative expression is

$$\text{NPMO} = \frac{\text{Number of non-conformities}}{(\text{no. of units}) \times (\text{no. of CTQCs})} \times 1\,000\,000$$

Example

An example of the application of this equation is now shown. Suppose 2000 similar units or items each with 10 CTQCs are subjected to inspection and test. If:

1 60 non-conformities are discovered;
2 One non-conformity is discovered.

Table 7.2 Relationship between Sigma and non-conformities per million, and per thousand, opportunities

Sigma value	0	0.1	0.2	0.3	0.4	0.5	0.6	0.7	0.8	0.9
▼ Non-conformities per million opportunities ▼										
6	3									
5	233	159	108	72	48	32	21	13	9	5
4	6210	4661	3467	2555	1866	1350	968	687	483	337
▼ Non-conformities per thousand opportunities ▼										
3	67	55	45	36	29	23	18	14	11	8
2	309	274	242	212	184	159	136	115	97	81
1	691	655	618	579	540	500	460	421	382	345

How many NPMOs are there? What is the Sigma level?

$$NPMO = \frac{\text{Number of non-conformities}}{(\text{no. of units}) \times (\text{no. of CTQCs})} \times 1\,000\,000$$

Regarding (1) NPMO = (60 × 1 000 000)/(2000 × 10) = 3000. Using Table 7.2, Sigma = 4.25. Regarding (2) NPMO = (1 × 1 000 000)/(2000 × 10) = 50. From Table 7.2, Sigma = 5.4.

The intention is that quoting NPMO in the way shown would provide a universal metric that could be applied to all products regardless of their relative complexity. How consistent is this metric likely to be in practice? A case study illustrates the approach required for successful application of this method.

Case study and conclusions

Take a tailored shirt of a particular style. The question as to how many and what critical-to-quality features there were in the shirt was put to two informed people, one the garment technologist involved and the other the shirt line examiner. They came up with two quite different results:

- The garment technologist listed 107 CTQCs. A selection is given in Table 7.3.
- The line examiner listed a maximum of 11 CTQCs. She did not consider all these as critical. She prioritized them for improvement action as shown in Figure 7.2.

Others, for example, customers, may take quite a different view. For instance, style characteristics may predominate in the case of customers in their choice of what, or what not, to purchase.

This indicates that if NPMO is to be a universal metric, as claimed, extreme care should be taken to reach a consensus on what is, and what is not, a CTQC.

Table 7.3   Critical-to-quality characteristics on a tailored shirt as determined by a garment technologist

Shirt component	No. of CTQCs	Examples of types of CTQCs
Body	25	Fabric; shading, marks, soiling. Stitches; grinning, slipped, … etc.
Placket	24	Buttons; type, size. Box; size, shape. Topstitching; position, pucker, … etc.
Collar	21	Fusing; delamination, discolouration. Symmetrical shape and points, … etc.
Sleeves	16	Dimensions; overarm, underarm, armhole, elbow width. Shade re. body, … etc.
General	11	Stitching; density, pucker. Thread; shade, type secured ends, … etc.
Cuffs	10	Seam bight. Shade. Dimensions; cuff opening, cuff depth, … etc.
Total	107	

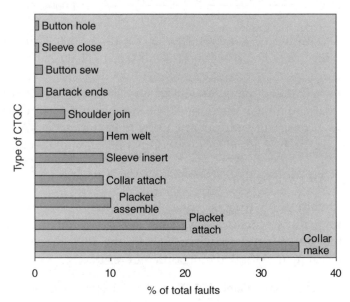

Figure 7.2   The critical-to-quality characteristics on the same tailored shirt as determined by a line examiner

This is because of the sensitivity of NPMO to number of CTQCs. It would be wise to reflect on why we are using CTQCs, in each case, and for what specific purpose. Take the shirt case for instance. The technologist's approach might well be applicable if one is preparing technical specifications for ranges of shirts. If, however, one is concerned with improvement projects on a particular shirt then, obviously, concentration would be on the vital few, identified by the line examiner, causing the bulk of current problems.

Chapter highlights

- The statistical model provides the marketing name for the Six Sigma improvement initiative. Its effectiveness is indicated by the tremendous interest shown in, and take-up of, the Six Sigma business process throughout the world. That Six Sigma has considerable substance is borne out by the fact of positive news-feed from organizations already committed to Six Sigma.
- A number of statisticians are extremely critical of some of the statistical features of the model. These criticisms have been aired in this chapter and positive responses given. These responses are intended to be helpful to those engaged, currently and potentially, in Six Sigma activities.
- It should be borne in mind that the five constructive criticisms made in respect of the statistical component of the Six Sigma initiative is not associated with, or detracts from the benefits gained by deployment of, the overall Six Sigma business improvement process itself.
  - One should be careful to distinguish between the universally used Greek term for standard deviation namely, *sigma*, and the Sigma used by Six Sigma practitioners. The smaller the value of standard deviation, *sigma*, the better the precision (performance) of a process. The larger the 'Sigma' the better the performance of the process.
  - It is recommended that anyone and everyone associated with Six Sigma use the accepted linkage between 'defects' per million opportunities and the Sigma measure purely for convenience in respect to what is now accepted common usage in the Six Sigma arena. They should, however, not be taken in by the very tenuous arguments put forward to justify this relationship.
  - The name Six Sigma is a marketing concept for a continual-improvement initiative that aims to provide a somewhat arbitrary amount of clear water between a 6 Sigma performance standard and current standard practice. A 6 Sigma standard is commonly said to represent a world-class performance of 3.4 'defects' per million opportunities.
  - The originators of Six Sigma use the term 'defect' to describe the universally accepted term 'non-conformities'. The perpetuation of this practice by many Six Sigma authors, trainers and practitioners is strongly discouraged. The International Standards Organization explicitly state that the term 'defects' should be used with extreme caution, primarily because of legal and product liability implications.

- In general Six Sigma practice, the term opportunity is said to apply to a critical-to-quality characteristic (CTQC). A Sigma level in a given situation is determined by the number of non-conformities per million opportunites (NPMO). If NPMO is to be a universal metric, as claimed, extreme care should be taken on what a CTQC is. This is because of the sensitivity of NPMO, and hence the Sigma level, to number of CTQCs.

Bibliography

BSI:SS/4 (2001). *BS 5702-1: Guide to SPC charts for variables*, London: BSI.
Shewhart, W. A. (1931). *Economic control of quality of manufactured product*, New York: Van Nostrand.
TC69/SC4 (1991). *ISO 8258: Shewhart control charts*, Geneva: ISO.

Chapter 8
Which Sigma should be used?

I realize that this upper case Greek letter sigma, Σ, means 'some of', but how do I know which ones to choose?

Undergraduate at a British University

Overview

Inferential statistics is about drawing conclusions about a body of data on the basis of taking a representative sample. As such it forms an important aspect of Six Sigma activities. This concept is illustrated as a process in Figure 8.1.

In Figure 8.1, a population refers to the totality of items or entities under consideration. [A]: It is statistical convention to symbolize a population parameter by lower case Greek letters in italics. For example, mean $= \mu$ (*mu*); standard

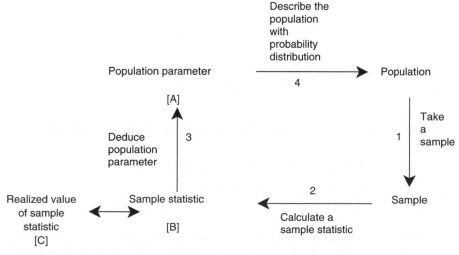

Figure 8.1   Process of statistical inference

deviation = σ (*sigma*). [B]: A population parameter is deduced from a sample statistic. It is statistical convention to symbolize a sample statistic by upper case Latin letters in italics. For example, mean = $\bar{X}$; standard deviation = S. [C]: It is statistical convention to symbolize a realized value of a sample statistic by lower case Latin letters in italics. For example, mean, $\bar{x}$ = 12.0; standard deviation, s = 1.0.

Of particular relevance to Six Sigma practitioners is the use of the *sigma* symbol as a measure of standard devation. This is because the Six Sigma 'Sigma' means something quite different. This sigma situation is compounded by two further aspects. First, the Six Sigma 'Sigma' is related in a peculiar and arbitrary way to the statistical *sigma*. Second, there is yet another sigma used by statisticians. This relates to the upper case Greek symbol for sigma, namely, Σ. By statistical convention this refers to 'the sum of'. These three quite different uses of sigma can cause confusion.

This has already been discussed, in part, at appreciation level in Chapters 1 and 7. Here, the discussion is opened up in both a logical and statistical sense in relation to measured data. This will enable the Six Sigma practitioner to make sound judgements on what measures to use to transmit performance information in a valid and transparent manner readily understandable to the many.

Three key statistical features

Three things are of vital importance in estimating capability and performance based on numerical data. These are:

1 *A measure of central tendency*. This could be the average (arithmetic mean), median (central value) or mode (most frequent value).
2 *A measure of variation*. This is usually the range (the difference between the largest and smallest value) or the standard deviation.
3 *The pattern of variation*. Often this approximates to the 'normal' (symmetrical bell shaped) form, 'log normal' (skewed) or 'negative exponential' for measured data. For discrete data it takes the form of 'Poisson' for counts of events (e.g. sales, errors, absentees) per given time period or unit of product and 'binomial' for binary (go/no go, ok/nok) data.

The statistical '*sigma*' and the 'normal' distribution

The normal distribution and its parameters

The normal distribution has just two parameters.[1] It is uniquely described by the mean and the standard deviation. Conventionally, in statistics, standard

---

[1] The word 'normal' is used generally to describe the Gaussian distribution. However, this is purely a name that has been given to a symmetrical bell-shaped pattern of variation. It should never be assumed that it is normal in the conventional sense of being usual.

deviation is symbolized by the lower case Greek letter *'sigma'*, that is, *'σ'*. The standard deviation is a statistical parameter that measures the spread, variability, dispersion or precision of a set of values. It is a measure of the average amount the values in a distribution deviate from the mean. The more widely the values are spread out the larger the standard deviation – the worse the performance. It is commonly used in conjunction with a measure of central tendency, the arithmetic mean, symbolized by the Greek lower case letter *'mu'*, that is, *'μ'*. These two together, when the underlying pattern of the data is 'normal', enables one to make predictions as what number of events per hundred, thousand or million opportunities are expected to lie above, below or within a particular value. An example is shown.

Example

The heights of a number of adult males are measured, as part of a size survey, by a major clothing retailer. Results are shown pictorially in Figure 8.2.

Figure 8.2 indicates that the pattern of variation is reasonably symmetrical and bell shaped. This is confirmed by superimposing a 'normal' distribution on the vertical line representation of the actual size data as indicated in Figure 8.3. This 'normal' distribution has a mean of 69 in. and a standard deviation of 3 in.

Properties and application of the standardized normal distribution

We have now established that the 'normal' model, with a mean and standard deviation of 69 and 3, respectively, is appropriate here. This enables us to use

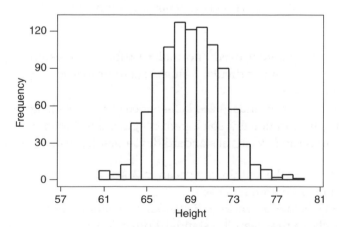

Figure 8.2 Frequency diagram of heights of adult males obtained in a size survey (units are in inches rather than in metric as round numbers are then involved. This simplifies the calculations)

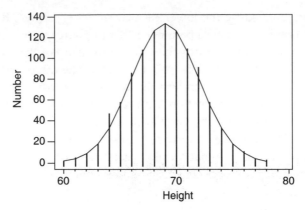

Figure 8.3   Normal distribution model fitted to actual survey data

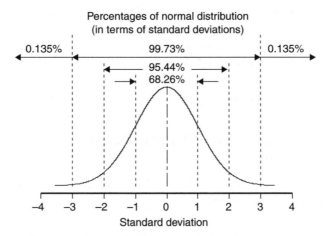

Figure 8.4   Basic features of a standarized normal distribution

the properties of a standardized[2] 'normal' distribution to estimate proportions above, below or within particular values. These properties are indicated conceptually in Figure 8.4.

Figure 8.4 shows the standardized bell-shaped curve that characterizes the normal distribution. Additionally, some percentages are included in relation to distances from the mean in terms of standard deviations. It illustrates pictorially that:

- 99.73% of values lie within the mean ±3 standard deviations (mean ±3 *sigma*). Of the remaining 0.27%:
  – 0.135% lie below the mean − 3 standard deviations, and
  – 0.135% above the mean + 3 standard deviations;

---

[2]A standardized normal distribution is one with a mean of zero and a standard deviation of 1.

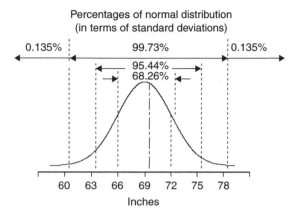

Figure 8.5 Use of the properties of the normal distribution to estimate clothing size ratios from survey data (the standardized mean of zero is replaced by the actual value of 69 in.; the horizontal scale is transposed from standard deviations to the actual equivalent of 3 in.)

- 95.44% of values lie within the limits: mean ± 2 standard deviations;
- 68.26% of values lie within the limits: mean ± 1 standard deviation.

This may now be applied to the size survey data as a basis for determining buying ratios for different garment sizes. All that needs to be done to achieve this is to substitute the actual mean and standard deviation (*sigma*) for the standardized values shown in Figure 8.4. This is shown in Figure 8.5.

Figure 8.5 demonstrates a simple but useful property of the mean and standard deviation, *sigma*. Such a diagram shows the effectiveness of the normal distribution in predicting, from a sample, the proportion of the whole lying within a specified range or above, or below particular limits. It illustrates pictorially that:

- 99.73% of the heights are expected to lie within 60 and 78 in. Of the remaining 0.27%:
  - 0.135% are shorter that 60 in.
  - 0.135% are taller than 78 in.
- 95.44% of the heights are expected to lie within 63 and 75 in.
- 68.26% of the heights are expected to lie within 66 and 72 in.

Whilst it is helpful in conveying certain principles, Figure 8.5 is, however, not usually of sufficient resolution to be of real value in practice. Table 8.1 provides this. It also extrapolates performance in terms of value expectation for a wider range of values of standard deviation.

Table 8.1 shows that for a characteristic centred between two limits with the limits placed at:

- mean ± 6 standard deviations, 0.001 values per million (VPM) are expected above the upper limit and 0.001 VPM below the lower limit;

Table 8.1 Proportion of values expected outside of an upper and lower limit in terms of standard deviations from the mean (for a normally distributed measured data characteristic)

No. of standard deviations, sigma, a limit is from the mean, or 3 Cpk	Values per million, or percentage outside upper/lower limits									
	0.0	0.1	0.2	0.3	0.4	0.5	0.6	0.7	0.8	0.9
6	0.001 VPM									
5	0.29 VPM									
4	32 VPM>	21	13	8.5	5.4	3.4*	2.1	1.3	0.8	0.5
3	1350 VPM>	988	687	483	337	233	159	108	72	48
2	2.3%	1.8	1.4	1.1	0.8	0.6	0.5	0.4	0.3	0.2
1	16%	14	12	10	8.1	6.7	5.5	4.5	3.6	2.9
0	50%	46	42	38	34	31	27	24	21	18

Values are rounded off and relate to stable measured data characteristics conforming to a normal distribution only.
* For a limit at 4.5 *sigma* from the mean: 3.4 VPM is expected outside of a limit.

- mean ± 5 standard deviations, 0.29 VPM are expected above and below the limits.

Effect of mean offset from nominal

Sometimes, the process or characteristic represented by the normal distribution may not be centred within the limits. This can occur, for instance, when the preferred value is not the nominal but when smaller is better, or larger is better. In such cases good practice obliges us to aim for preferred value, or as close to it as possible, taking into account the consequences of contravening specification limits. This could be expressed as a design intent in the form of 100^{+0}_{-2} or 100^{+2}_{-0}.

Example

Suppose the mean and standard deviation of a normally distributed process is given by mean = 50 and standard deviation = 1.0. The specified tolerance is 48–54. This situation is illustrated pictorially in Figure 8.6. As the:

- lower limit, L, is 2 standard deviations (2 *sigma*) from the process mean, Table 8.1 shows that 2.3% are expected below the lower limit, L;

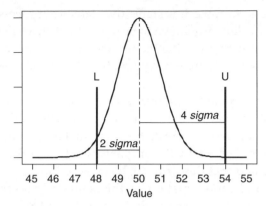

Figure 8.6 Characteristics of a particular normally distributed process offset by one standard deviation from the mean

● upper limit, U, is 4 standard deviations (4 *sigma*) from the process mean, Table 8.1 shows that 32 values per million opportunities are expected above the upper limit, U.

The 'Sigma' measure used by the originators of Six Sigma

So far in this chapter the term *sigma* has been used in its generally accepted, and internationally defined, sense as standard deviation. We now discuss the reasoning behind the adoption of a different sigma as coined by the originators of the Six Sigma initiative. This is distinguished here from conventional '*sigma*', where a lower case italic text is used, by an initial upper case S, and lower case regular text thus, 'Sigma'.

> In Six Sigma activities it is vitally important to distinguish between the 'Sigma' measure used by the originators of Six Sigma and now commonly used in Six Sigma activities on the one hand and the *sigma* symbol for standard deviation as internationally defined and adopted by statisticians world-wide.

The differences between 'Sigma' and '*sigma*' are now discussed from a statistical viewpoint.

Sigma versus *sigma*

Overview

First take a measured data process, centred on nominal, with a mean 6 standard deviations (6 *sigma*) from each of the upper and lower specification limits.

With such a process, suppose it is stable (by statistical process control criteria) and the individual values are shown to be normally distributed. We would then enter Table 8.1 at column 1 (giving the number of *sigma* the mean is from each limit), namely, 6. The estimate would then be 0.001 values per million outside of each limit.

In the Six Sigma standard philosophy, this is considered to be an idealized situation only realized in the short term. It is acknowledged that whilst this is representative of short-term performance it is usual for processes to drift some-what over time. It is claimed, by the originators of the Six Sigma initiative, that research has indicated that this drift can be expected to be 1.5 *sigma* in a single direction. A pictorial representation of this shift in process mean, or drift, towards the upper limit, U, is shown in Figures 8.7 and 8.8.

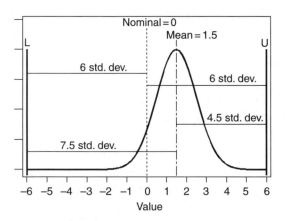

Figure 8.7   Representation of a 6 Sigma process

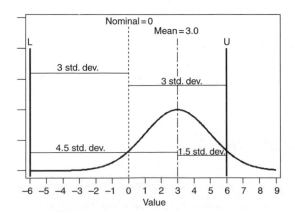

Figure 8.8   Representation of a 3 Sigma process

The 6 Sigma process

A 6 Sigma process is shown in Figure 8.7.

Conventionally, we would say that the process, shown in Figure 8.7, is now 4.5 standard deviations (4.5 *sigma*) in from the upper specification limit. Table 8.1 would be entered at 4.5 to read an expected 3.4 values per million opportunities above the upper specification limit, U. Similarly, entering Table 8.1 at 7.5 standard deviations (7.5 *sigma*), less than 0.001 values per million opportunities would be expected below the lower limit, L.

The originators of Six Sigma, in their assessment of this process, would deem it to have a Sigma value of 6.0. However, this does not affect the end result in terms of values outside of specification limits. Consequently, a Sigma table is constructed, as in Table 8.2, which is displaced in column one by 1.5 standard deviations (1.5 *sigma*) from that in Table 8.1.

Consequently, the same result is achieved as before by entering Table 8.2 at 6.0 to estimate some 3 (3.4 as rounded in table) values per million opportunities outside of the specification limit.

The 3 Sigma process

Figure 8.8 shows the representation of a 3 Sigma process.

In Figure 8.8, the process has a standard deviation of 2.0 and is set 1.5 standard deviations higher than nominal.

The performance of the process can be estimated in a number of ways. The first two would only be used in this way from actual data, provided the process related to a measured feature was deemed to be stable (using a control

Table 8.2 Relationship between Sigma value and proportion of values outside of specification

Sigma value	0	0.1	0.2	0.3	0.4	0.5	0.6	0.7	0.8	0.9
▼ Non-conformities per million opportunities ▼										
6	3									
5	233	159	108	72	48	32	21	13	9	5
4	6210	4661	3467	2555	1866	1350	968	687	483	337
▼ Non-conformities per thousand opportunities ▼										
3	67	55	45	36	29	23	18	14	11	8
2	309	274	242	212	184	159	136	115	97	81
1	691	655	618	579	540	500	460	421	382	345

chart) and the distribution of individuals were predetermined to be normal:

1 *Conventional sigma (standard deviation) method.* Using Table 8.1, the mean is 1.5 standard deviations from the upper limit. Thence, 6.7% of values are expected above the upper specification limit, U. The mean is 4.5 standard deviations from the lower specification limit, L. Thence, 3.4 values per million are expected below the lower specification limit.

2 *Conventional Cp and Cpk method.* We have seen in Chapter 5 that the *Cp* and *Pp* families provide universal indices of capability and performance. For a normally distributed measured data characteristic, as here:

$$Cp = \frac{\text{Specified tolerance}}{6 \text{ standard deviations}} = \frac{U - L}{6 \text{ standard deviations}}$$

$$= 12 / (6 \times 2) = 1.0$$

$$Cpk_U = \frac{U - \text{mean}}{3 \text{ standard deviations}}$$

$$= (6 - 3)/(3 \times 2) = 0.5$$

Enter Table 8.1 at 3 Cpk_U to give 6.7% above U

$$Cpk_L = \frac{\text{Mean} - L}{3 \text{ standard deviations}}$$

$$= (3 + 6)/(3 \times 2) = 1.5$$

Enter Table 8.1 at 3 Cpk_L to give 3.4 values per million below L.

3 Sigma *method.* Using Table 8.2, the nominal is 3 standard deviations from the specification limits with the mean, deemed by supposition, to be offset by 1.5 standard deviations from it. Hence, Sigma = 3.0. Thence, from Table 8.2, 6.7% of values are expected above the upper specification limit.

Relationship between Sigma and proportion of values outside of each limit

Table 8.3 shows the relationship between values per million (VPM) outside of particular limits in terms of 'Sigma' values.

Preferred measures of capability and performance (BSI:SS/3, 2000)

Measured data

The *Cp* and *Pp* family of indices are of universal application in assessing the capability and performance of measured data processes from real data. They are preferred to that of Sigma measures particularly for technical uses and when groups of characteristics are concerned. For singular characteristics,

Table 8.3 Relationship between Sigma value and non-conformity to specification

Sigma *value*	*VPM above upper limit*	*VPM below lower limit*	*Total VPM non-conforming*
1	691 462	6297	697 759
2	308 538	233	308 771
3	66 807	3.4	66 810
4	6210	Near 0	6210
5	233	Near 0	233
6	3.4	Near 0	3.4

Columns 2 and 3 are transposed if the shift in mean is in the negative direction.
This table is valid only for normally distributed measured data with bilateral specification limits symmetrical about the nominal.
The Sigma values relate to a process deemed to be offset 1.5 standard deviations from the mean.
Some Six Sigma texts assume non-conformities only against the limit to which the process has shifted.
VPM = values per million.

either the conventional standard deviation method, based on real data, or the *Cp* or *Pp* method is preferred to the Sigma approach in technical situations. The method of calculating these indices has already been shown. The use of Table 8.1 in estimating proportions of values expected outside of each specification limit has also been illustrated. Here, the advantages associated with their deployment are discussed. These indices are extremely useful when a quality profile is required for a complex entity such as a steering system, an engine or a manufacturing machine shop area. Such entities usually consist of a large number of specific quantitative characteristics each with their individual preferred values, tolerances and measurement units. Their value is indicated in an extract of a steel works quality health profile shown in Table 8.4.

It is seen that Table 8.4 gives a wealth of information in standardized format. Column 2 relates to the preferred value, maximum, nominal or minimum is best. Column 3 indicates whether the process is stable or not by statistical process control criteria. Column 4 shows the shape of the underlying pattern of variation of individual values of the characteristic, normal, log normal, bi-modal, exponential, etc. Column 5 provides a three-component assessment of the behaviour of the characteristic. The value of *Cp* gives a measure of the inherent precision of the process. The minimum acceptable value for *Cp* will depend on contractual requirements or self-imposed benchmarks in a given sector or organization. Cpk_U and Cpk_L indicate the direction and degree to

Table 8.4   First-time quality profile for part of a steelworks

Characteristic	Aim	Stable process?	Type of distribution	Capability indices		
				Cpk_L	Cp	Cpk_U
Silicon	Nominal	Yes	Skew	1.3	1.0	0.9
Aluminium	Nominal	Yes	Normal	1.4	1.5	1.6
Teeming temperature	Nominal	Yes	Normal	1.3	1.3	1.3
Teeming time	Nominal	Yes	Normal	1.6	1.7	1.8
Injuries per week	Minimum	Yes	Attribute		0.73%	
Cobbles	Minimum	Yes	Attribute		0.14%	
Billet rhomboidity	Minimum	Yes	Normal	2.4	–	–
Time to charge	Minimum	No	Bi-modal	Disparity between steelment*		

* Subject of investigation.

which the process is actually off-centre and its implications in terms of out-of-specification values.

Some contractual requirements specify just a minimum *Cpk*. However, quoting this value on its own provides no information of the direction in which the process is biased, if at all. This is particularly relevant if the penalty of transgressing one limit is different from transgressing the other. An example is if an outer diameter is too large as opposed to being too small. One may involve inexpensive rework and the other expensive scrap or material rebuilding. Neither does it indicate the extent of the variation. Hence, it provides sparse information even for indicative let alone improvement purposes. The same criticism applies to the use of the Sigma value by Six Sigma practitioners.

Attribute data

For attribute data one should always aim for preferred state or condition. The capability of a stable process is estimated directly from the mean of the statistical process control chart. The conversion of proportion of non-conformities or events outside of specification to Sigma values is a matter of choice for the Six Sigma practitioner. A word of caution may not be amiss here. One should be careful in arriving at conclusions from a single set, or small number of sets, of samples. Stabilization of the process is required before arriving at a credible result. This is illustrated in the lower diagram of Figure 8.9. The lower diagram is a plot of the cumulative average up to the point plotted. It is seen that a reliable estimate of the process capability is not feasible until about sample number 35 (a batch of 25 constitutes each sample). At this point it appears reasonable to calculate the process capability as 0.101 faults per unit.

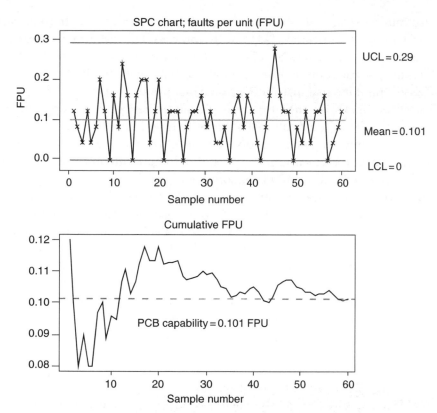

Figure 8.9 SPC chart for printed circuit board faults together with process capability assessment

Chapter highlights

- There are a number of metrics that can be used to determine the capability and performance of process parameters and product characteristics. Two basic statistical measures are the average and the standard deviation. Examples of derived metrics are Sigma, and the process capability indices, *Cp* and *Cpk*. All these are, at best of limited value, and at worst highly misleading, without a knowledge of:
  - the underlying pattern of variation (distribution shape);
  - the stability of the process (using statistical process control charts).
- The relationship between mean, standard deviation and expected proportion lying outside of specification limits for measured characteristics are well established for the symmetrical, bell-shaped, distribution generally called the 'normal' or Gaussian distribution. Here, the word 'normal' is not necessarily used in its colloquial sense as usual or customary.
- It is a basic tenet in optimizing process performance to: 'aim (the mean) at preferred value and minimize variation (standard deviation – *sigma*)'. One is

also cautioned against assuming any particular underlying pattern of varia-tion without specific knowledge of the process. For instance, features with a natural zero are likely to follow a skew distribution, counts of events a 'Poisson' distribution and yes/no data a 'binomial' distribution. Both the Poisson and binomial distributions take on various shapes.

- The relationship between Sigma and non-conformities per million opportunities, however, is based on a 'normal' distribution with an offset of 1.5 standard deviations from nominal. This does not affect the use of Sigma as a general, but quite arbitrary, measure; however, the dubious attempt at justifying the underlying rationale should be ignored.

- Whilst the Sigma measure can well be used for general end communication and motivational purposes it should not be used in a technical sense.

- Technically, one is advised to aim for preferred value and minimize variation. For measured data where specification limits are concerned the use of the Cp or Pp family of standardized indices are recommended. These indices allow one to focus on the estimation of consequences at each limit, upper and lower. Being universal they also facilitate capability/performance com-parisons between unlike process characteristics. This enables quality health profiles to be generated for complex products, or large areas, in terms of the relative ability of individual characteristics to hit preferred value and to meet both upper and lower specification limits.

- The Cp family of indices should be used when process stability has been established and the Pp family when it is not. This will ensure transparency and clarity of understanding. In all cases the underlying pattern of variation needs to be stated, for example, 'normal'. A Cpk (or Ppk)$_{minimum}$ of 1.5 equates to a Sigma value of 6.

- For attribute data one should always aim for preferred state. The conversion of proportion of conconformities or events outside of specification to Sigma values is a matter of choice for the Six Sigma practitioner.

Bibliography

BSI:SS/3 (2000). *BS 600: Guide to the application of statistical methods*, London: BSI.

Appendix A
Relationship between critical-to-quality characteristics and system performance

'AND' systems and the product rule

If a system is made up of a number of elements and it is necessary for all those elements to operate for the system to operate, we then have what is termed:

a series or 'AND' system.

Such a system is displayed in its simplest form in Figure A1 by two elements, A and B, in series. This denotes that it is necessary for both A and B to operate for the system to be functional.

The 'product rule' applies to such a series or 'AND' system. System reliability is determined by multiplying together the reliabilities of all the series elements. If, in Figure A1, the reliability (R) of A is 0.9 (90%) and that of B is 0.8 (80%). Then

$$\text{System reliability} = R_{\text{system}} = R_A \times R_B = 0.9 \times 0.8 = 0.72 \ (72\%)$$

If, on the other hand, both elements had the same reliability, say 0.7 (70%), the system reliability $= 0.7 \times 0.7 = 0.49$ (49%). This could alternatively be expressed as

$$\text{System reliability} = 0.7^2 = 0.49 \ (49\%)$$

The principle is now applied to quantifying the sensitivity of:

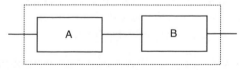

Figure A1   A simple series or 'AND' system

- number of CTQCs (critical-to-quality characteristics) on product performance;
- *Sigma* level on product performance.

Case study 1

The effect of the difference in number of CTQCs in a product are portrayed in Scenarios 1 and 2.

Scenario 1: Product with 1000 CTQCs, or opportunities for non-conformity, each at the 6 *Sigma* performance level.

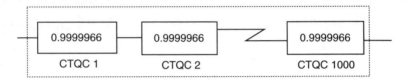

A 6 *Sigma* performance level equates to 3.4 non-conformities per million opportunities. This equates to a success rate of $1 - 0.0000034 = 0.9999966$:

$$0.9999966^{1000} = 3 \text{ non-conformities per 1000 products}$$

Scenario 2: Product with 5000 rather than 1000 CTQCs

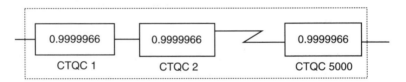

$$0.9999966^{5000} = 2 \text{ non-conformities per 100 products}$$

Comparison of the results of the two scenarios, namely, 3 per 1000 compared with 2 per 100, indicate the sensitivity to number of CTQCs, each with a constant *Sigma* value.

Case study 2

The effect of the difference in *Sigma* level for a given number of CTQCs in a product are portrayed in Scenarios 3–6.

Scenarios 3–6 consider the issue from another perspective, in terms of constancy of CTQCs and varying *Sigma* capability of a given product. For 100 CTQCs per product and a changing *Sigma* level:

– *Scenario 3*: *Sigma* level = 3; gives 99.9% non-conforming products.
– *Scenario 4*: *Sigma* level = 4; gives 46% non-conforming products.

– *Scenario 5*: *Sigma* level = 5; gives 2.3% non-conforming products.
– *Scenario 6*: *Sigma* level = 6; gives 0.03% non-conforming products.

Scenarios 3–6 indicate that for a product of this complexity going from:

- 3 *Sigma* to 4 *Sigma* gives a 2:1 improvement ratio;
- 4 *Sigma* to 5 *Sigma* gives a 20:1 improvement ratio;
- 5 *Sigma* to 6 *Sigma* gives a 77:1 improvement ratio.

Summary

When a process is made up of a number of stages the overall process performance is dependent on each individual stage performance. A similar situation exists for a product that has a number of different opportunities to fail. Either is known as an 'AND' system where the process overall probability of success is the product of individual stage probabilities of success.

1 For a 10-stage process with each stage operating at 3 Sigma (93.32% yield), the overall process performance, or yield, is given by: $0.9332^{10} = 50\%$.
2 For a 100-component unit (or unit with 100 opportunities for failure) with each component operating at:
   – 4 Sigma (99.38%), the overall unit probability of success is given by: $0.9938^{100} = 54\%$;
   – 5 Sigma (99.98%), this becomes $0.9998^{100} = 98\%$.
   – 6 Sigma (99.99966), this becomes virtually 100%.

This indicates the need for very high Sigma values in terms of opportunities.

Index

Robust design, 74, 83, 85–6, 90, 113–14, 171
Rolled throughput yield (RTY), 132, 137